THE
GUITAR
GRIMOIRE®

BY ADAM KADMON

THE EXERCISE BOOK

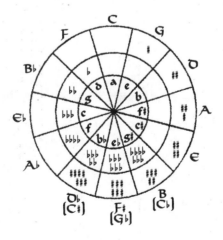

Produced by

☆®METATRON INC.

for

CARL FISCHER®

65 Bleecker Street, New York, NY 10012

GT100

ISBN 0-8258-2171-1

For more information on **The Guitar Grimoire®** Series and other music instructional products
by Adam Kadmon check out the following websites:
http://www.guitargrimoire.com
http://www.adamkadmon.com

INTRODUCTION

A few years back, in one of the guitar magazines, I saw an ad for a book that said something like, "Play lightning fast now without practicing any useless scales or exercises." The only thing more stupid than that ad were the poor suckers who bought that book. Needless to say, neither the book nor the ad exist anymore. To tell a young student of guitar that they can learn to play lightning fast without practicing scales or exercises is like telling a 98 pound weakling they can have a body like Schwartzenegger by drinking a potion without lifting weights, working out or exercising.

Scales and exercises are the crux, the apex, the foundation of the players playing. Over time they build strength, endurance, dexterity and technique. They also improve control, dynamics, timing and help to develop style and a command over one's instrument that can only come with years of daily repetition and drilling.

The exercises in this book are written in odd timings so that the notation works hand in hand with the diagrams to help demonstrate the pattern involved with each exercise. Start slow, after all you will be doing these for the rest of your life, become familiar with them. After you get comfortable with them start using a metronome at a slow speed gradually working your way faster. You can even do scales and exercises while watching TV or movies.

Whether you want to be a star, a recording artist or just play for yourself you need to practice scales and exercises. Too many kids today are caught up in tab and transcription books. Learning other peoples stuff is good, but if you really want to become a unique player this is where it's at.

Have fun,

ADAM KADMON

CONTENTS

CONTENTS CONTINUED

CONTENTS CONTINUED

PART ONE

MAJOR SCALE EXERCISES

PRACTICING THE SCALES

We are going to start with the F Major scale. The reason we are starting with F is because the patterns connect nicely staring with pattern 1. What I mean is, other keys may start with pattern 5 for instance, and connect thus: 5, 6, 7, 1, 2, 3, 4. But we will get to that later, for now just concern yourself with F Major.

Below we have figure 1 demonstrating the key of F Major as it applies to the fretboard. The fretboard to the far left shows every note possible, and the fretboards to the right of that show how to break it down into patterns making it easier for us to play since we don't have 30 fingers on our hands.

Below that the individual patterns are expanded to demonstrate the fingering used to play each pattern.

F MAJOR

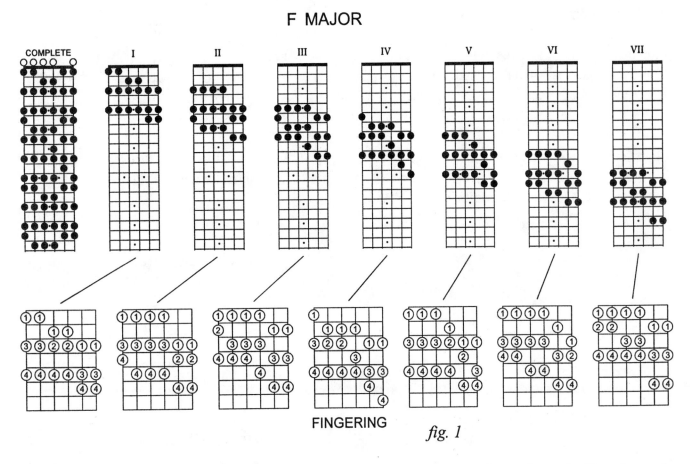

FINGERING

fig. 1

Though the notes may change when you move the position of the pattern to change keys, the fingering and the intervallic relationship remain the same (fig. 2). If you don't understand intervals we recommend **The Guitar Grimoire Scales & Modes.**

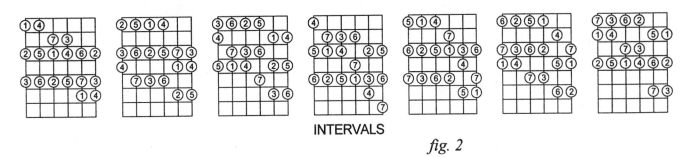

INTERVALS

fig. 2

The notes in F Major for the patterns are as follows.

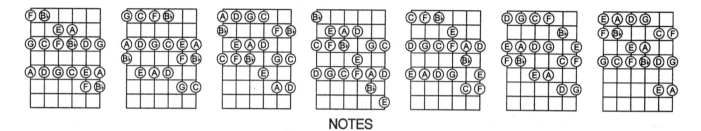

NOTES

Now before we start the excercises we will cover picking. We will use V for the down stroke and we will use Λ for the upstroke. These are the ascending picking patterns, in other words, from the lowest note to the highest note consecutively. Notice as you change strings there are two downstrokes in a row. This is to conserve energy. This technique was originally called economy picking. More recently it has been called speed picking, sweeping or shredding.

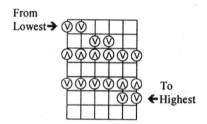

From Lowest →

To Highest ←

Note that all seven patterns are the same as far as down, up, down, down, up, down, etc. even though they are fingered differently. In fact, once mastered, you use the same patterns for any of the seven tone exotic scales from the **Guitar Grimoire Scales & Modes.**

I   II   III   IV   V   VI   VII

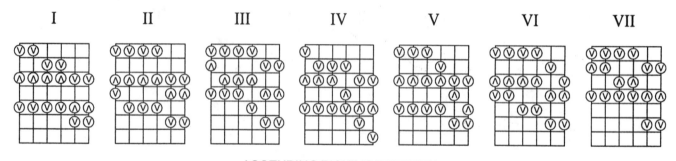

ASCENDING PICKING PATTERN

PATTERNS IN F MAJOR (ascending)

I notated this exercise in 18/8 time so you can see the strings in 3 note groups and so the entire pattern would fit in one measure.

Observe the picking pattern above the notes.

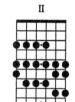

Pick the notes evenly and smoothly. Remember that the picking pattern is the same for each fingering pattern in each measure.

4

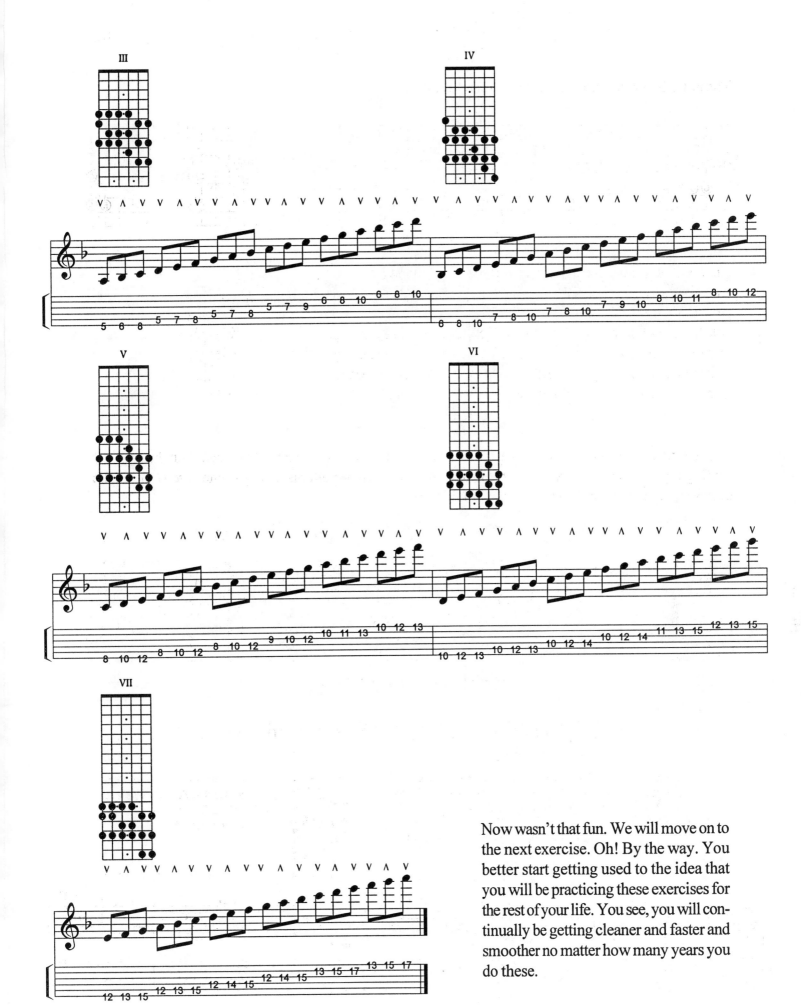

Now wasn't that fun. We will move on to the next exercise. Oh! By the way. You better start getting used to the idea that you will be practicing these exercises for the rest of your life. You see, you will continually be getting cleaner and faster and smoother no matter how many years you do these.

Next we go to the descending picking patterns. In this case we go from the highest note to the lowest.

Just as with the ascending, the picking pattern for all seven fingering patterns is the same.

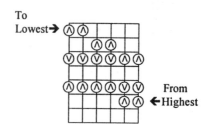

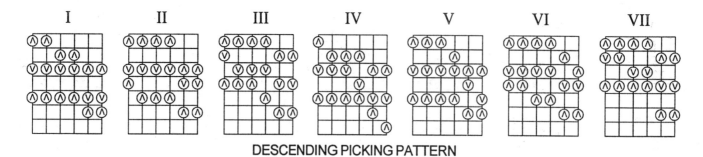

DESCENDING PICKING PATTERN

PATTERNS IN F MAJOR (descending)

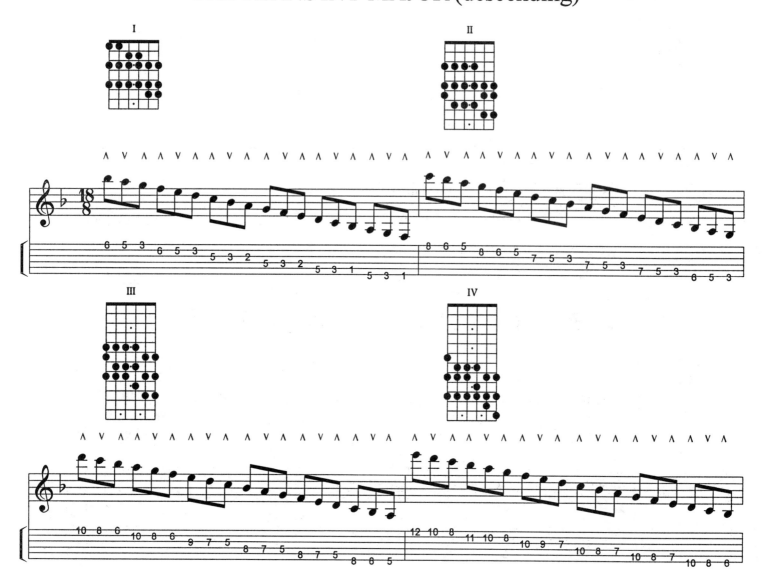

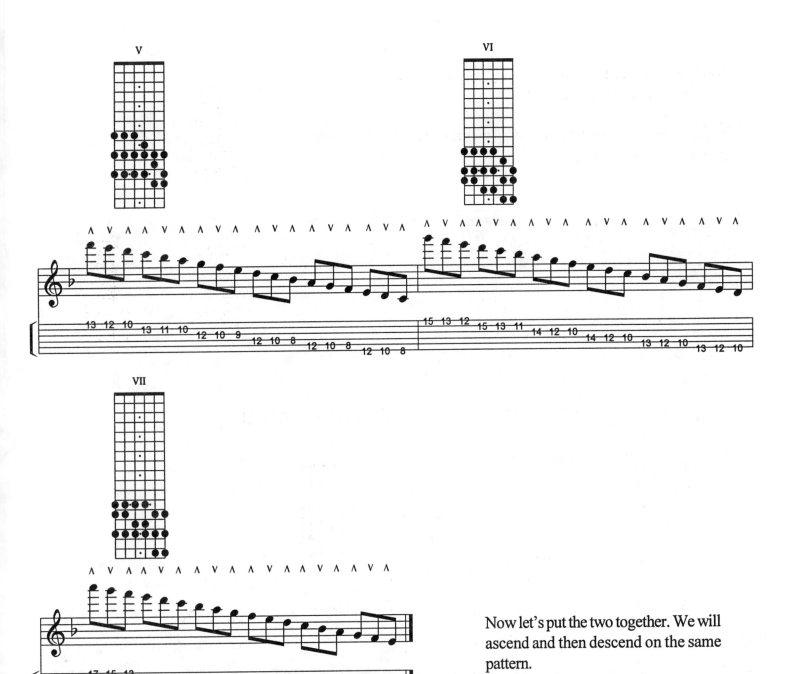

Now let's put the two together. We will ascend and then descend on the same pattern.

PATTERNS IN F MAJOR (ascending & descending)

We use the ascending picking here.

We use the descending picking here.

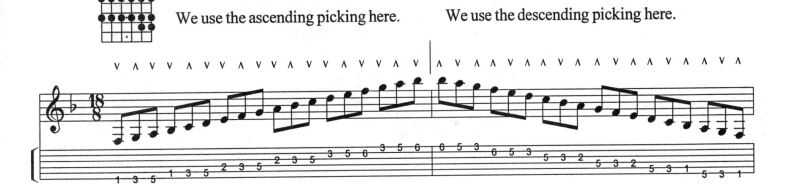

7

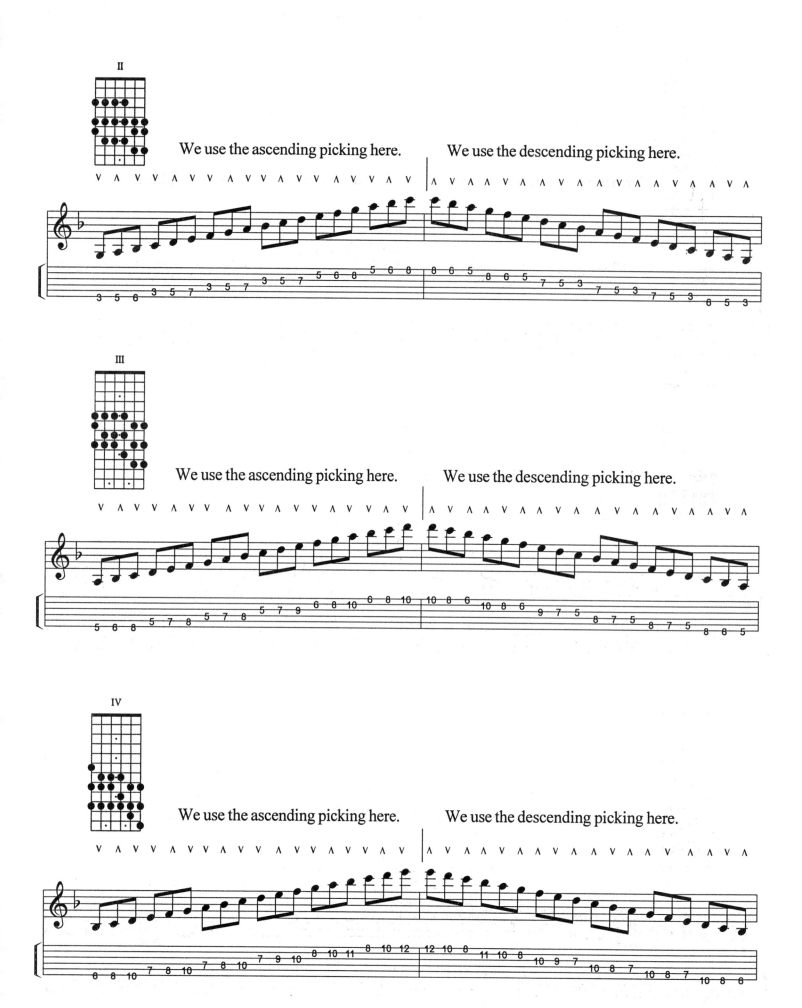

We use the ascending picking here.   We use the descending picking here.

We use the ascending picking here.   We use the descending picking here.

We use the ascending picking here.   We use the descending picking here.

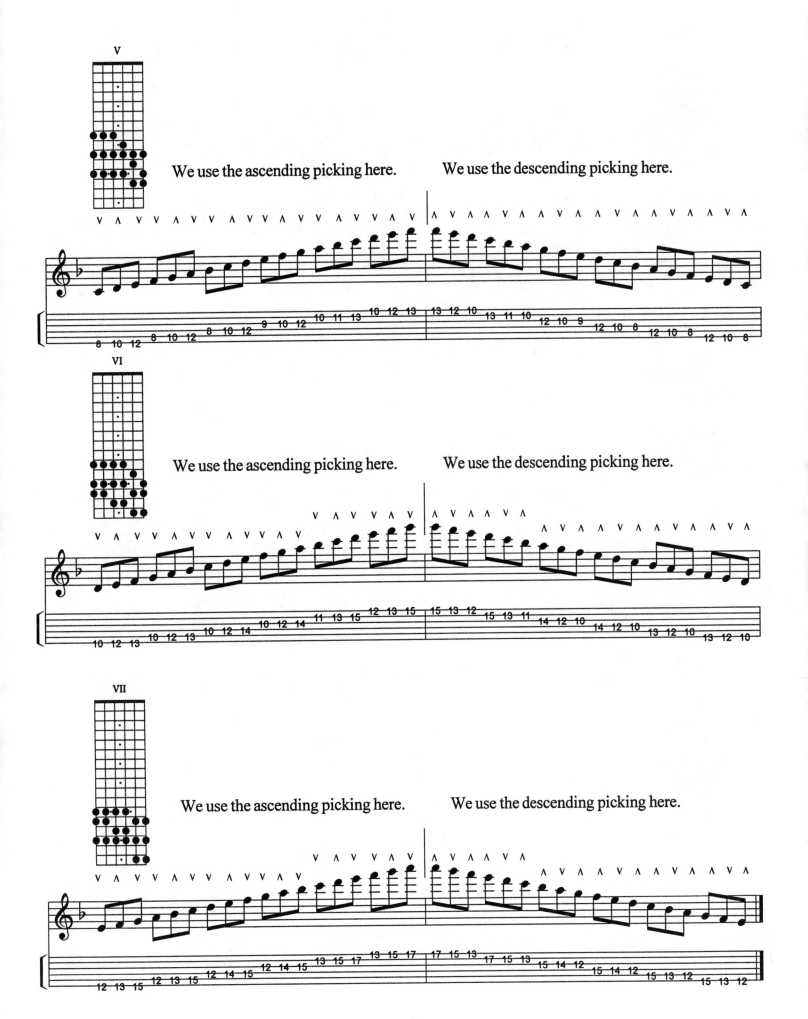

9

PATTERNS IN F MAJOR (ascending & descending - alternating)

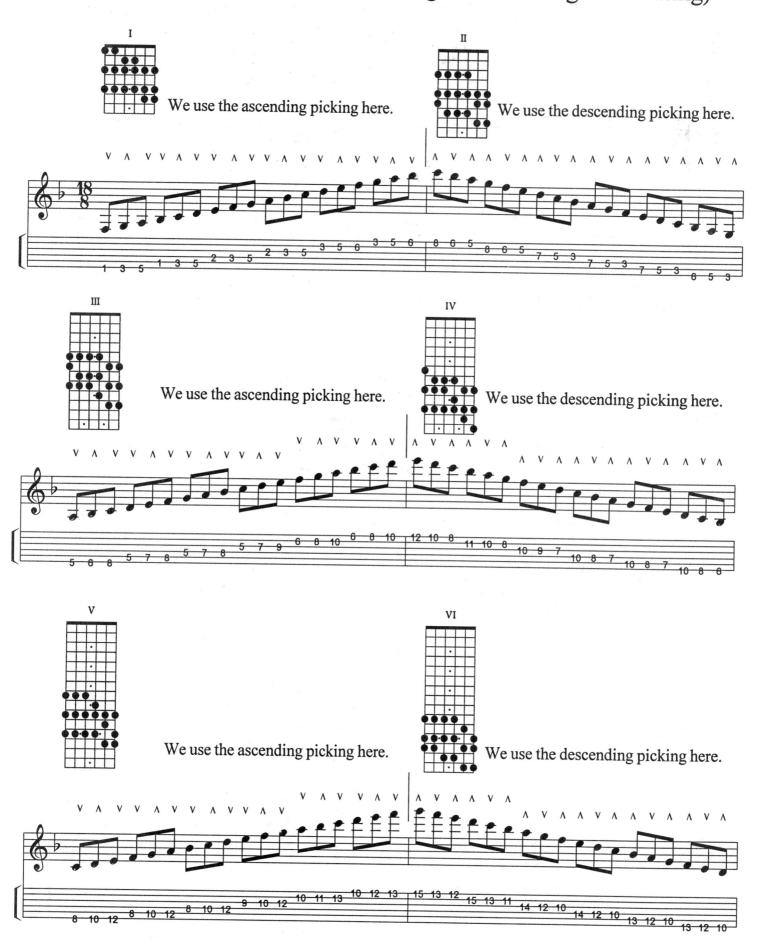

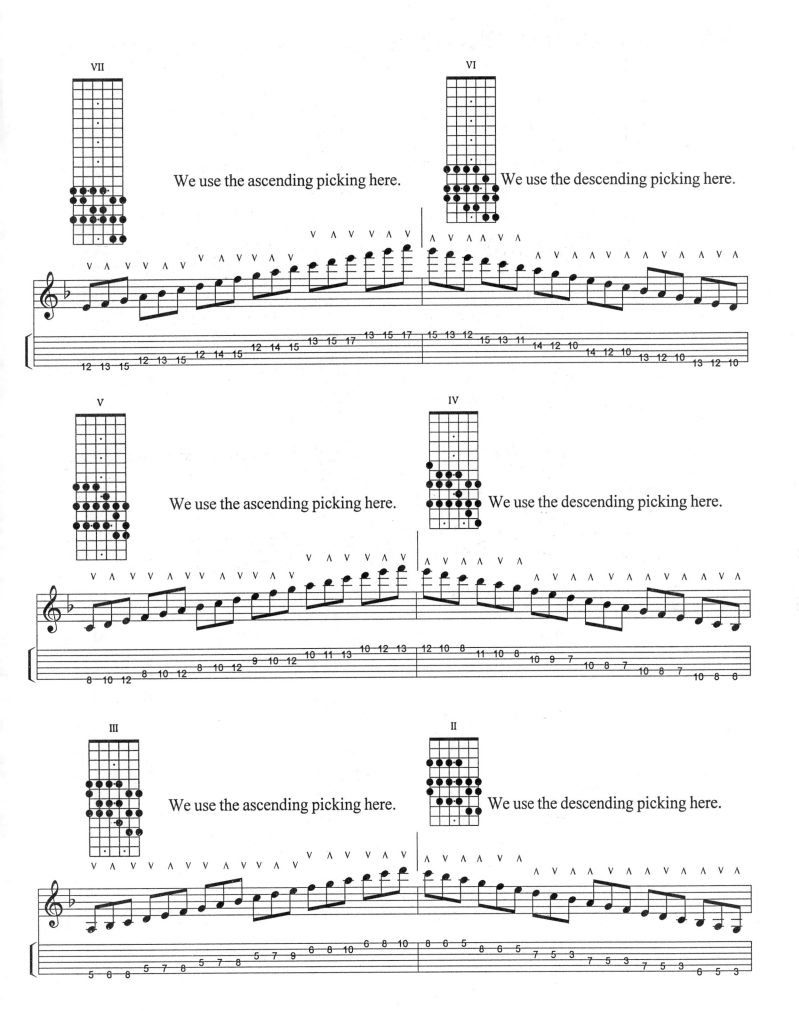

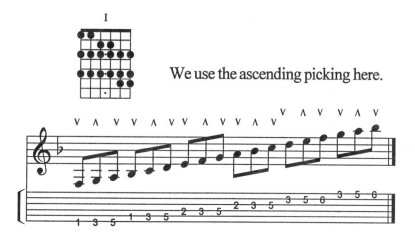

We use the ascending picking here.

COILS

Now we are going to cover coils. First of all let's discuss what a coil is for those of you who have never heard of them. Some texts have called them spirals and others by other names. In a nutshell coils ascend or descend in groups of three or four or even five or six. The following group starts on the second tone of the group preceding it. It will make more sense once we start.

First we have to learn the picking patterns. Again, we will use economy picking for ultimate speed in the long run. In order to learn the picking pattern for each fingering pattern we have to break it up into "mini " patterns. The notes darkened in the fretboard pattern above each measure are the notes used from the fingering pattern for that measure.

Once learned and mastered, coils add style when thrown into your solos. We are going to start with three note coils.

THREE NOTE COIL ASCENDING PICKING PATTERNS

We are going to start by breaking down pattern one of the Major scale in three note coil format. Below, each group of three represents a "mini" pattern of two strings. Each group also represents measures in the excercise with a oddball pattern for the last measure of each line. I notated these in 9/8 time with an oddball of 3/8 time so each measure could clearly demonstrate each "mini" picking pattern. Notice the picking pattern of ∨∧∨ ∧∨∨ ∨∨∧ repeats with each measure and the odd ball pattern is ∨∧∨. Remember that the picking is identical for all the patterns of the Major scale.

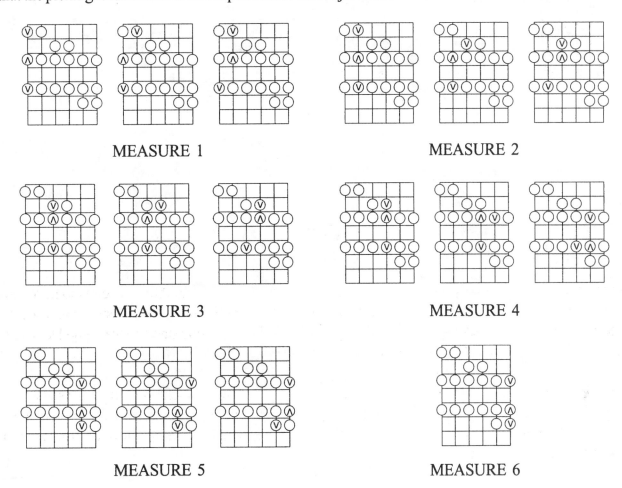

MEASURE 1   MEASURE 2

MEASURE 3   MEASURE 4

MEASURE 5   MEASURE 6

THREE NOTE COILS IN F MAJOR (ascending)

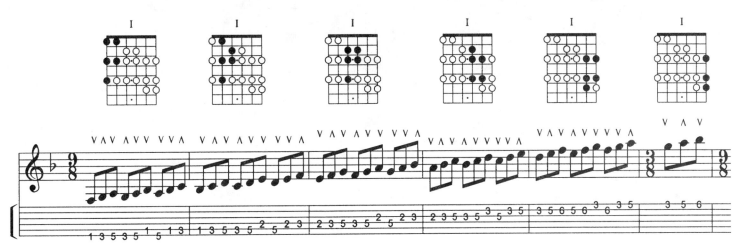

13

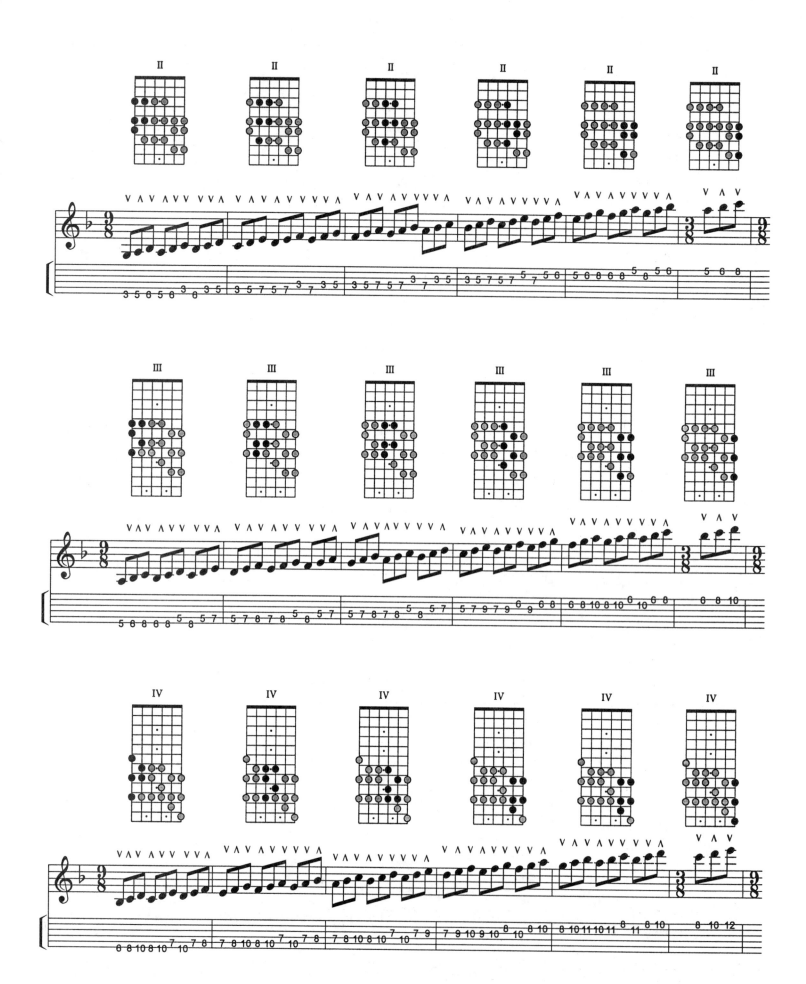

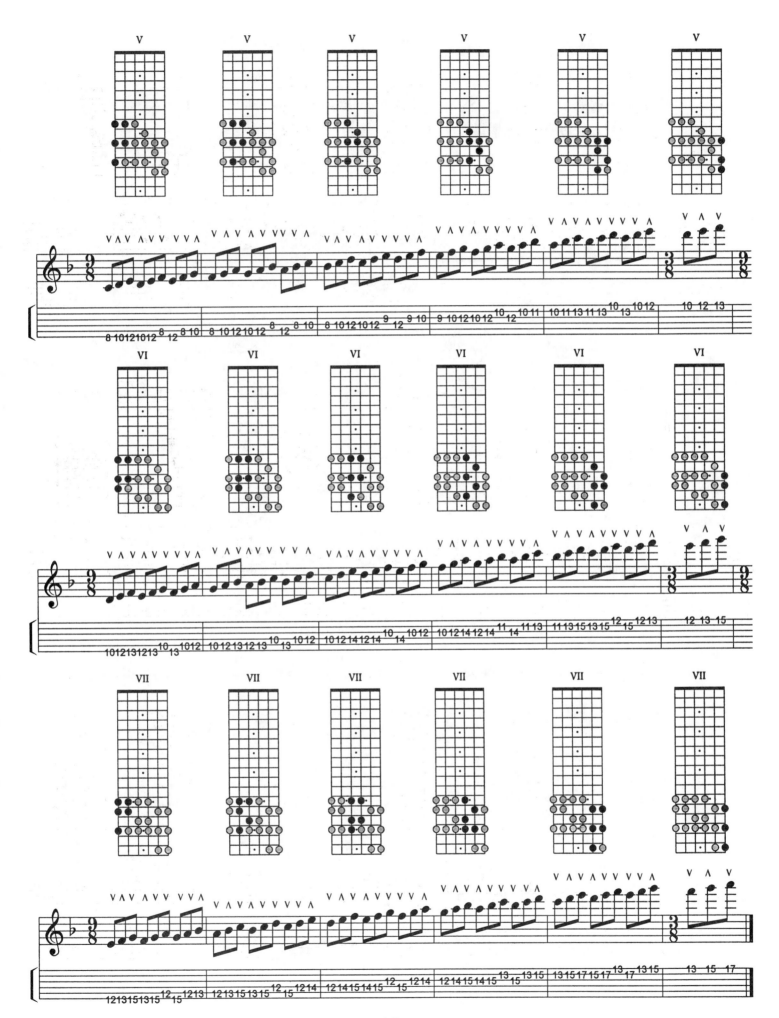

THREE NOTE COIL DESCENDING PICKING PATTERNS

The picking pattern for the three note coils descending is the same as ascending just in reverse.

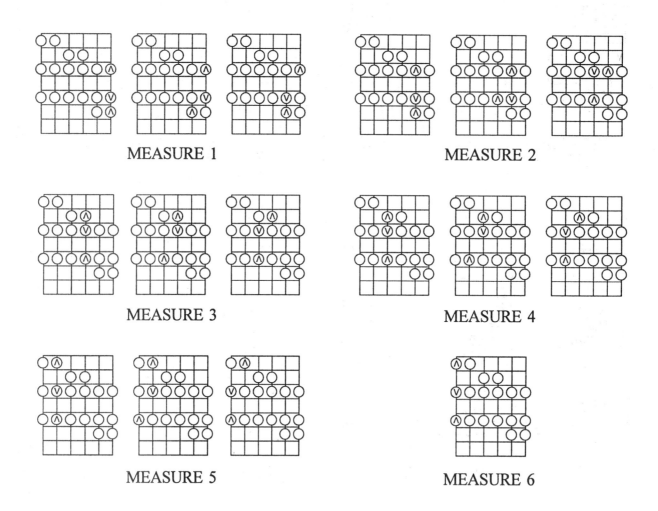

MEASURE 1   MEASURE 2

MEASURE 3   MEASURE 4

MEASURE 5   MEASURE 6

THREE NOTE COILS IN F MAJOR (descending)

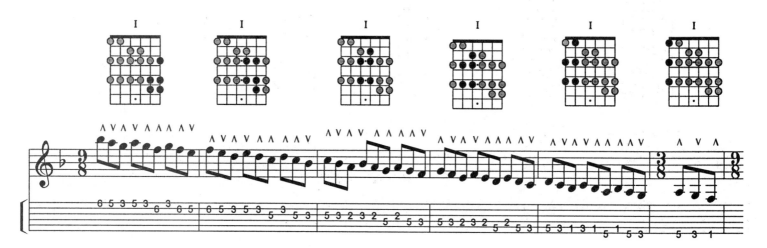

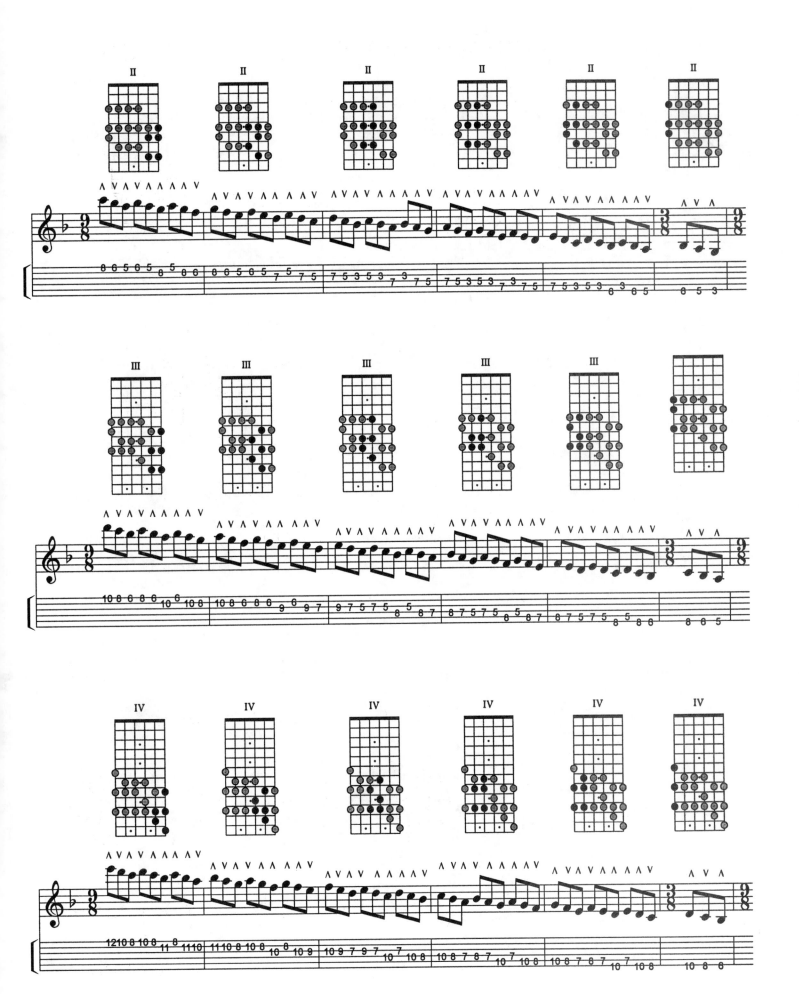

17

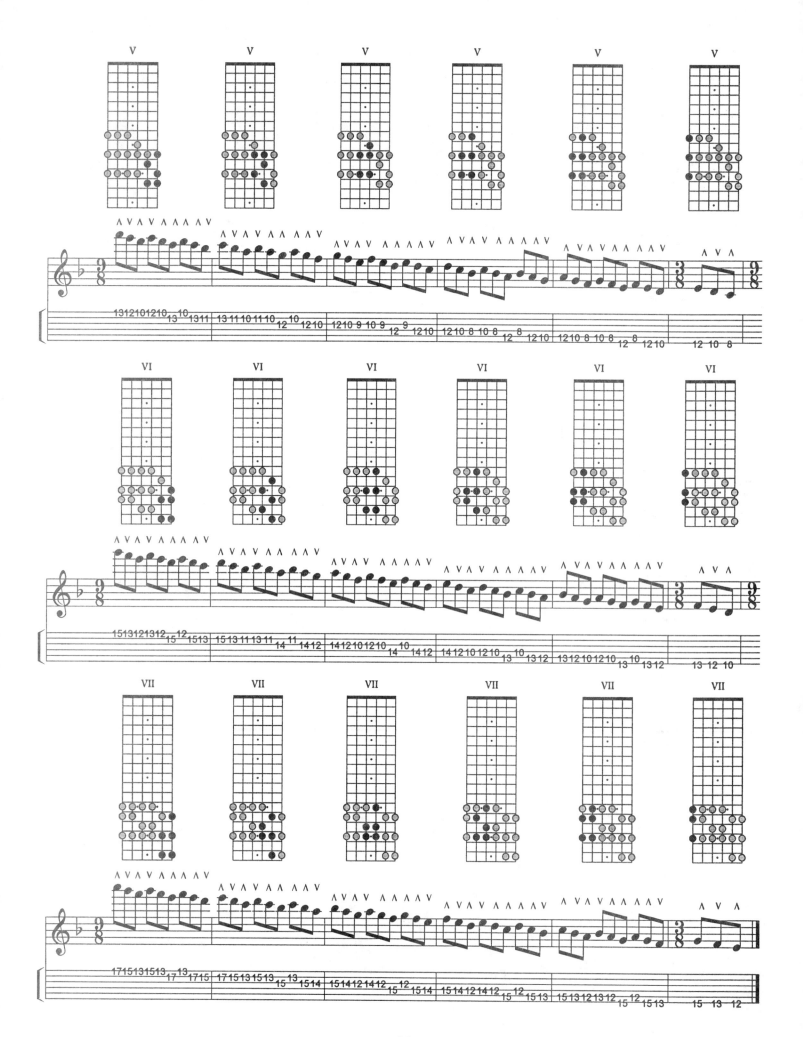

18

THREE NOTE COILS IN F MAJOR (ascending & descending)

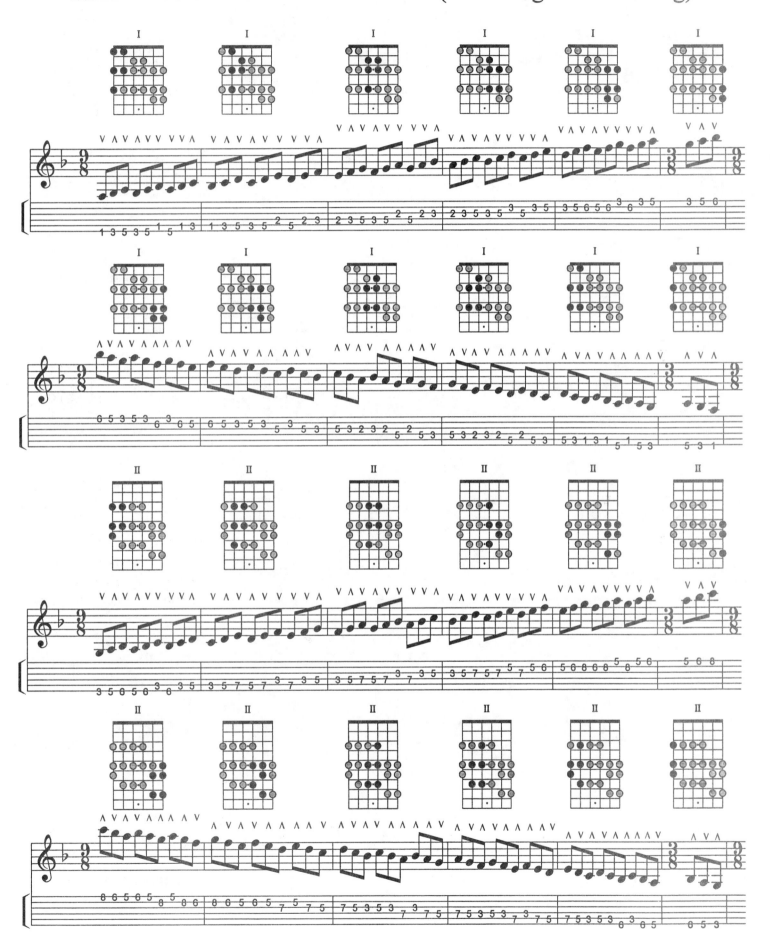

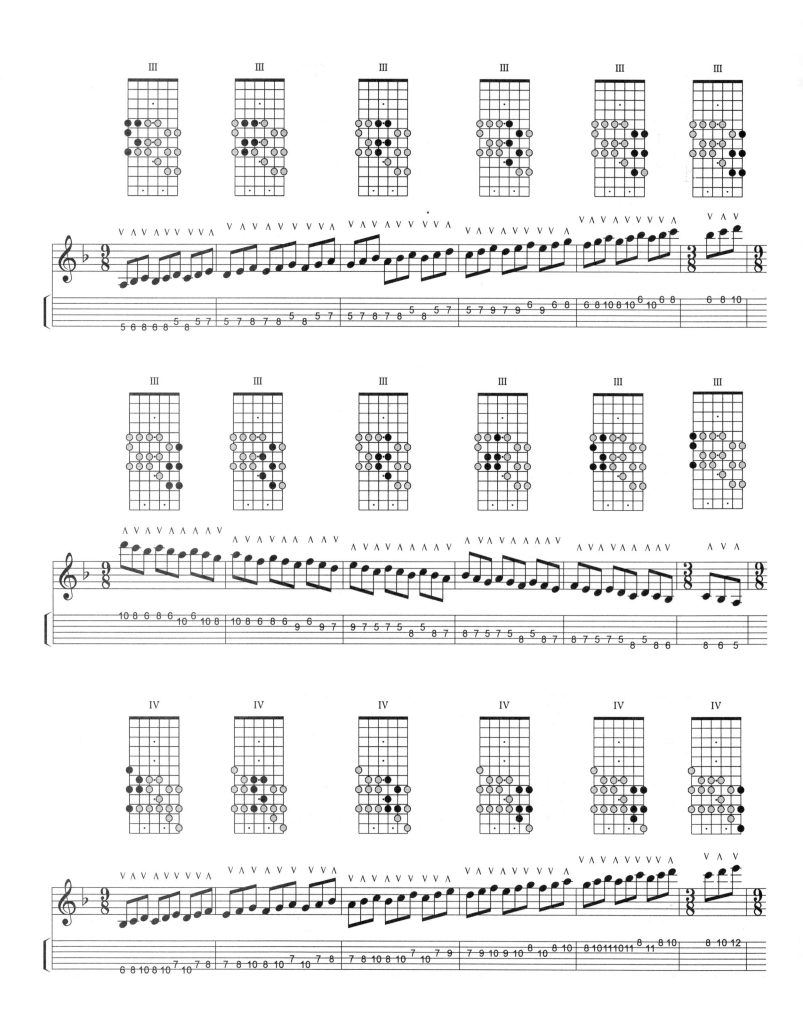

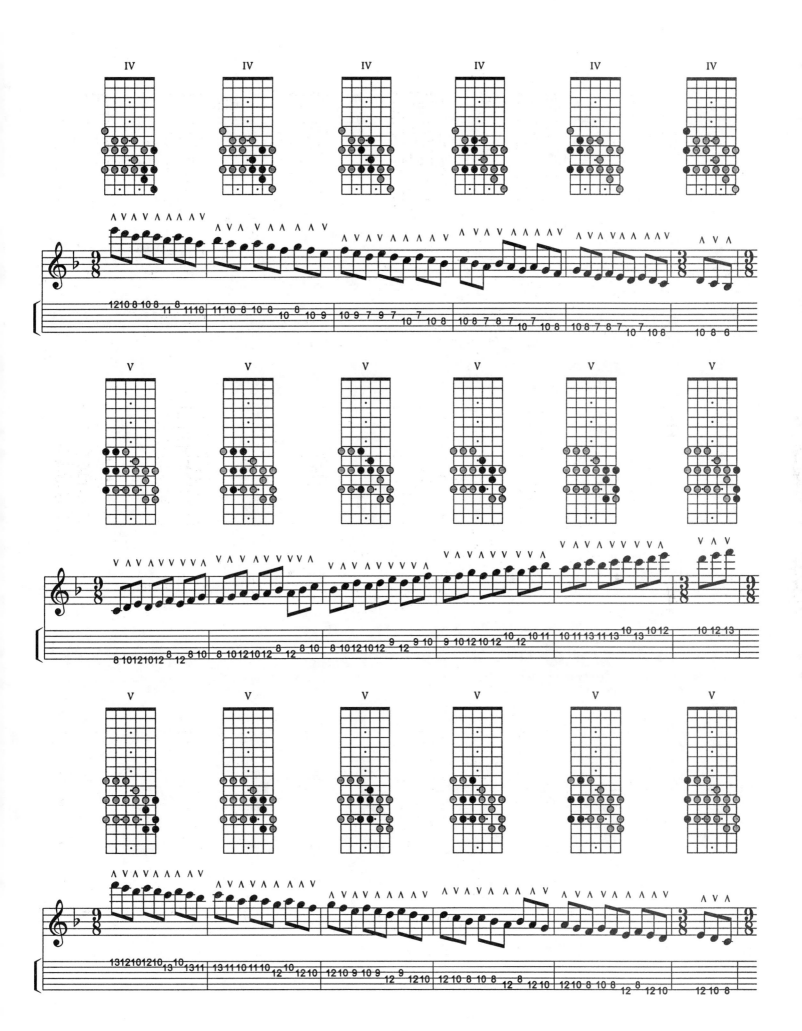

21

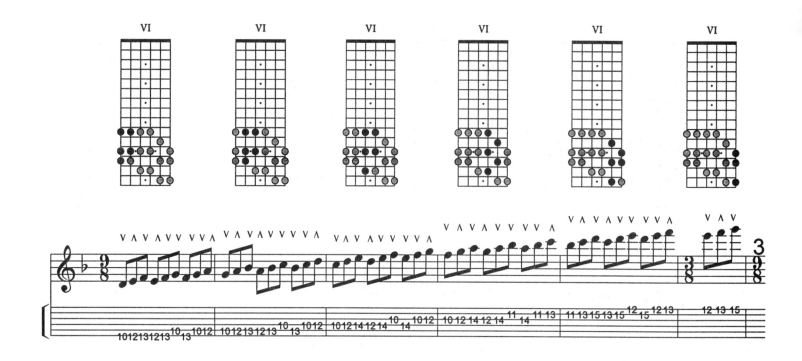

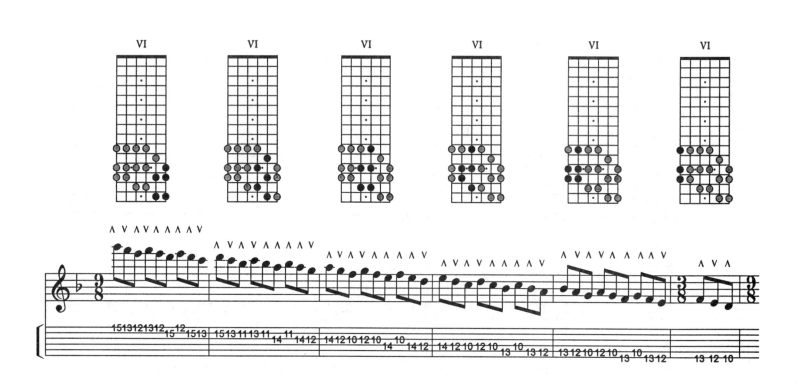

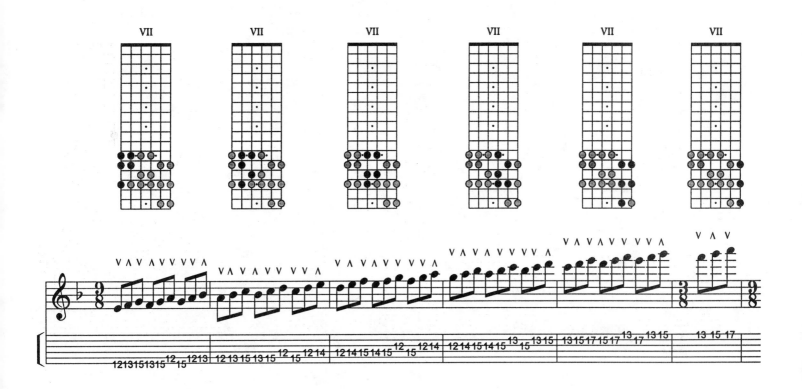

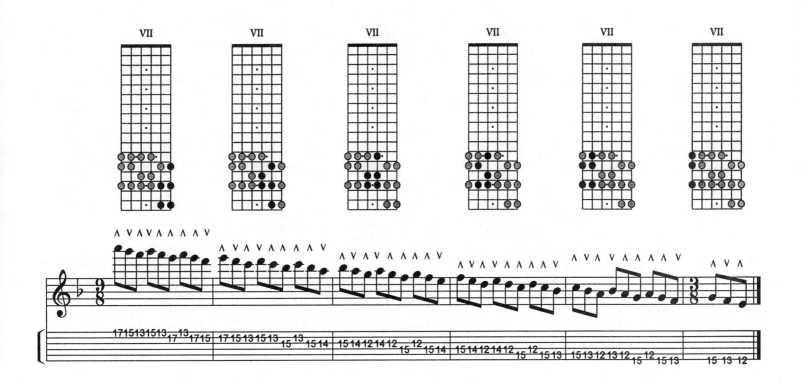

THREE NOTE COILS IN F MAJOR
(ascending & descending - alternating patterns)

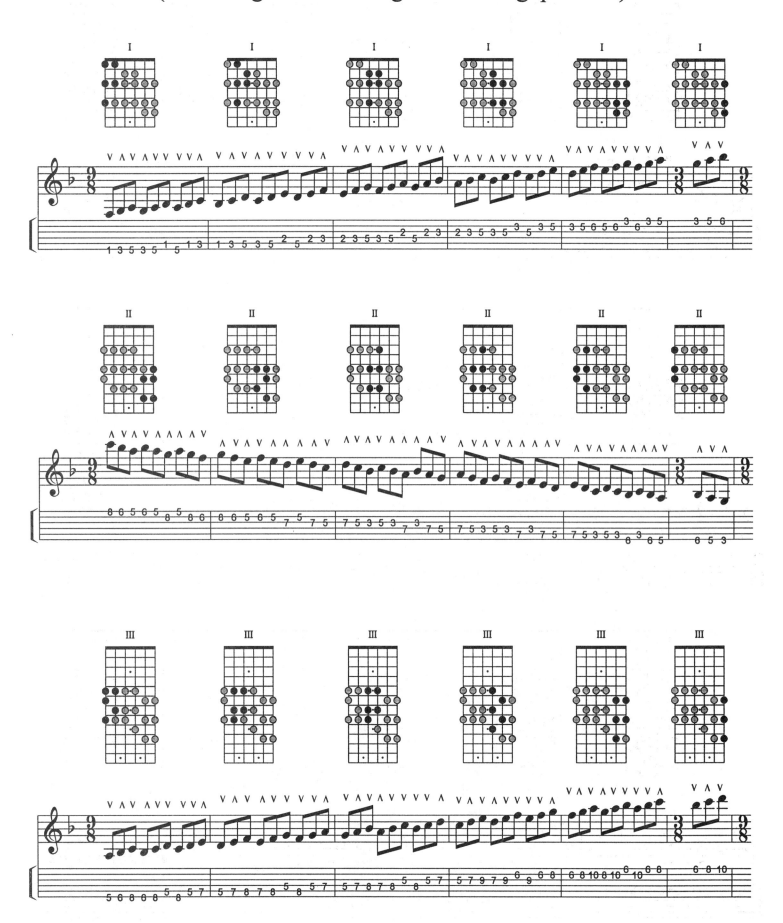

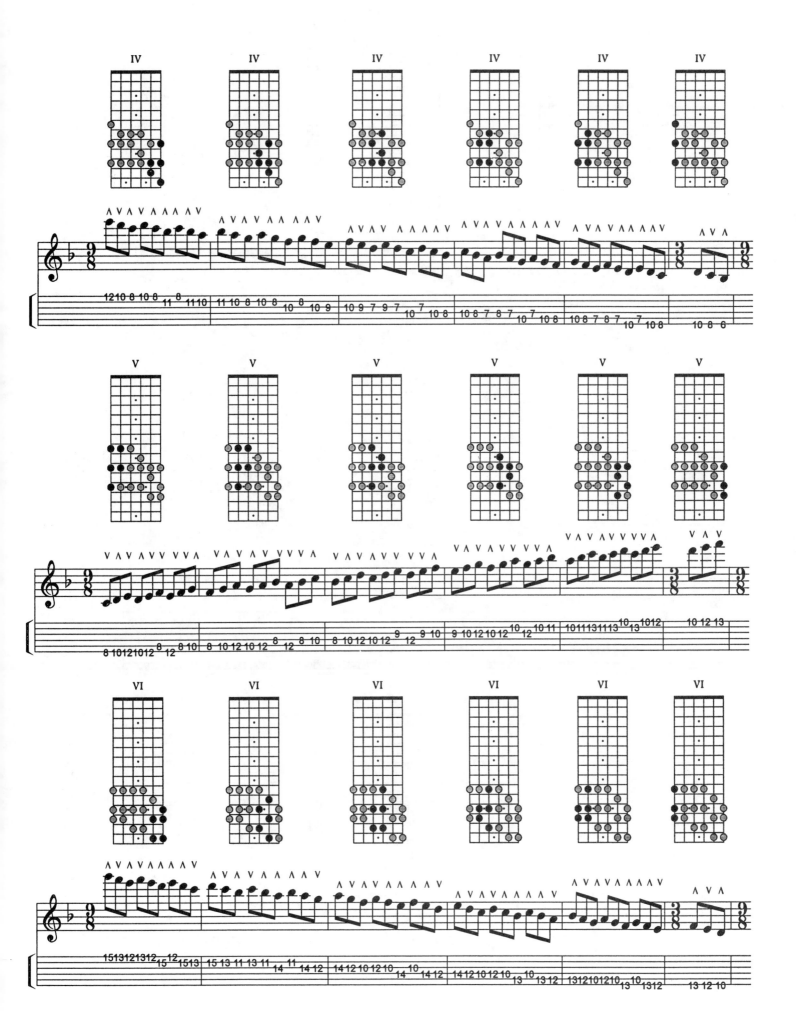

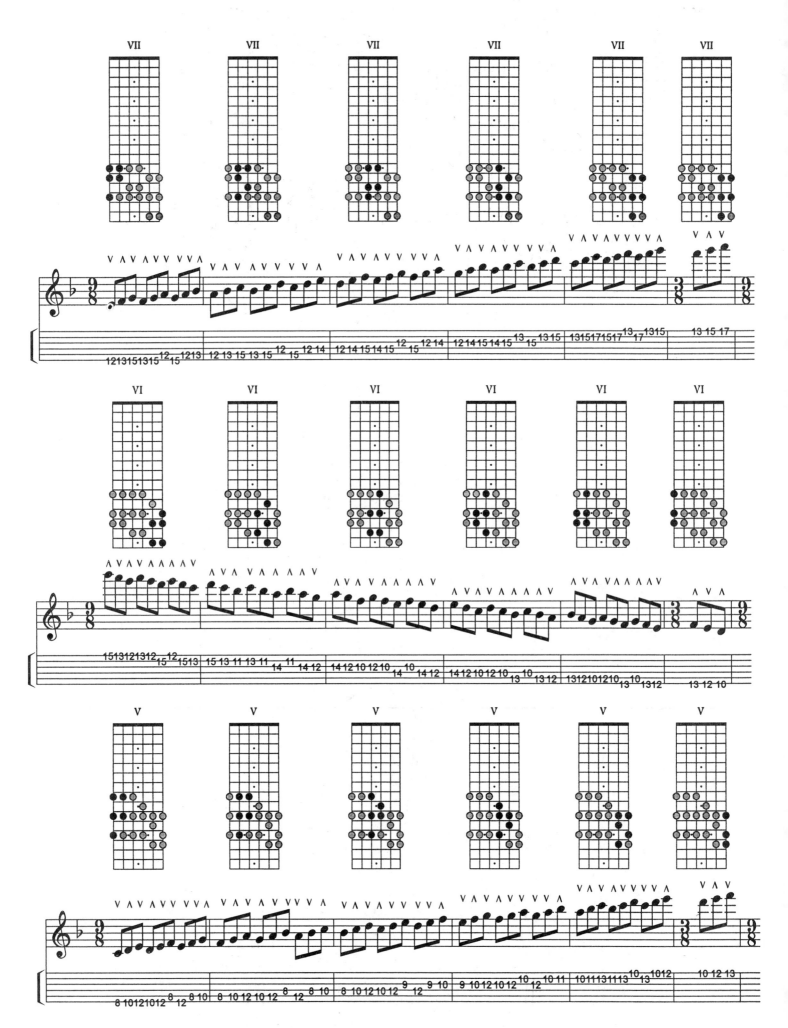

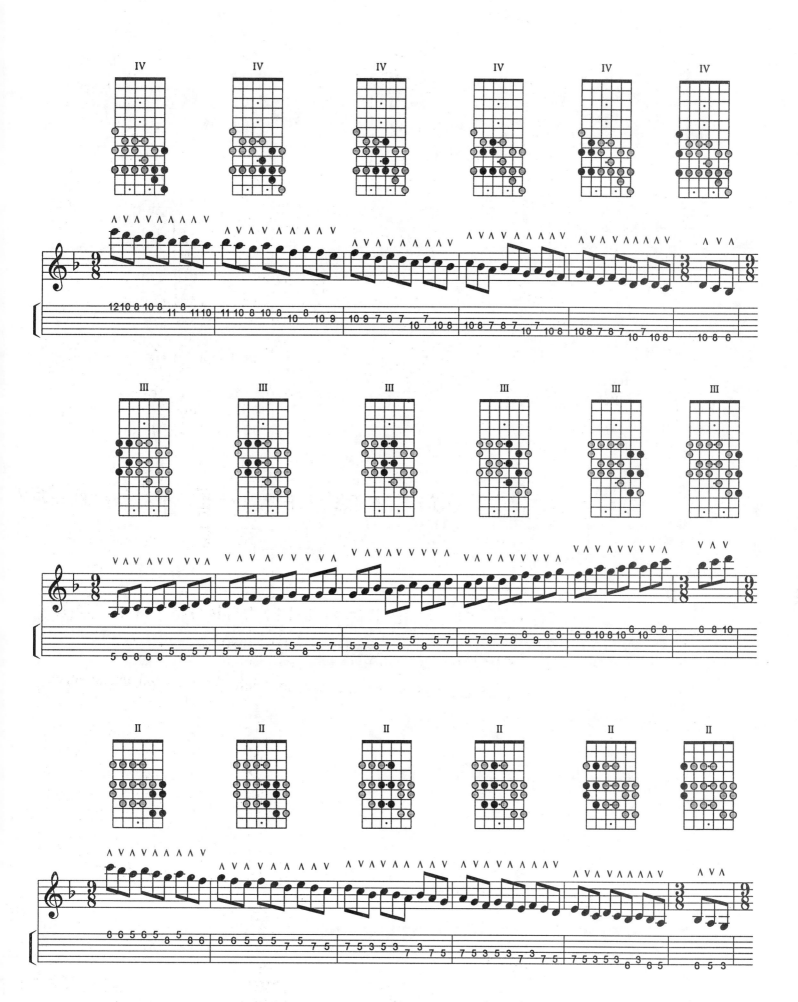

27

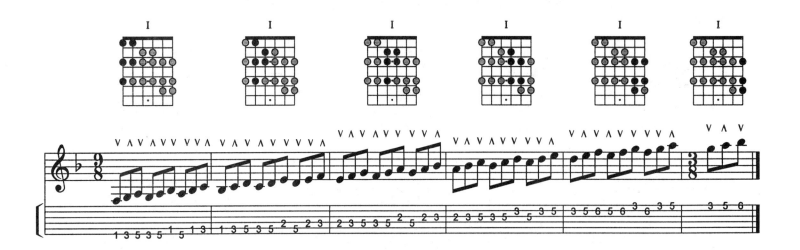

FOUR NOTE COIL ASCENDING PICKING PATTERNS

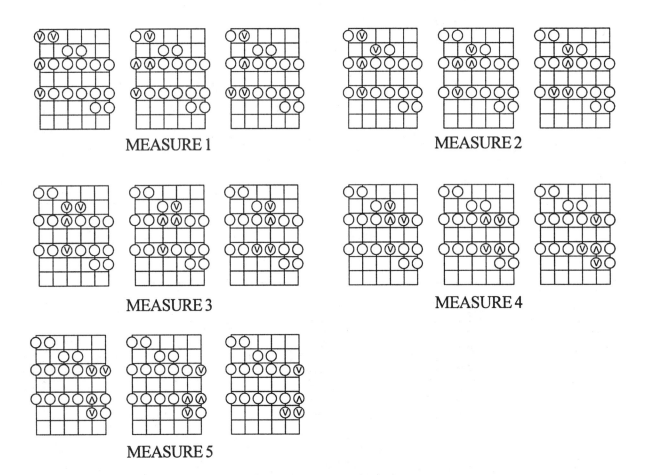

MEASURE 1

MEASURE 2

MEASURE 3

MEASURE 4

MEASURE 5

The same approach is used for the four note coils as in the three note coils. The only difference is you have four note groups rather than three note groups.

FOUR NOTE COILS IN F MAJOR (ascending)

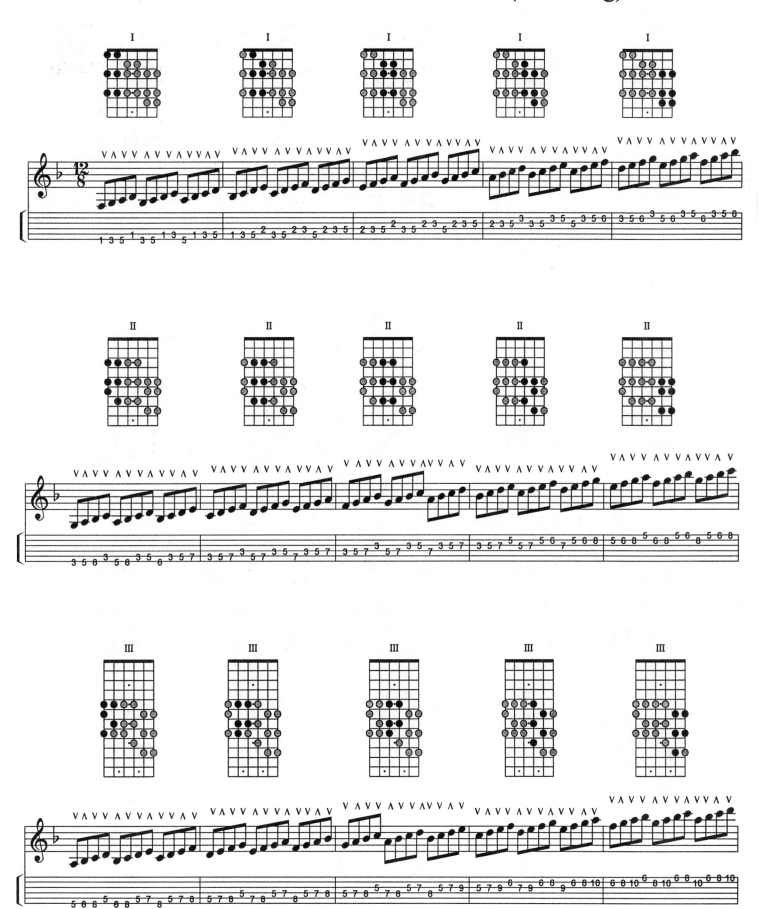

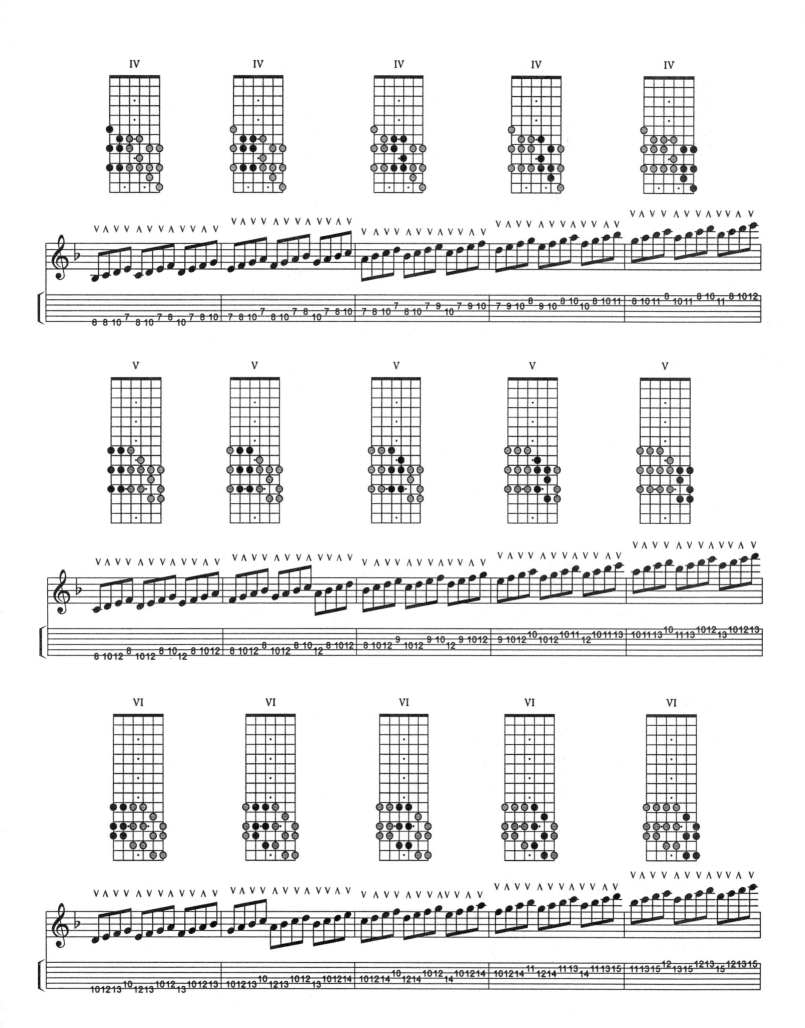

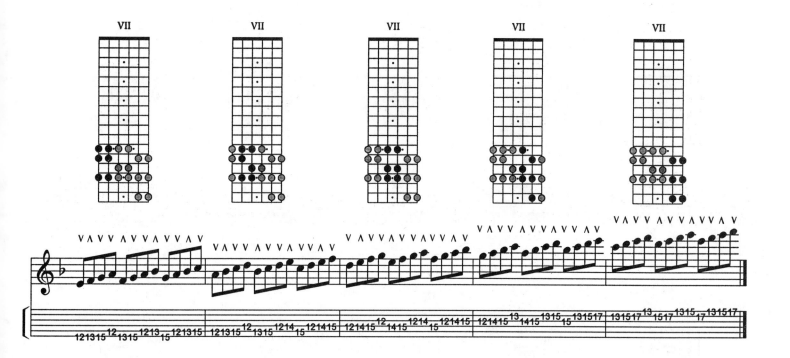

FOUR NOTE COIL DESCENDING PICKING PATTERNS

By now you should be familiar with this. So here is the breakdown of the picking pattern for the four note coils.

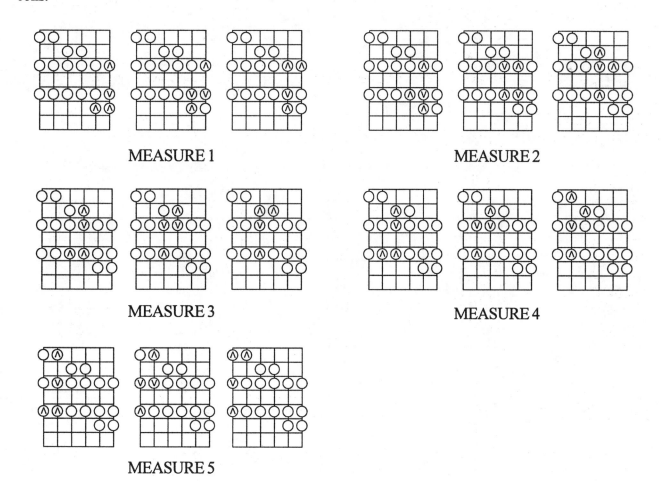

MEASURE 1

MEASURE 2

MEASURE 3

MEASURE 4

MEASURE 5

FOUR NOTE COILS IN F MAJOR (descending)

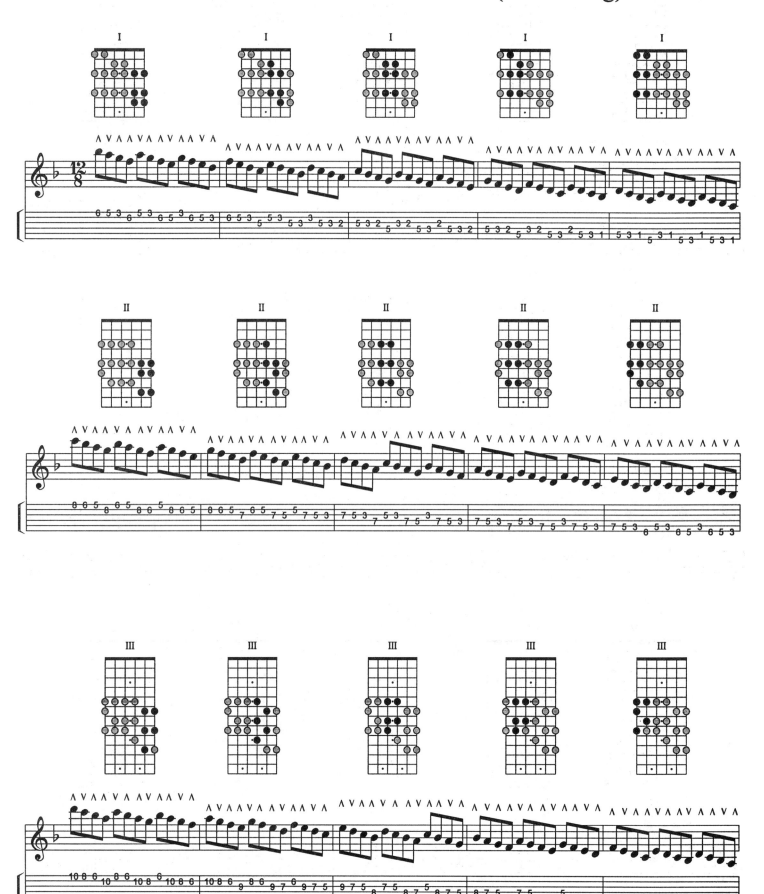

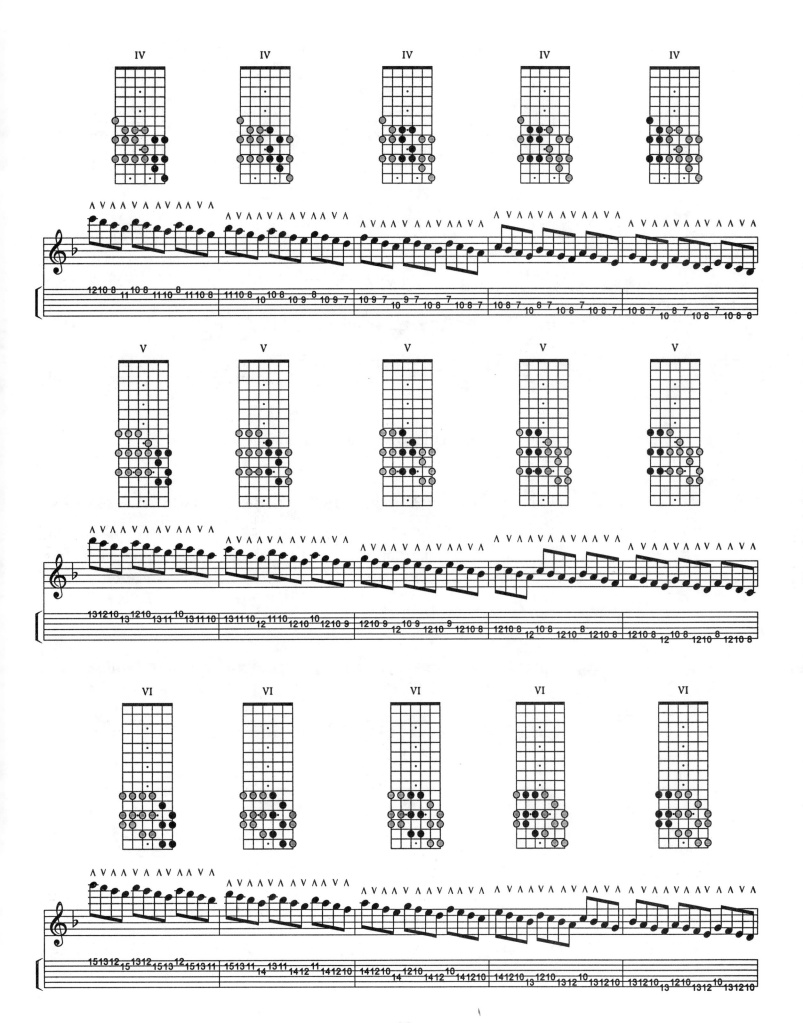

33

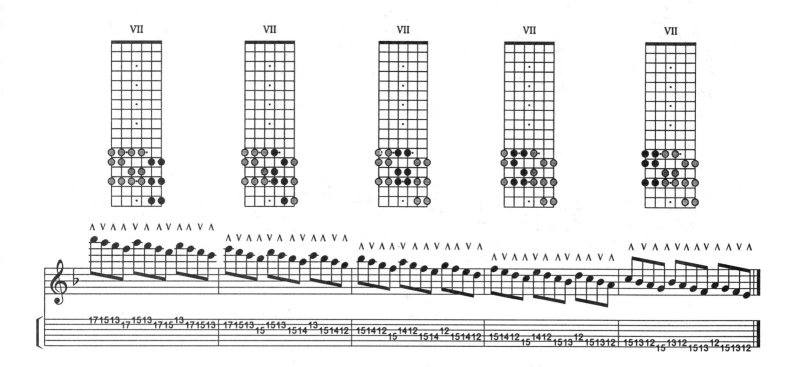

Now we will put the two together for ascending and descending with four note coils.

FOUR NOTE COILS IN F MAJOR (ascending & descending)

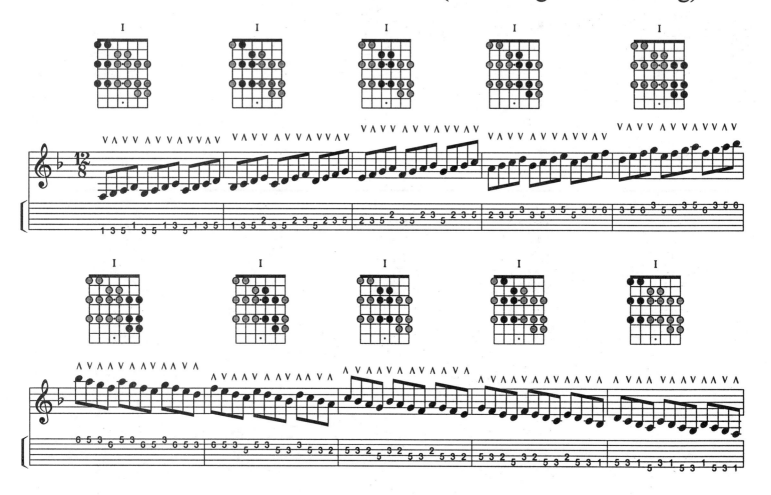

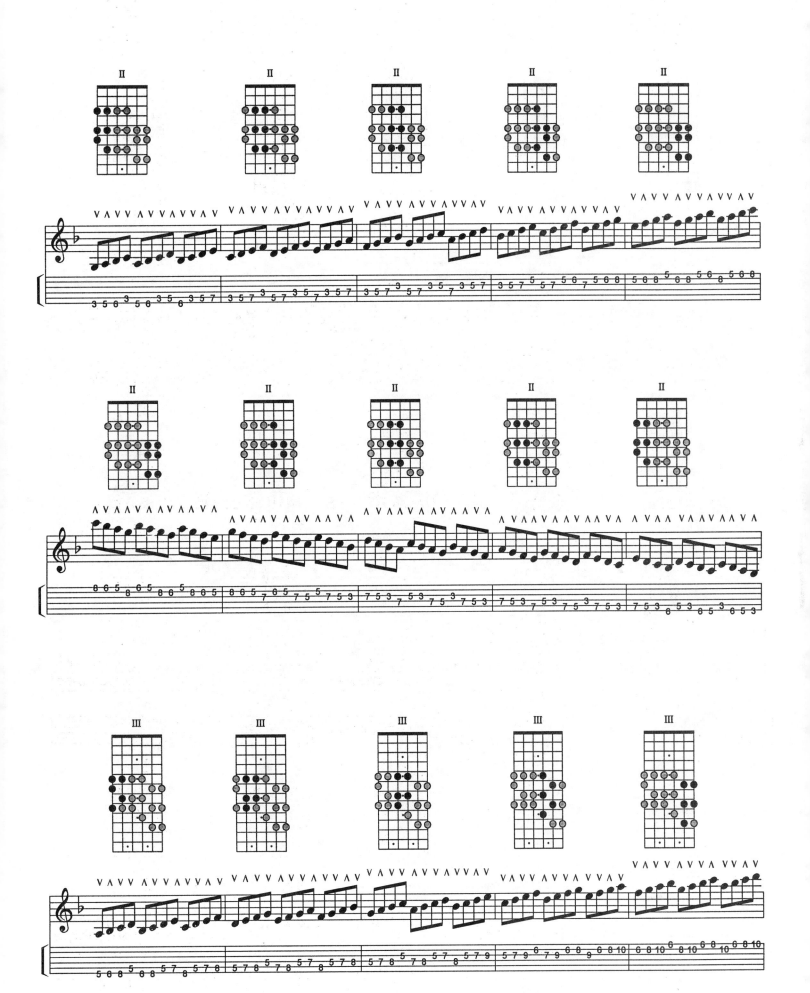

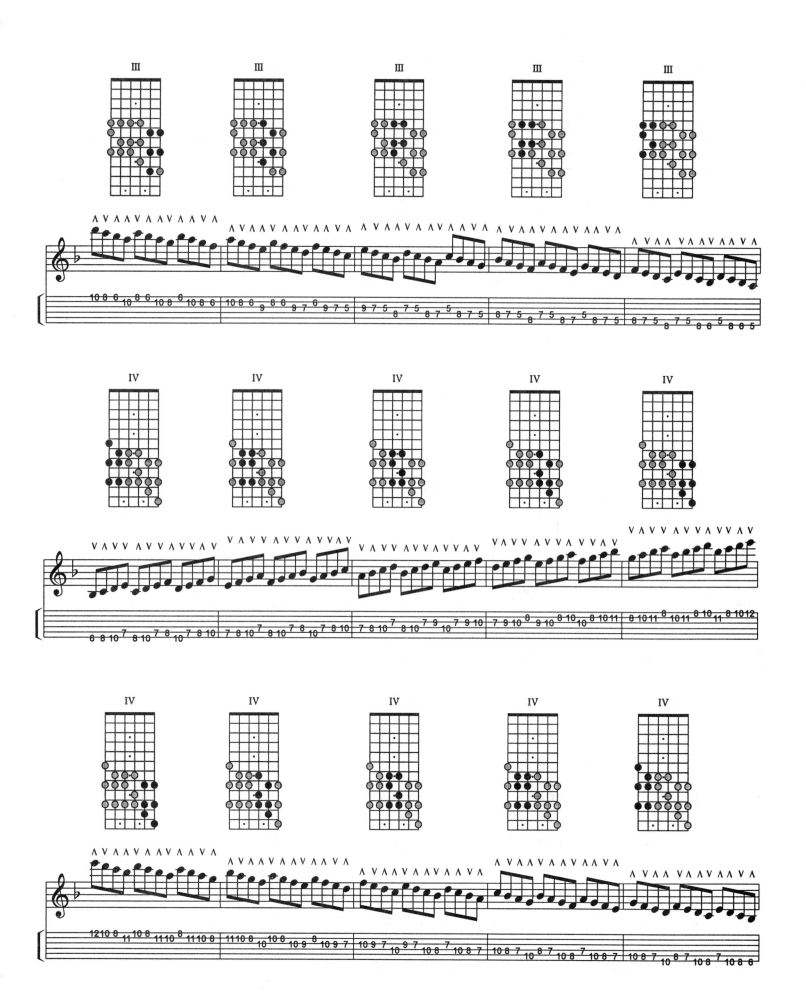

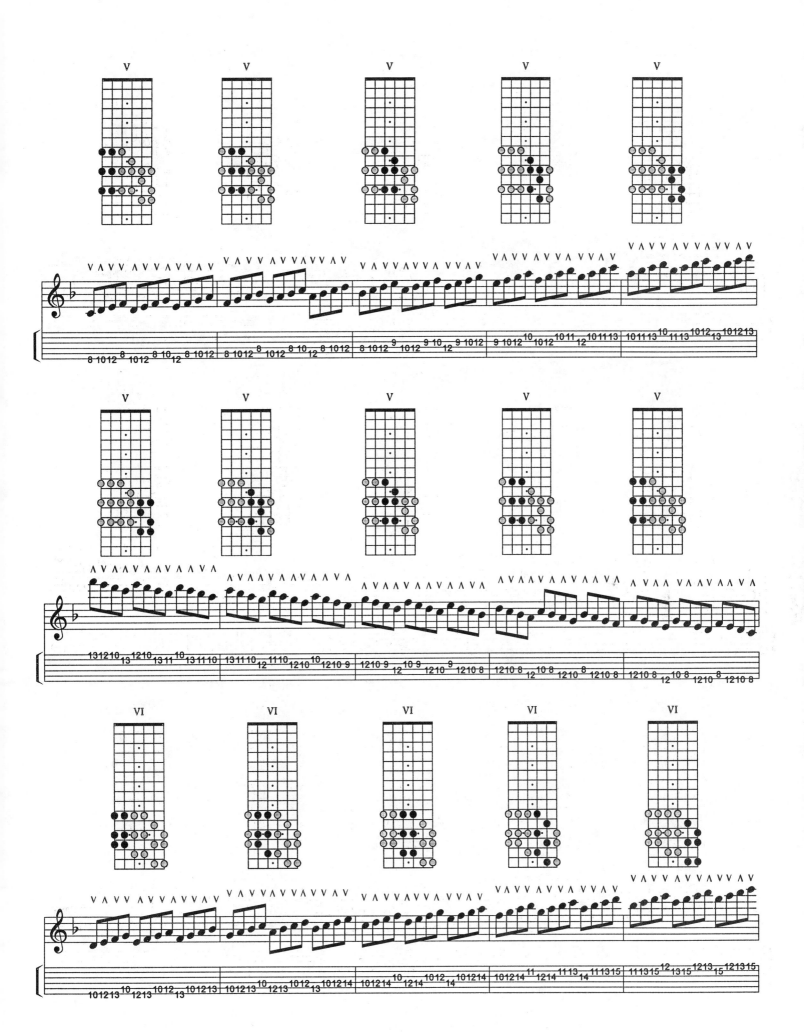

37

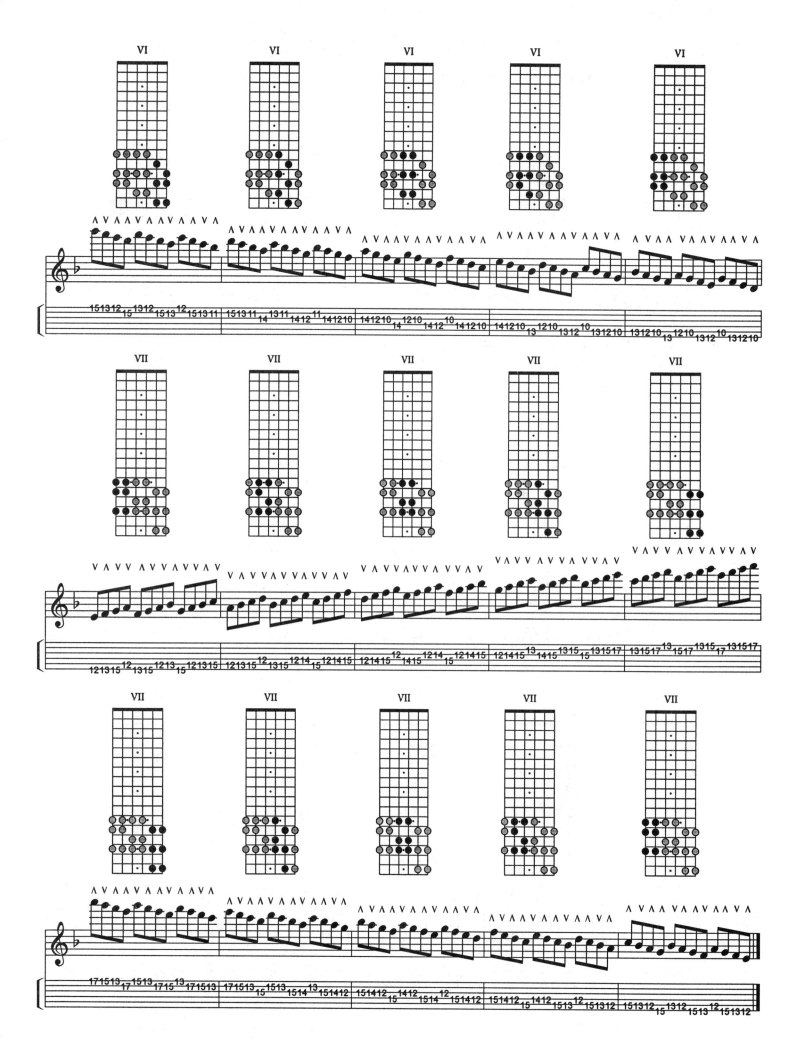

FOUR NOTE COILS IN F MAJOR
(ascending & descending - alternating patterns)

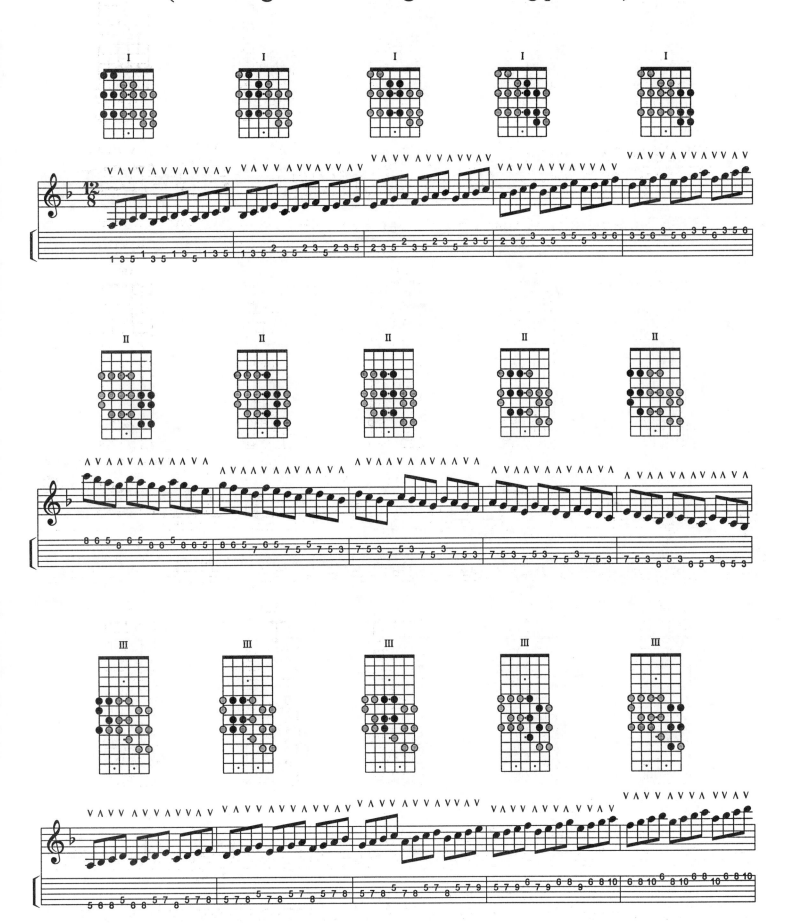

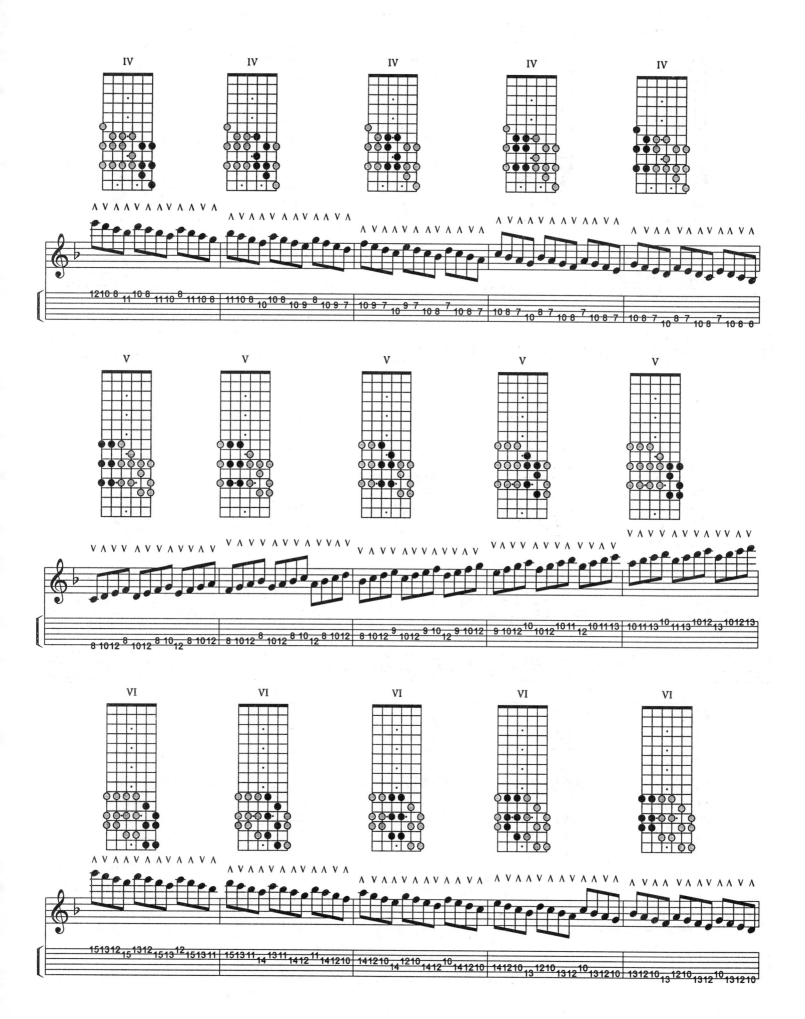

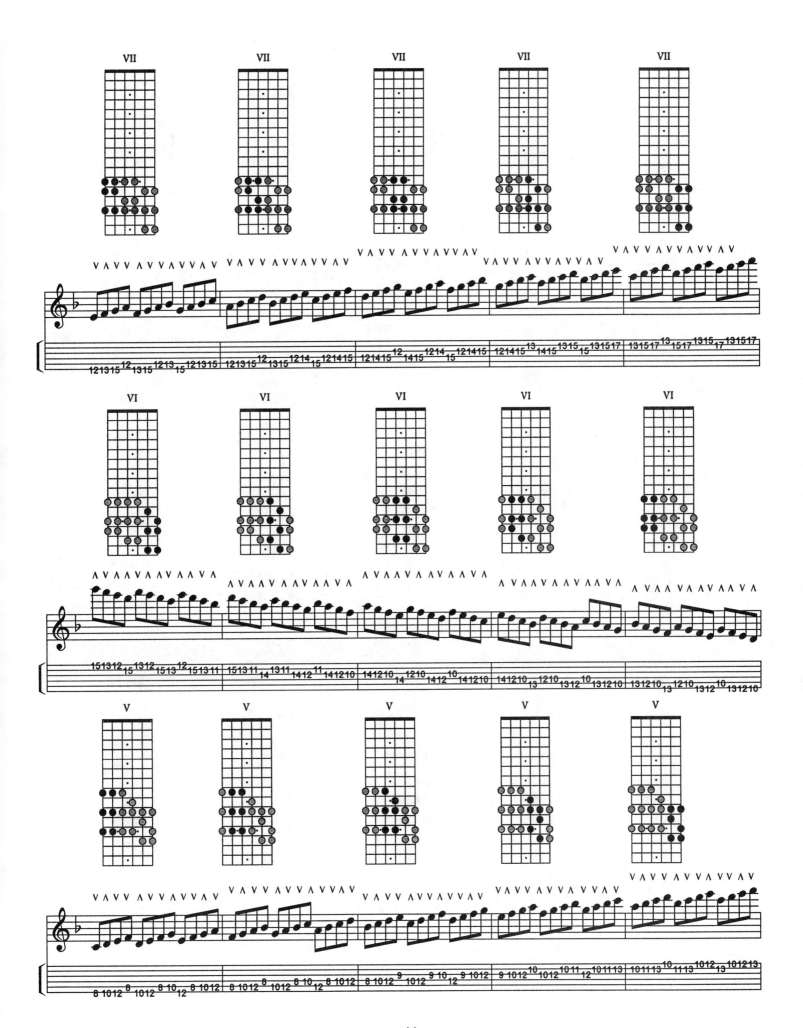

41

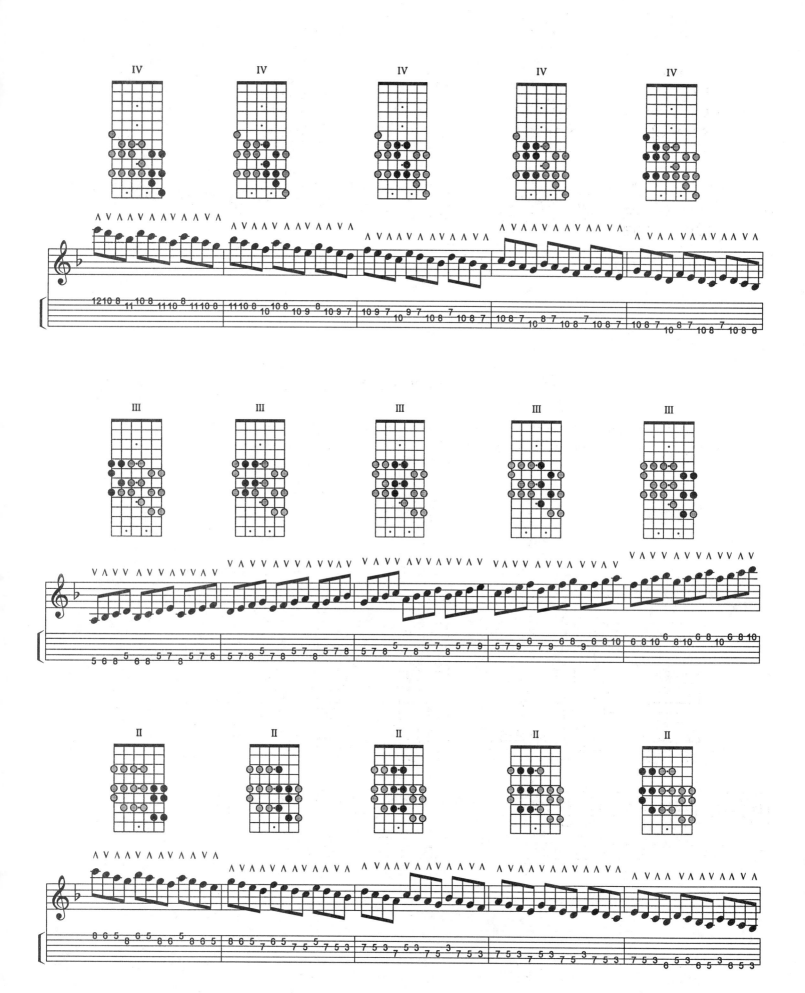

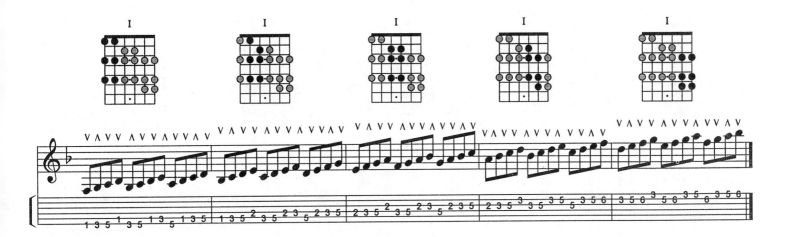

SINGLE STRING EXERCISES

These single string exercises are designed to give the ability to change patterns from any string. The picking pattern of ∨ ∧ ∨, ∨ ∧ ∨ etc. can also be played as ∨ ∧ ∨, ∧ ∨ ∧, ∨ ∧ ∨, ∧ ∨ ∧ etc. or ∧ ∨ ∧, ∧ ∨ ∧ etc.

6th String

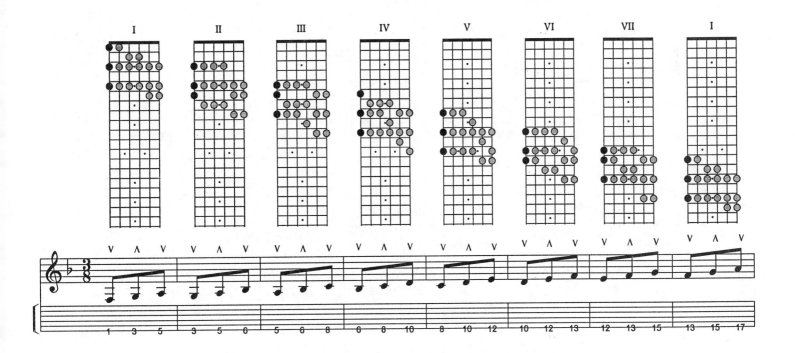

5th String

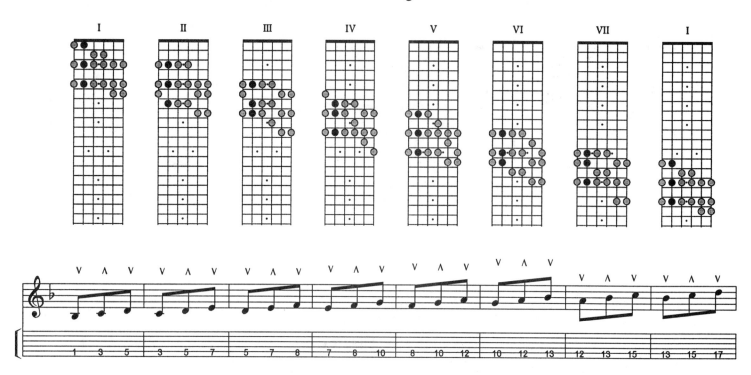

4th String

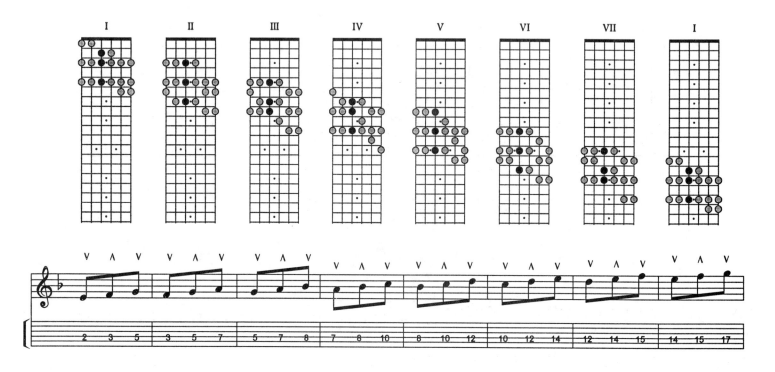

3rd String

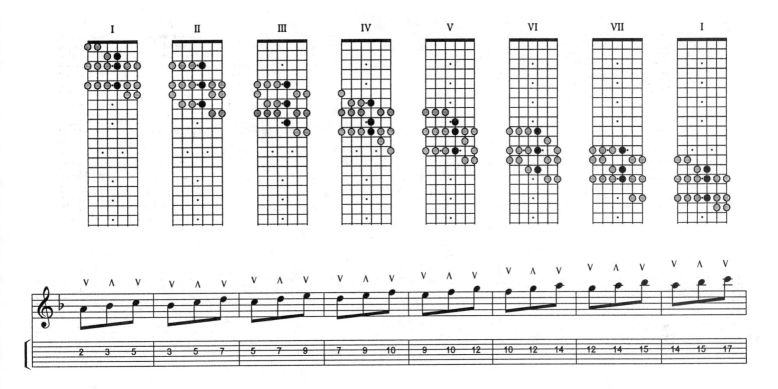

2nd String

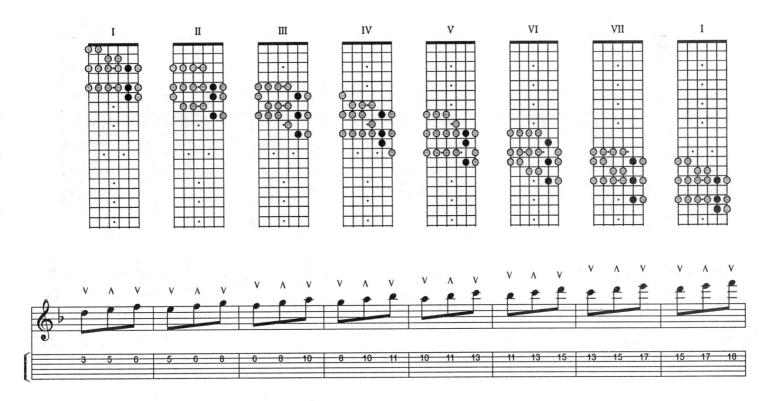

1st String

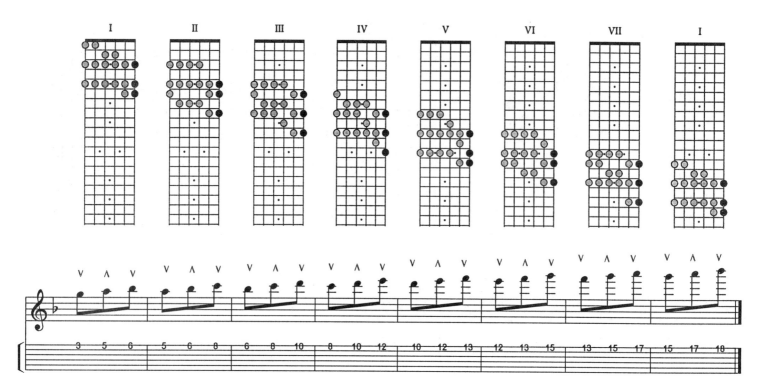

TWO STRING EXERCISES

This next bunch are two string exercises. They're also designed to develop inner pattern changing using two strings. After you learn these you can then do them in groups of five (quintuplets) or groups of six (sextuplets).

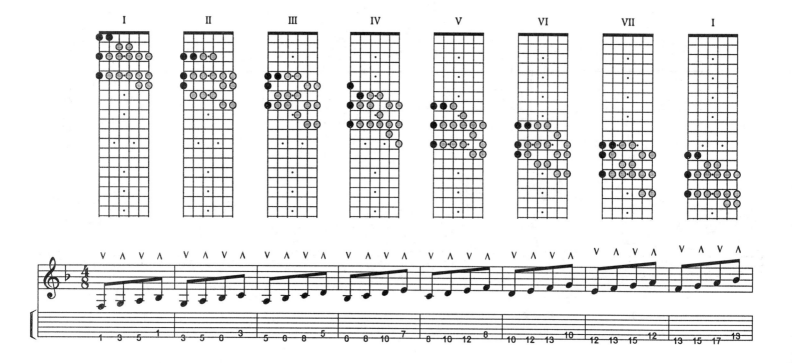

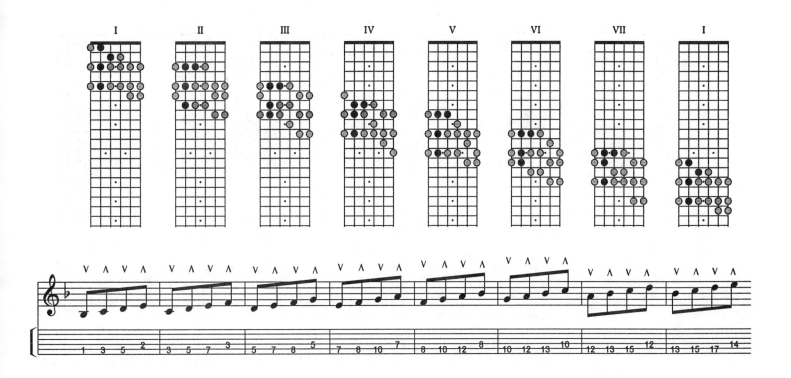

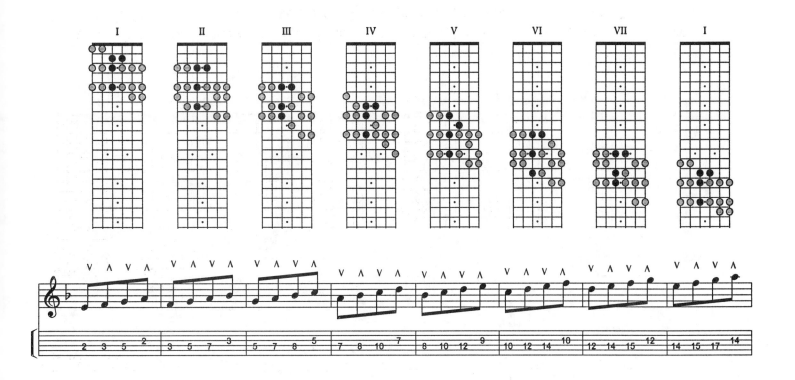

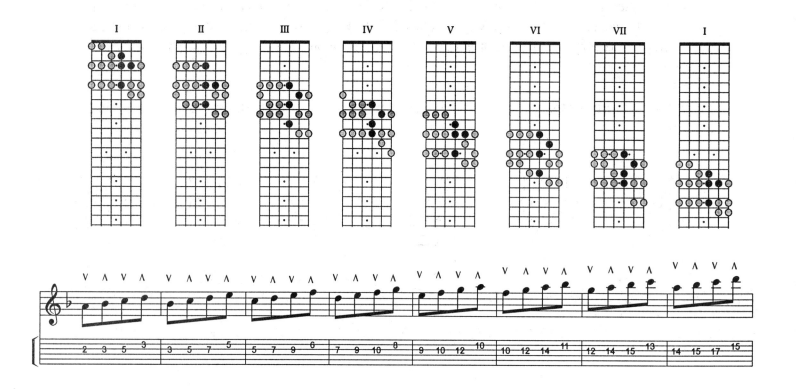

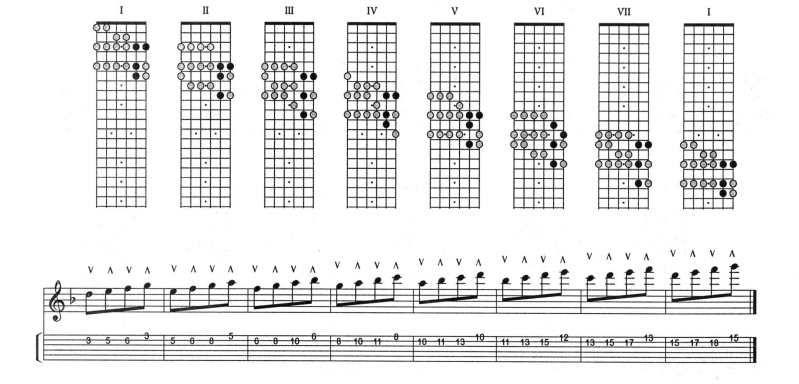

SCALE TONE THIRDS IN F MAJOR (ascending)

The next exercise is scale tone thirds. The reason it is called scale tone thirds is that you are using every other note of the scale, in this case the Major scale in F. By doing so some of the thirds are minor thirds as well as major thirds. If you you used straight major thirds the whole time you would be using the whole-tone scale.

The picking pattern for this one remains a constant down, up, down, up, down, up, etc. even when descending

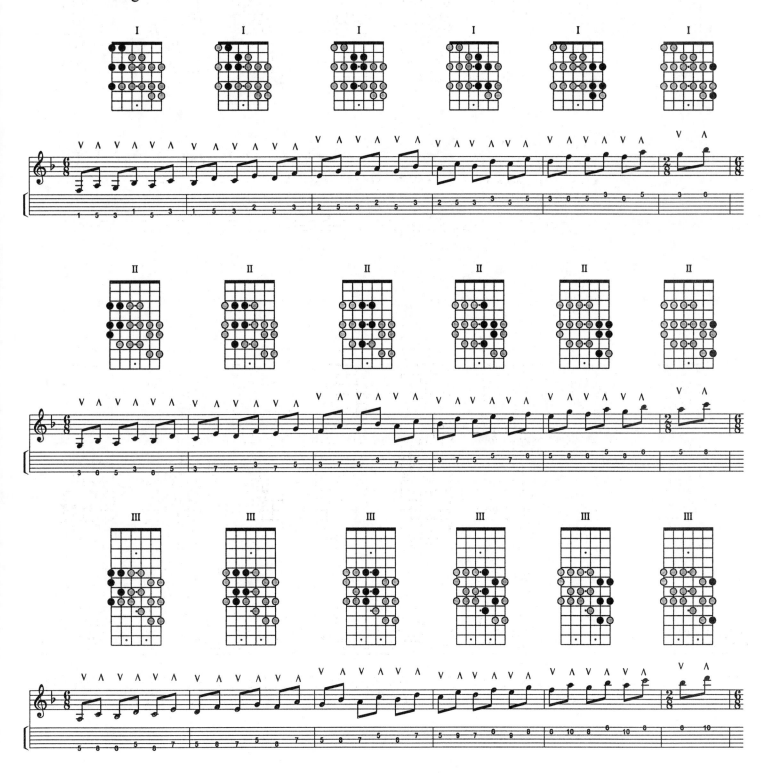

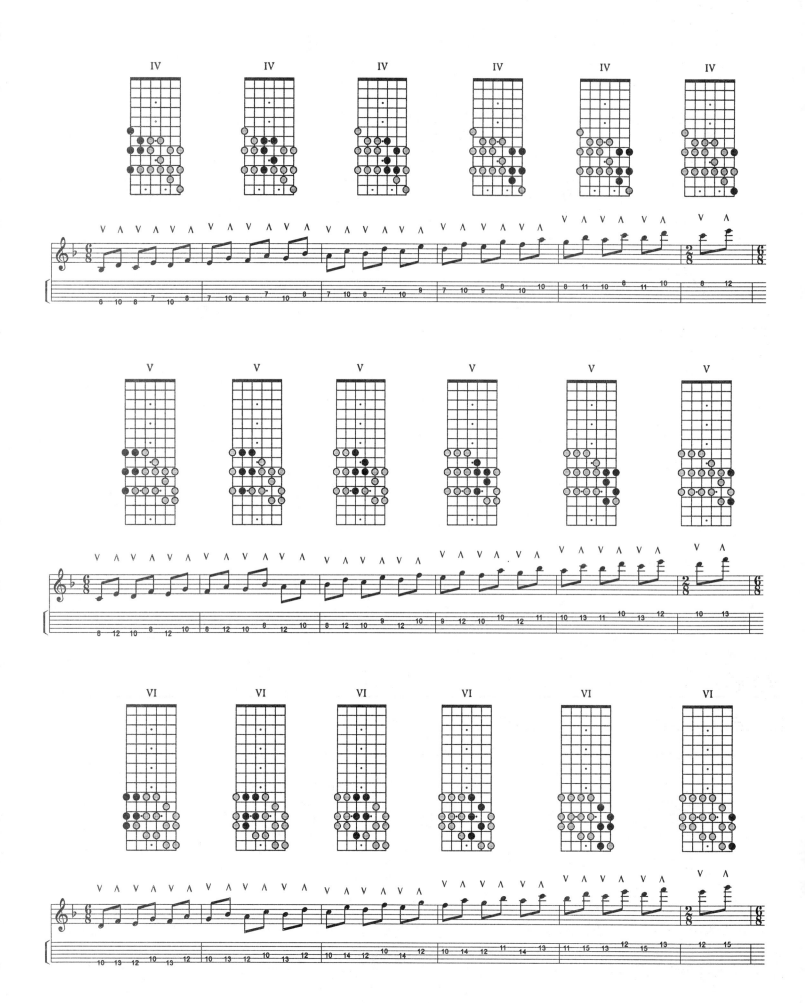

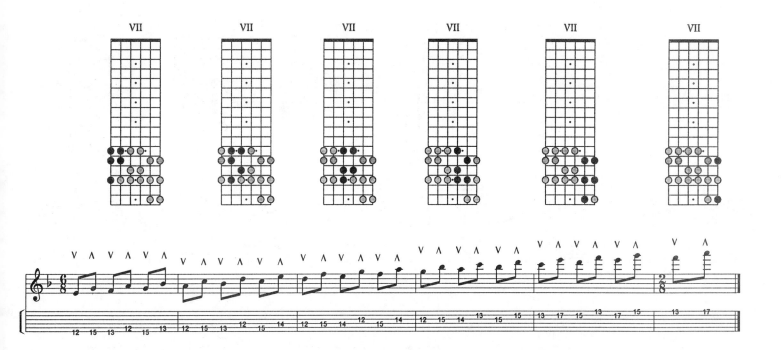

SCALE TONE THIRDS IN F MAJOR (descending)

Now we learn the same thing descending. The picking pattern to descend is also down, up, down, up, down, up etc.

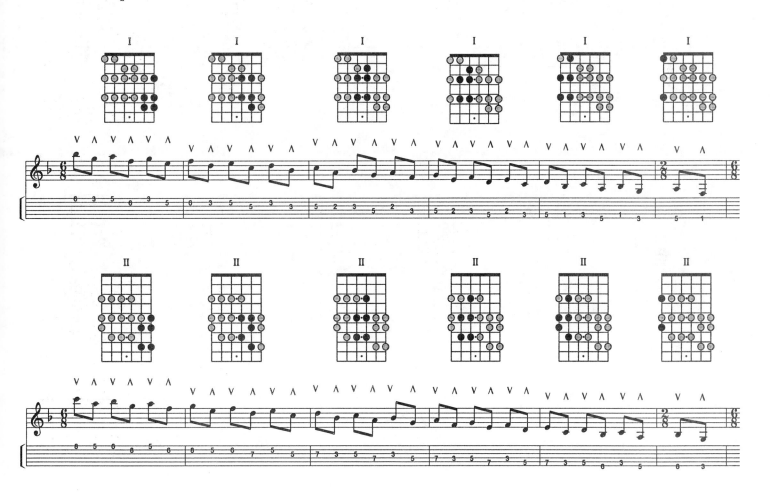

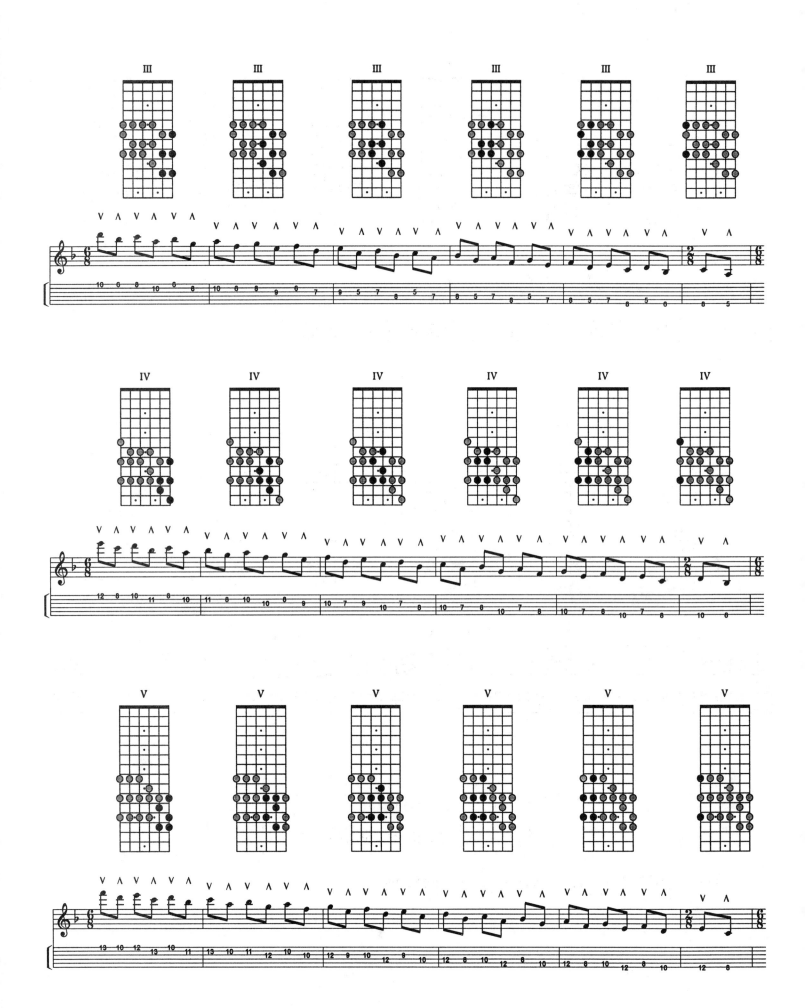

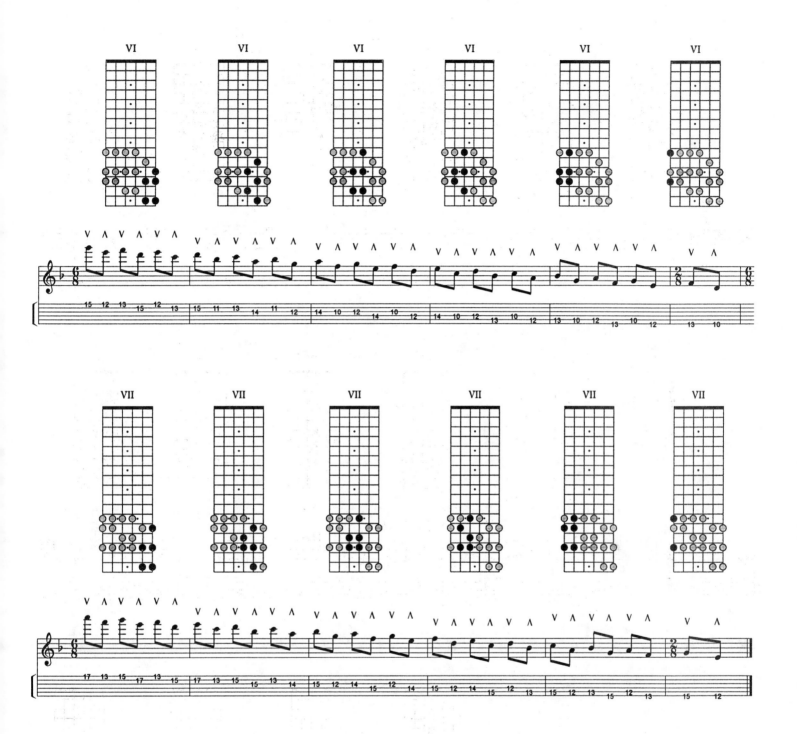

SCALE TONE THIRDS IN F MAJOR
(ascending & descending)

Now we put the two together ascending and descending.

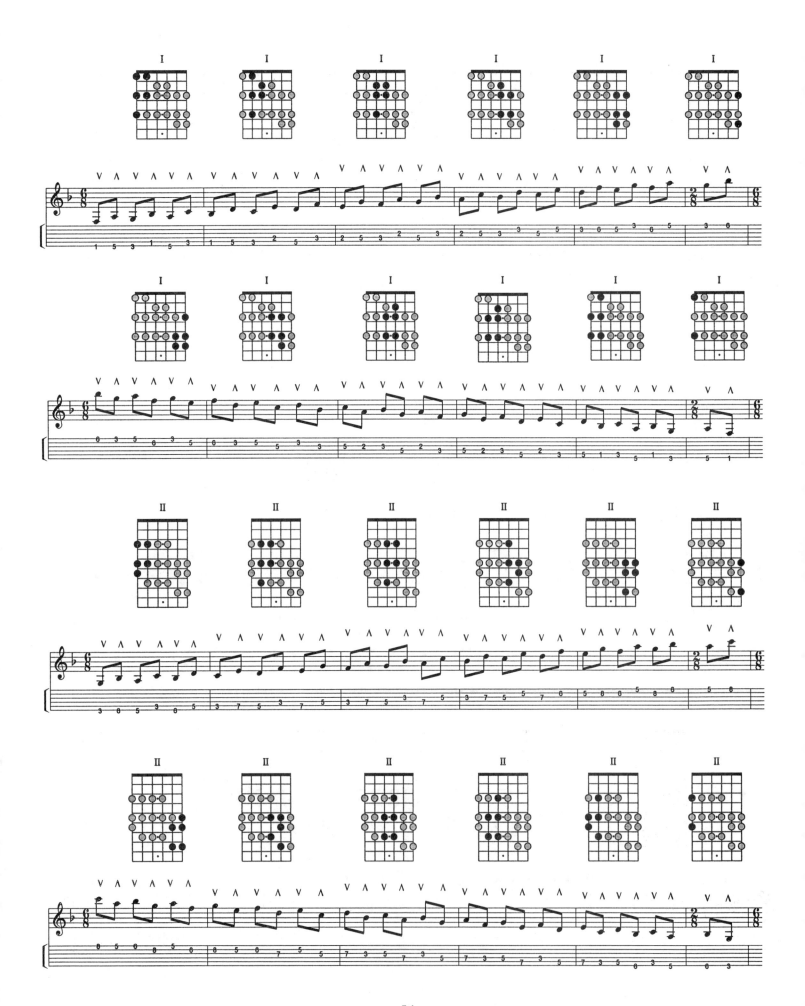

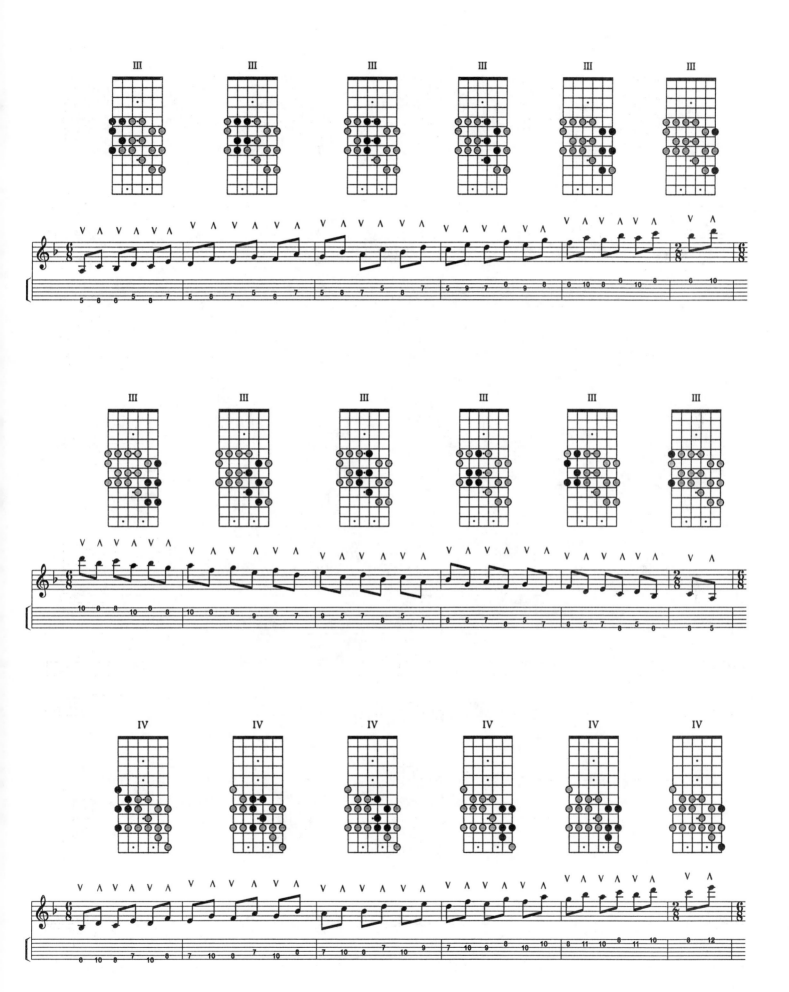

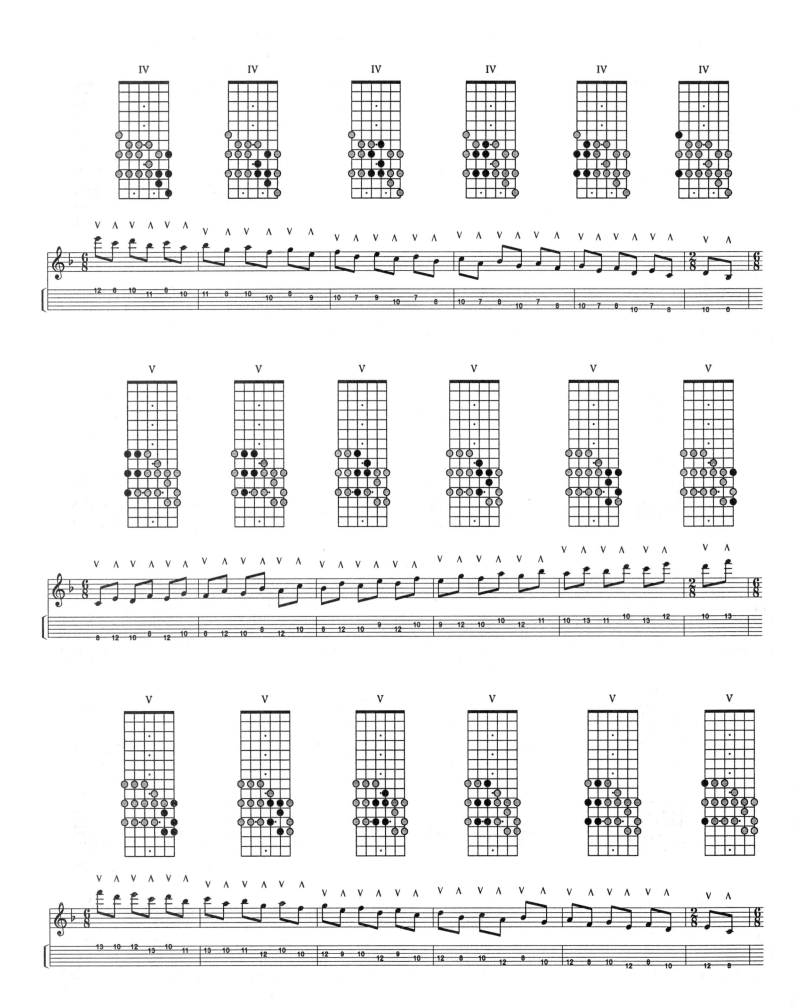

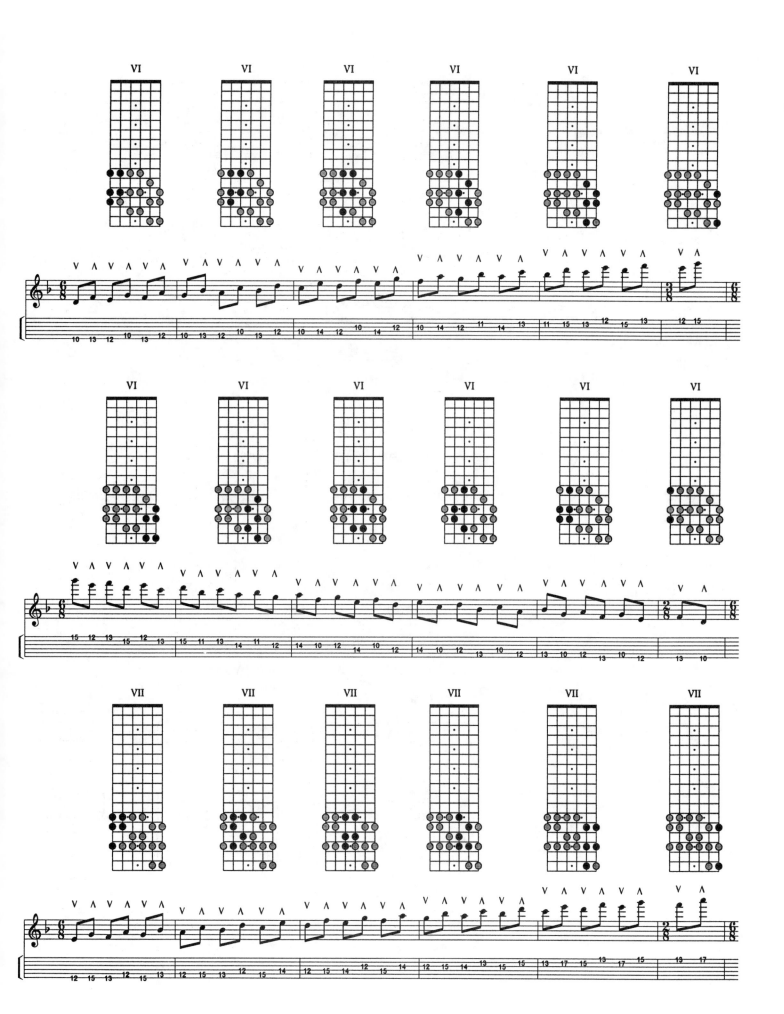

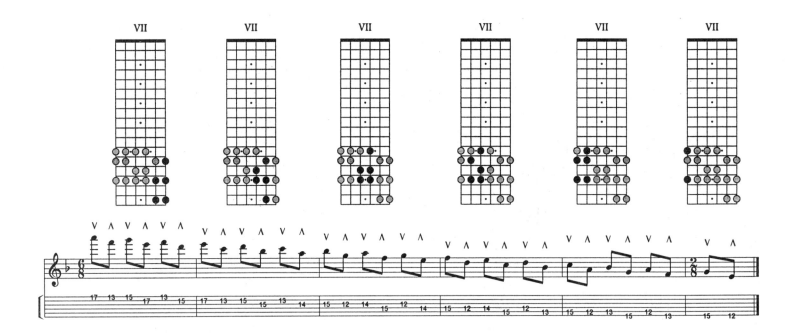

SCALE TONE THIRDS IN F MAJOR
(ascending & descending - alternating)

Now we ascend and descend while alternating the patterns. The picking pattern down, up, down, up remains the same.

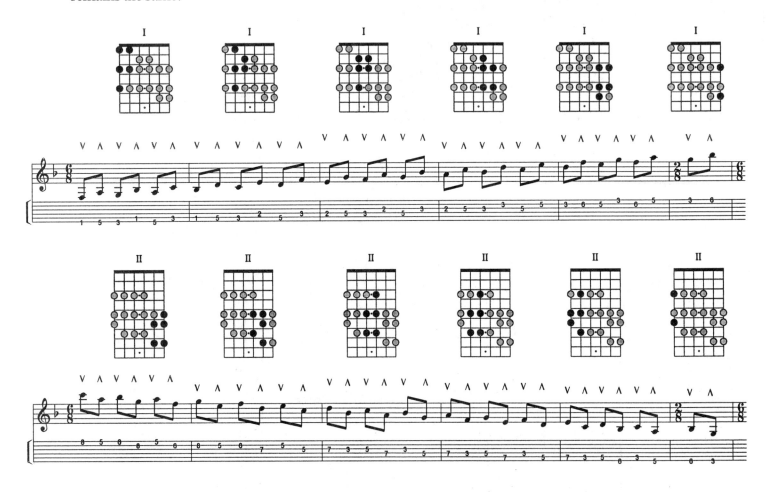

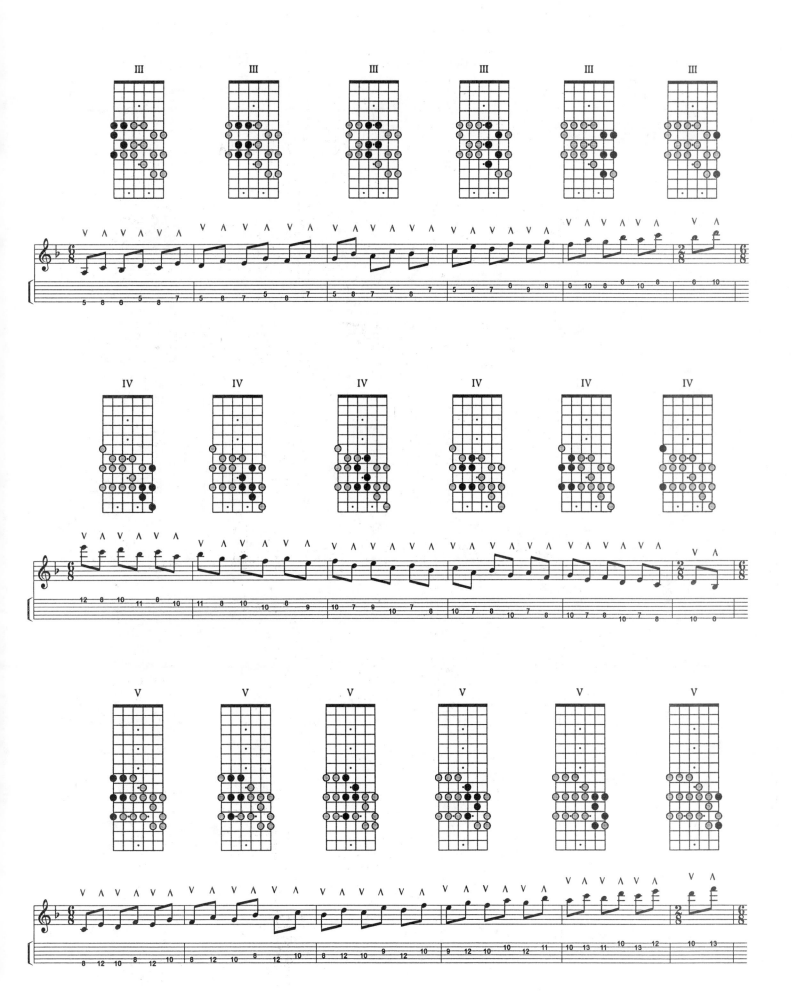

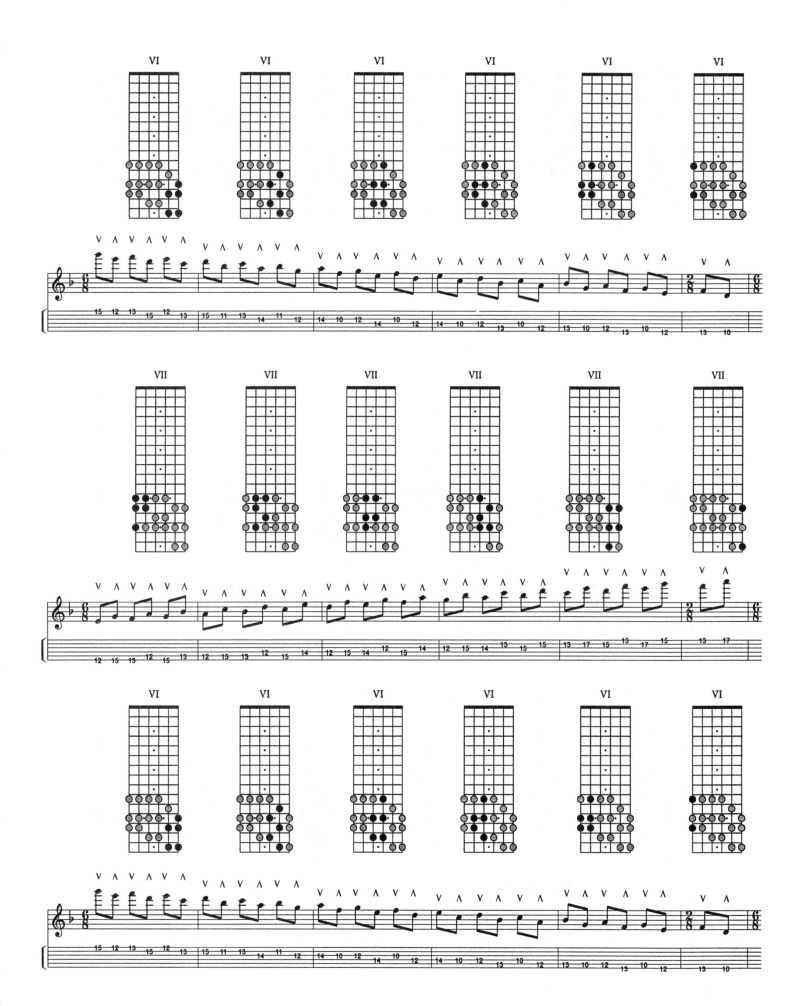

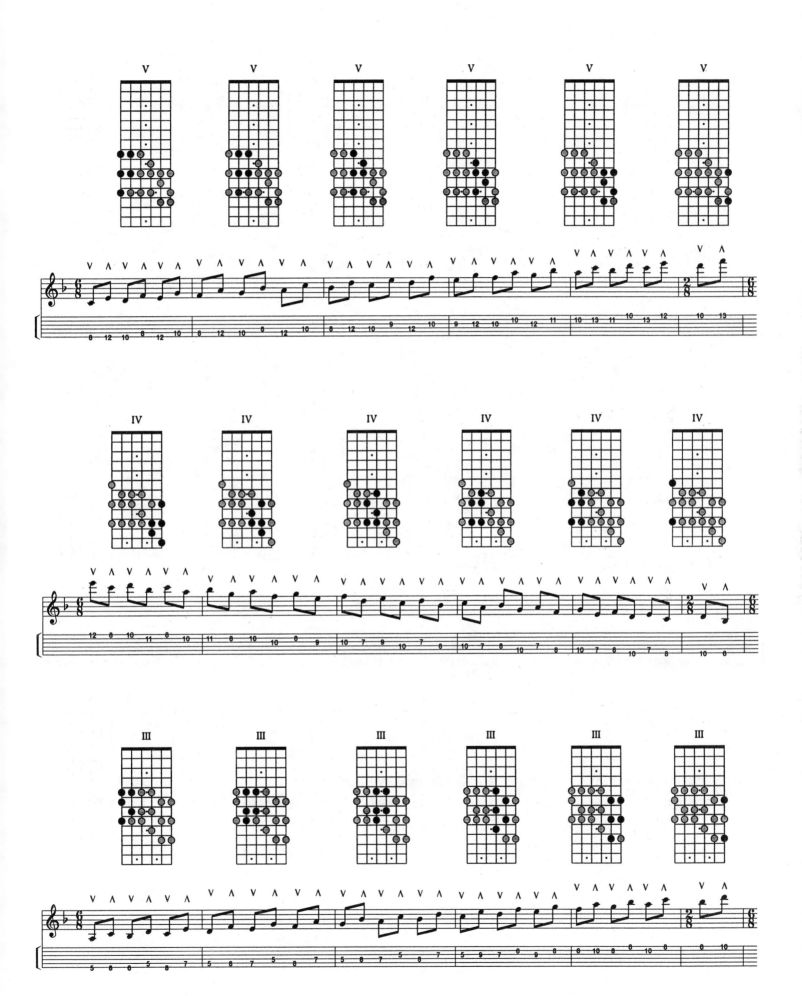

61

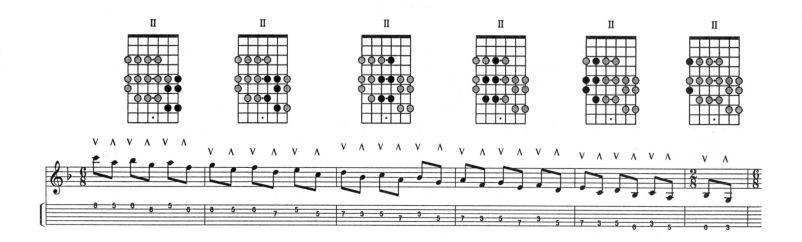

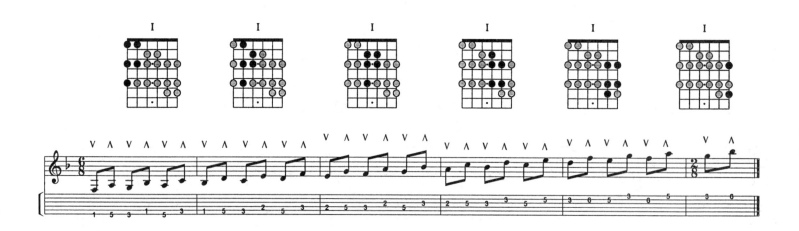

The following pages show the patterns in all the other keys. Every exercise you have learned in F will work in all the keys. Now you will see what I was talking about earlier on page 3 that the other keys don't start with pattern 1.

F# MAJOR

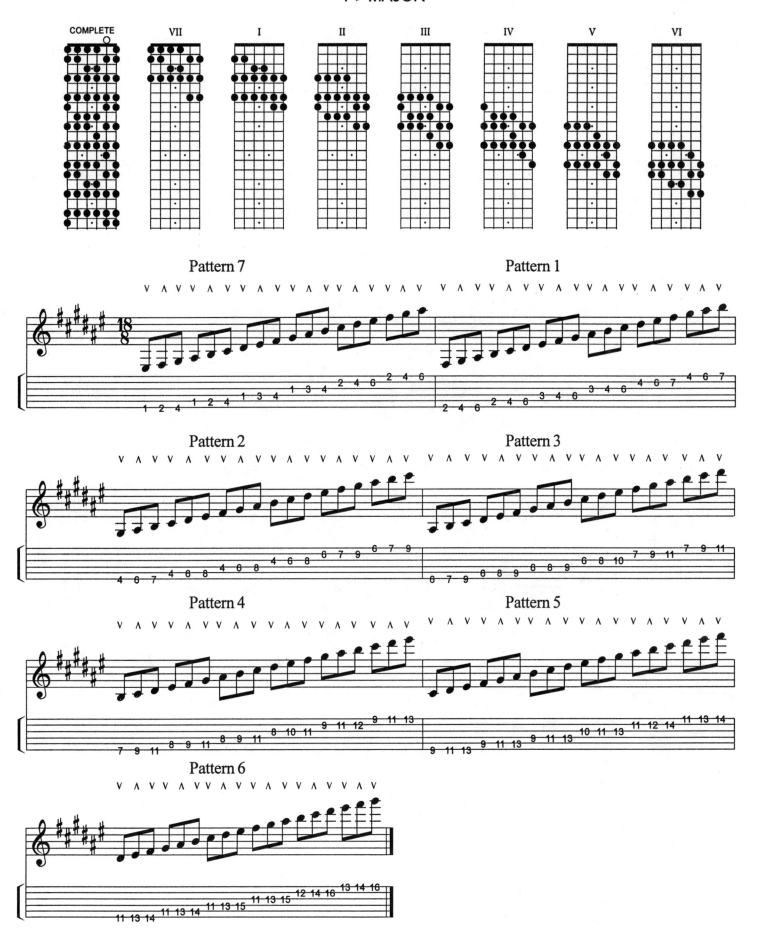

G♭ MAJOR

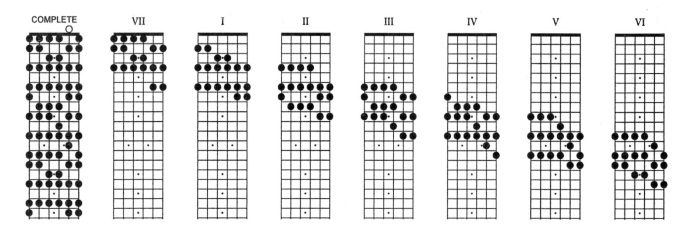

Pattern 7   Pattern 1

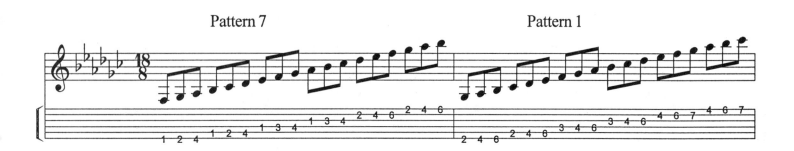

Pattern 2   Pattern 3

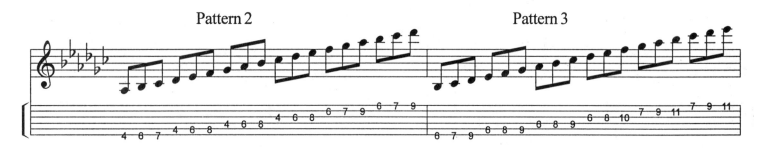

Pattern 4   Pattern 5

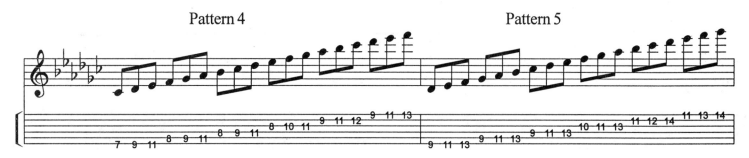

Pattern 6

G♭ Major is the same as F♯ Major. It is included here for the sake of studying the notation.

G MAJOR

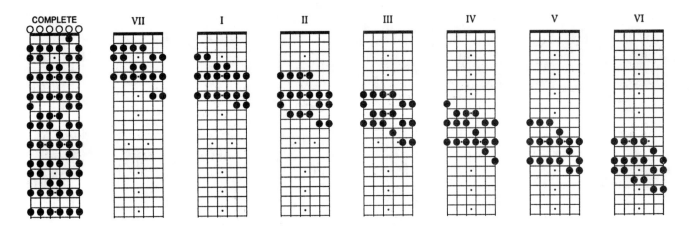

Pattern 7   Pattern 1

Pattern 2   Pattern 3

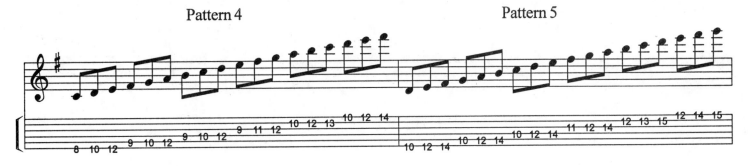

Pattern 4   Pattern 5

Pattern 6

A♭ MAJOR

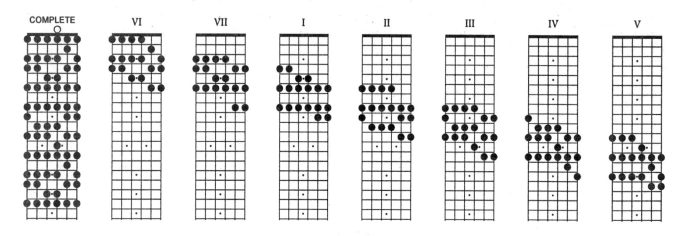

Pattern 6
Pattern 7

Pattern 1
Pattern 2

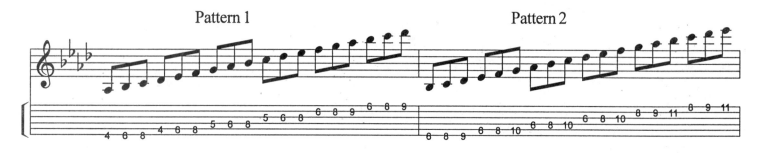

Pattern 3
Pattern 4

Pattern 5

A MAJOR

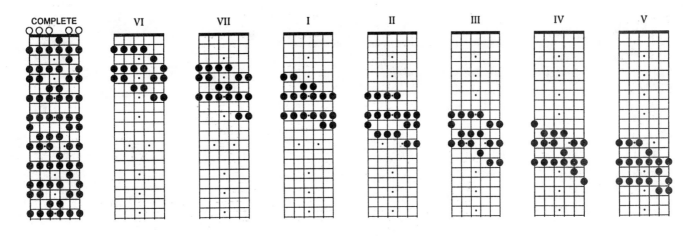

Pattern 6

Pattern 7

Pattern 1

Pattern 2

Pattern 3

Pattern 4

Pattern 5

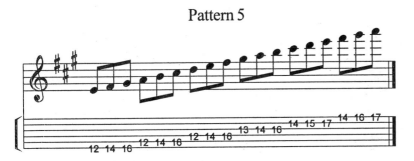

Bb MAJOR

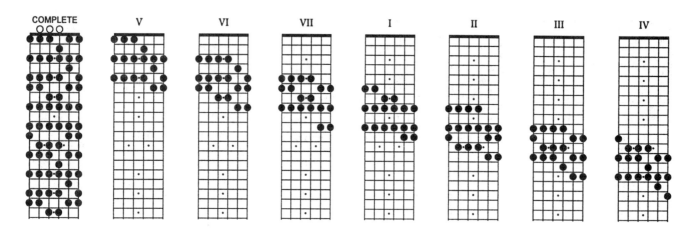

Pattern 5   Pattern 6

Pattern 7   Pattern 1

Pattern 2   Pattern 3

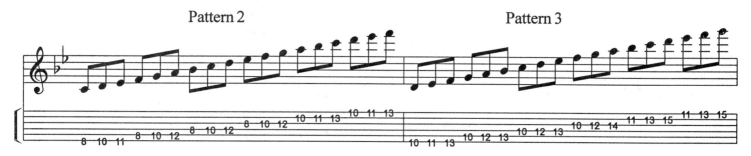

Pattern 4

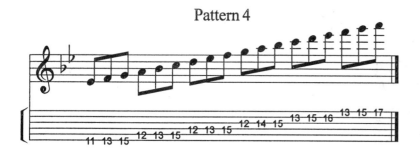

B MAJOR

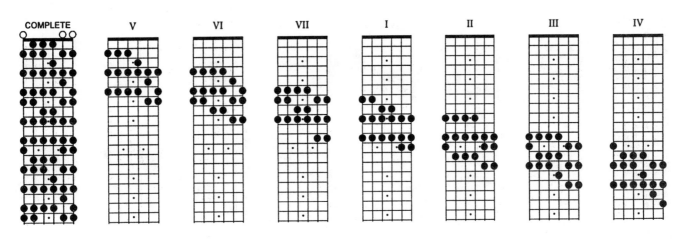

Pattern 5
Pattern 6

Pattern 7
Pattern 1

Pattern 2
Pattern 3

Pattern 4

C♭ MAJOR

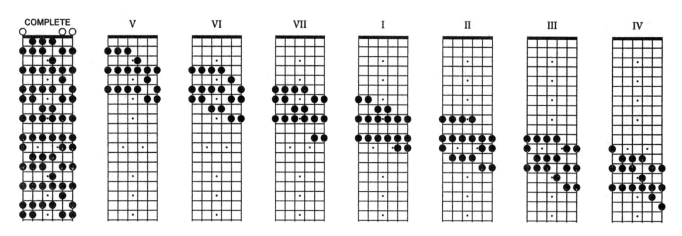

Pattern 5
Pattern 6

Pattern 7
Pattern 1

Pattern 2
Pattern 3

Pattern 4

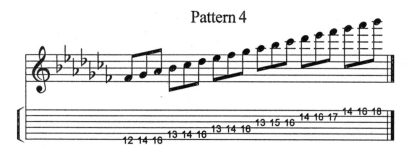

C♭ Major is the same as B Major. It is included here for the sake of studying the notation.

C MAJOR

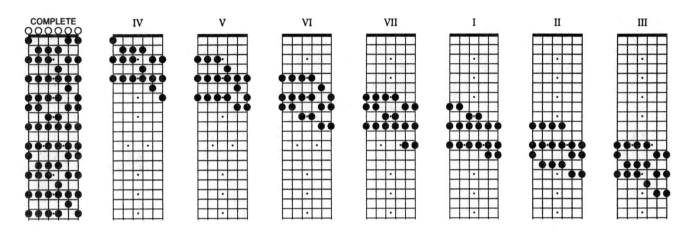

Pattern 4   Pattern 5

Pattern 6   Pattern 7

Pattern 1   Pattern 2

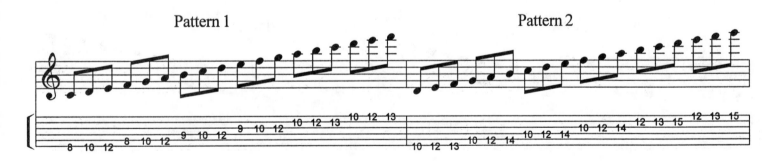

Pattern 3

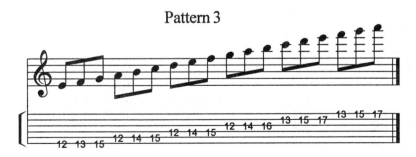

C♯ MAJOR

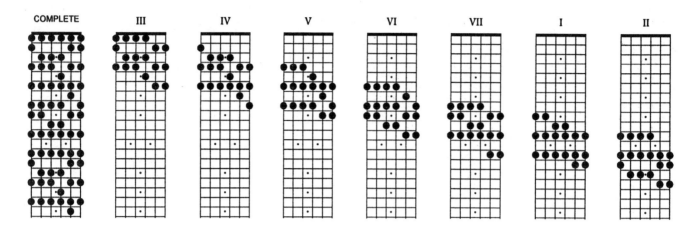

Pattern 3　　　　　　　　　　　　　　Pattern 4

Pattern 5　　　　　　　　　　　　　　Pattern 6

Pattern 7　　　　　　　　　　　　　　Pattern 1

Pattern 2

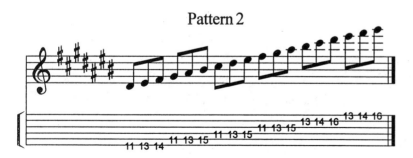

Db MAJOR

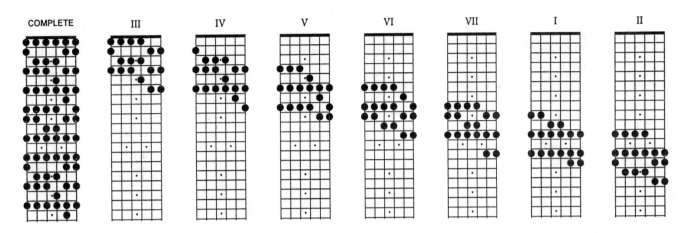

COMPLETE   III   IV   V   VI   VII   I   II

Pattern 3   Pattern 4

Pattern 5   Pattern 6

Pattern 7   Pattern 1

Pattern 2

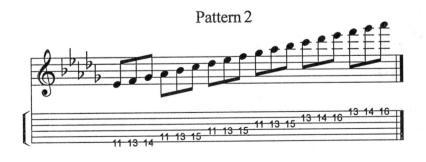

Db Major is the same as C# Major. It is
included here for the sake of studying the
notation.

D MAJOR

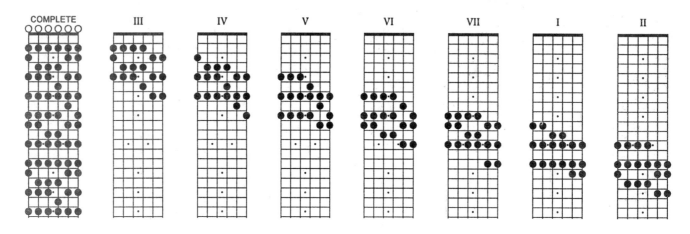

Pattern 3　　　　　　　　　　　　　　　Pattern 4

Pattern 5　　　　　　　　　　　　　　　Pattern 6

Pattern 7　　　　　　　　　　　　　　　Pattern 1

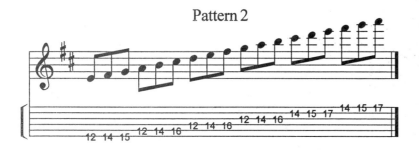

Pattern 2

E♭ MAJOR

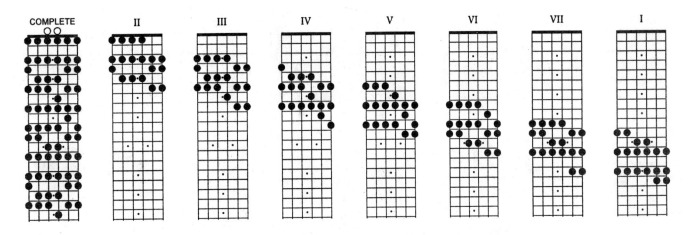

Pattern 2   Pattern 3

Pattern 4   Pattern 5

Pattern 6   Pattern 7

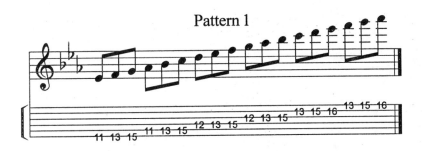

Pattern 1

75

E MAJOR

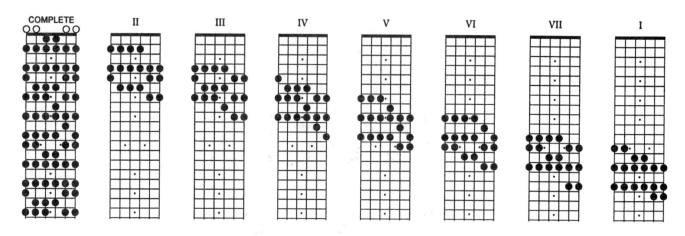

Pattern 2

Pattern 3

Pattern 4

Pattern 5

Pattern 6

Pattern 7

Pattern 1

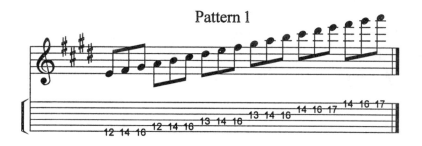

PART
TWO

MINOR PENTATONIC
EXERCISES

PRACTICING THE PENTATONICS

Next we learn how to practice the pentatonics. Most of the ground work as to how to practice these scales has been done when you learned the Major scales.

Just like the Major scale breakdown we do the same thing for the Minor Pentatonic. In figure 3 below, the fretboard on the left shows every note possible for the F Minor Pentatonic. The fretboards to the right of it break it down into patterns at various positions.

Below that the patterns are expanded to show what fingerings are used to play the patterns.

F MINOR PENTATONIC

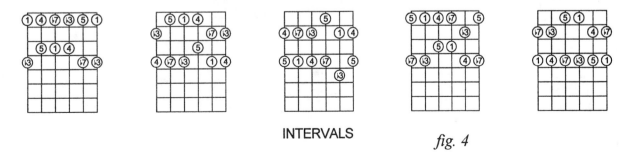

In figure 4 below are the intervals of the patterns of the pentatonic. Just as with the patterns of the Major scale, the intervallic relationship always remains constant even when the notes change after changing keys.

79

The notes for the Pentatonic patterns in F Minor are as follows:

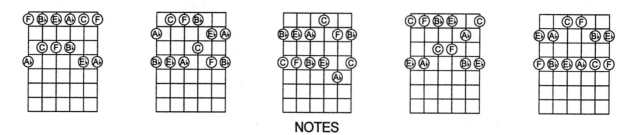

NOTES

The picking for the Pentatonic Patterns is quite easy. For the ascending from lowest to highest note of the pattern it is down, up, down, up etc. That is it. The same holds true for all five patterns.

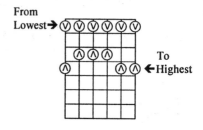

| I | II | III | IV | V |

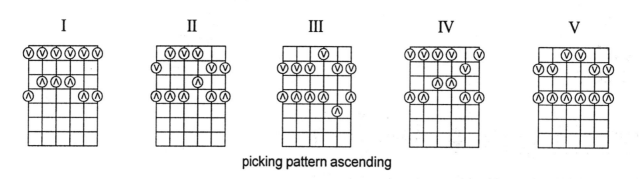

picking pattern ascending

F MINOR PENTATONIC (ascending)

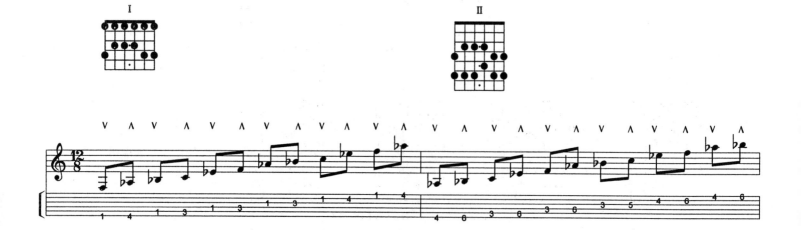

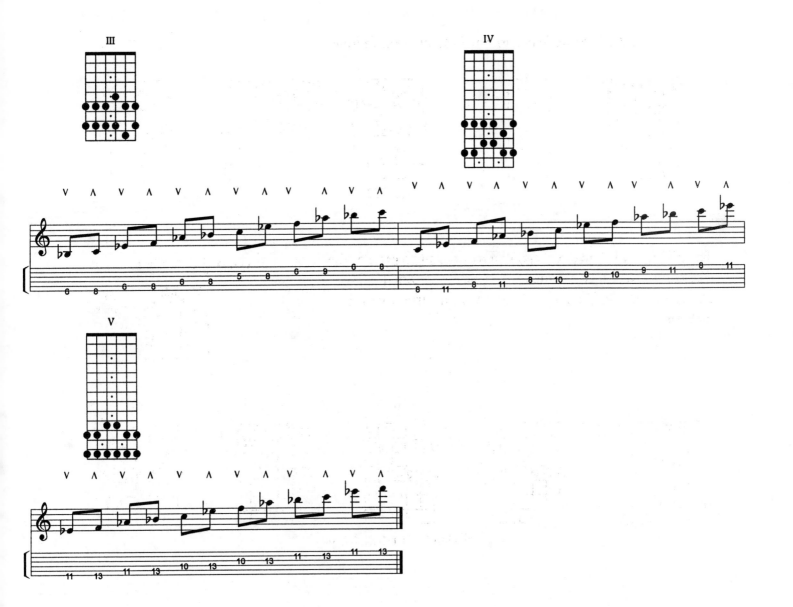

The picking pattern for descending the pentatonic is also down, up, down, up.

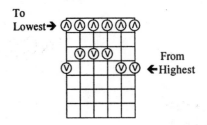

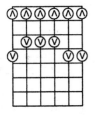 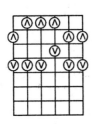 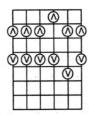 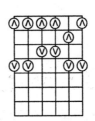 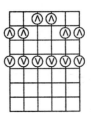

picking pattern descending

F MINOR PENTATONIC (descending)

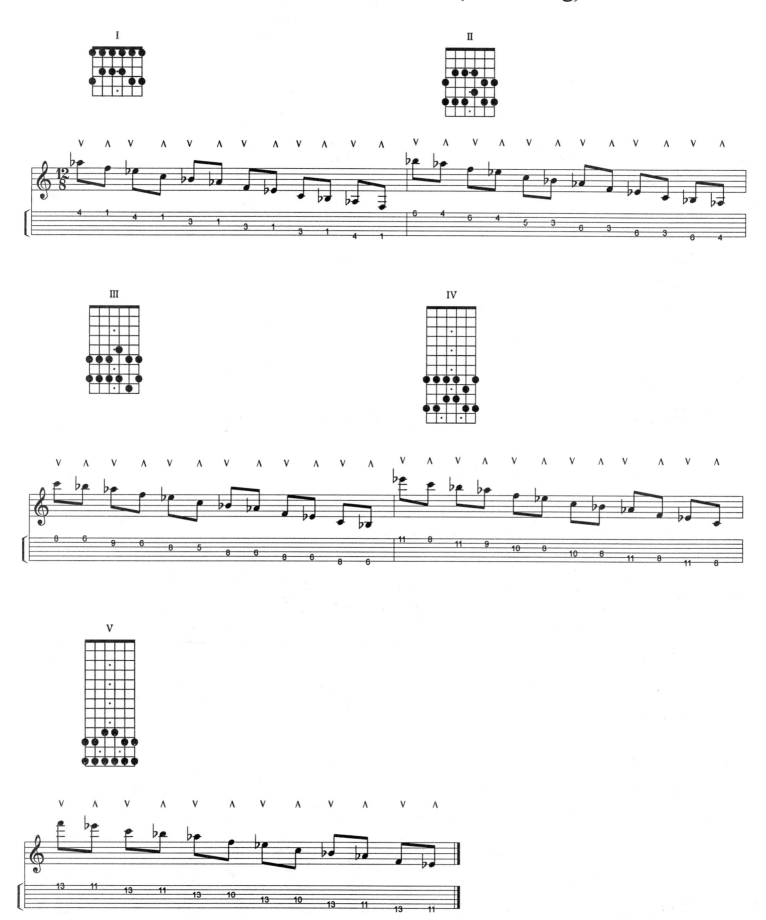

F MINOR PENTATONIC (ascending & descending)

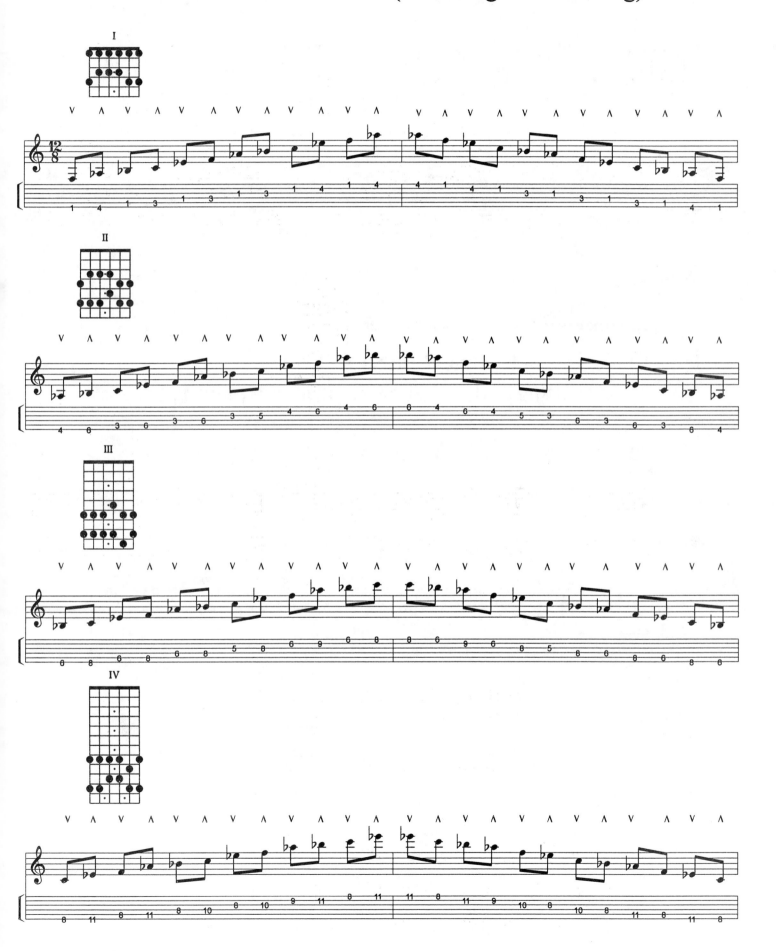

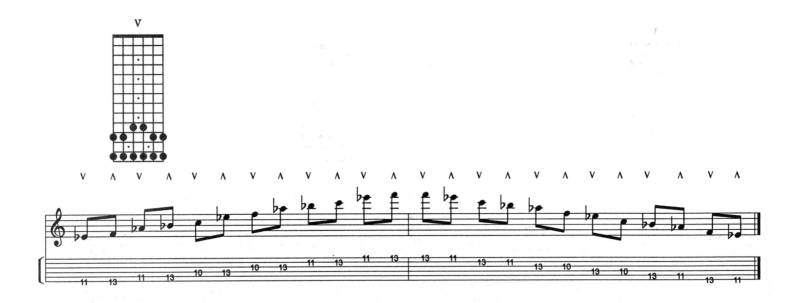

Now we ascend and descend while alternating the patterns.

F MINOR PENTATONIC
(ascending & descending - alternating patterns)

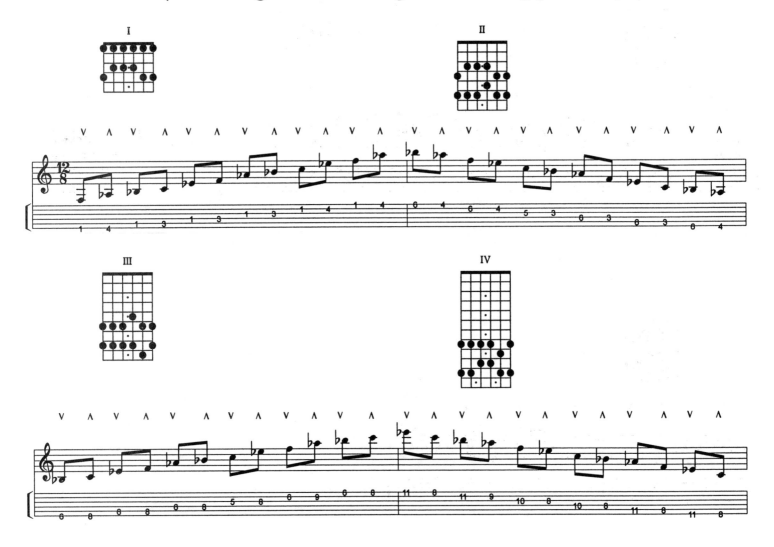

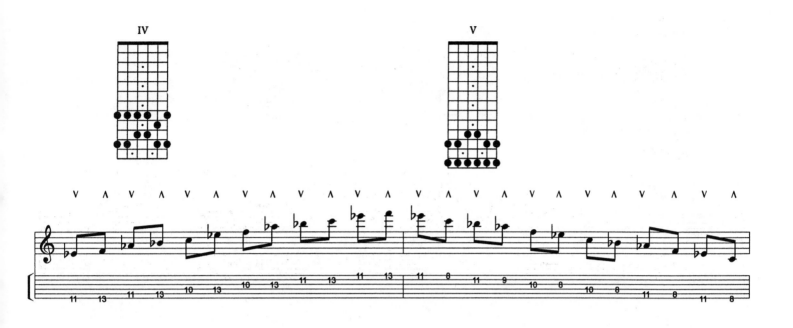

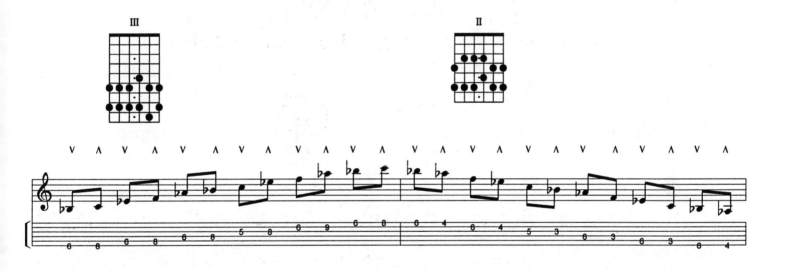

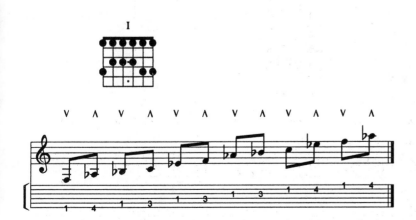

THREE NOTE COIL ASCENDING PICKING PATTERNS
(for pentatonic)

By now we should be familiar with the format used to present these exercises. Just go with the flow of the continuity. The picking is broken up for you using these two pattern groups. Each group represents the picking action taking place in a measure. The direction of the pick is listed with a ʌ for upstroke or a v for a down stroke. Once learned the same picking pattern applies to all of the pentatonic patterns.

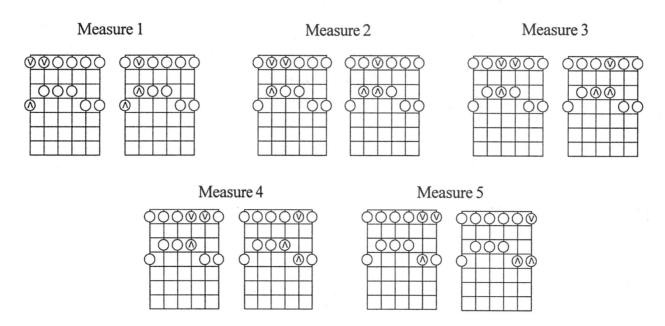

THREE NOTE COILS IN F MINOR PENTATONIC (ascending)

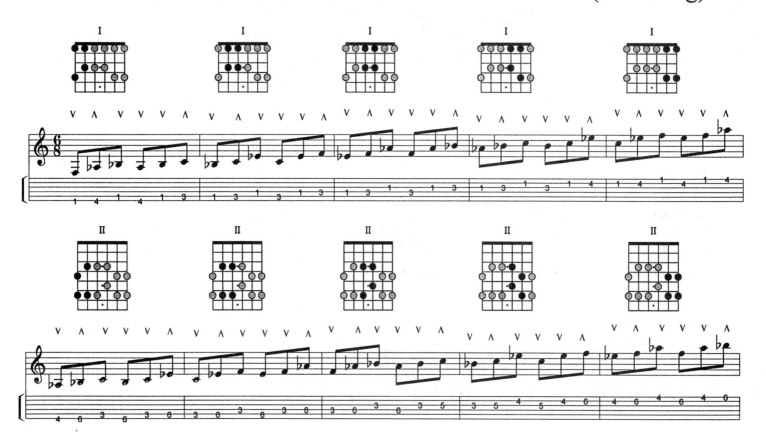

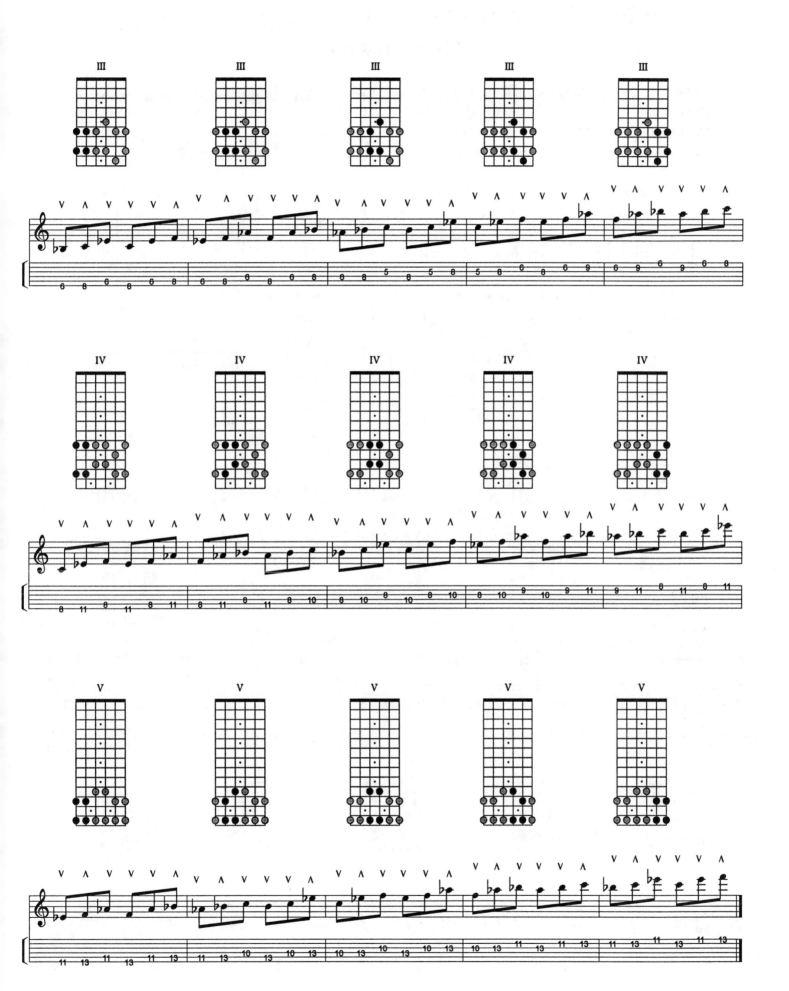

87

THREE NOTE COIL DESCENDING PICKING PATTERNS
(for pentatonic)

OK! Now we learn to descend the pentatonic three note coils. Learn the picking pattern and go to it.

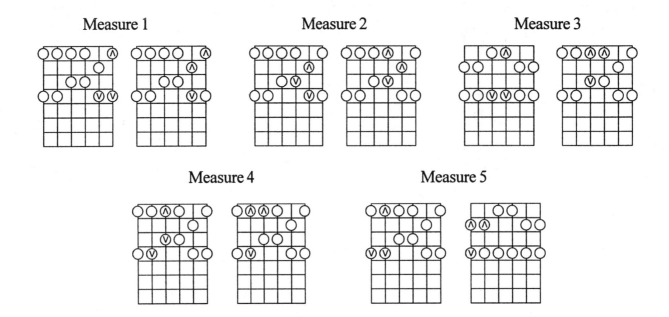

THREE NOTE COILS IN F MINOR PENTATONIC (descending)

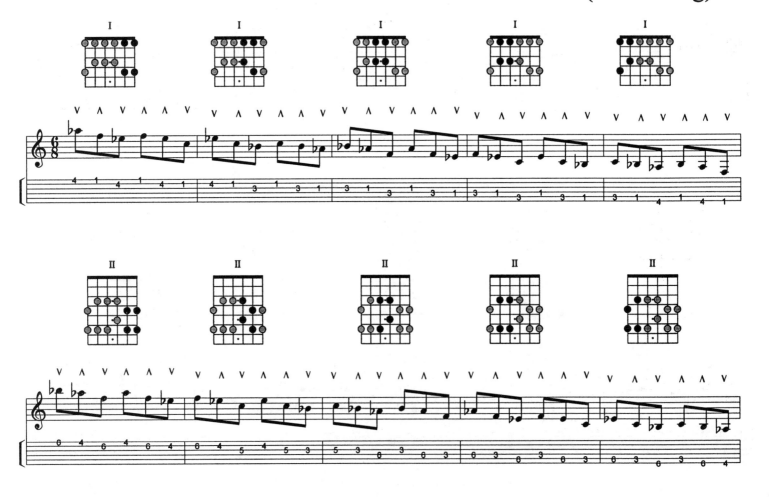

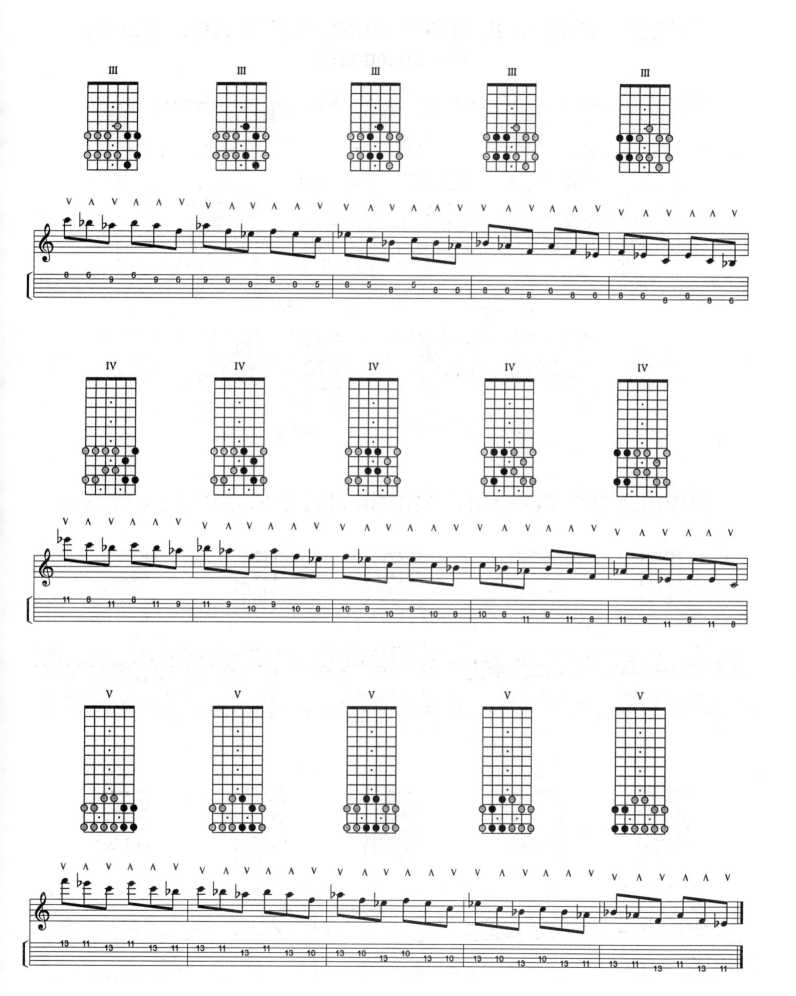

89

THREE NOTE COILS IN F MINOR PENTATONIC
(ascending & descending)

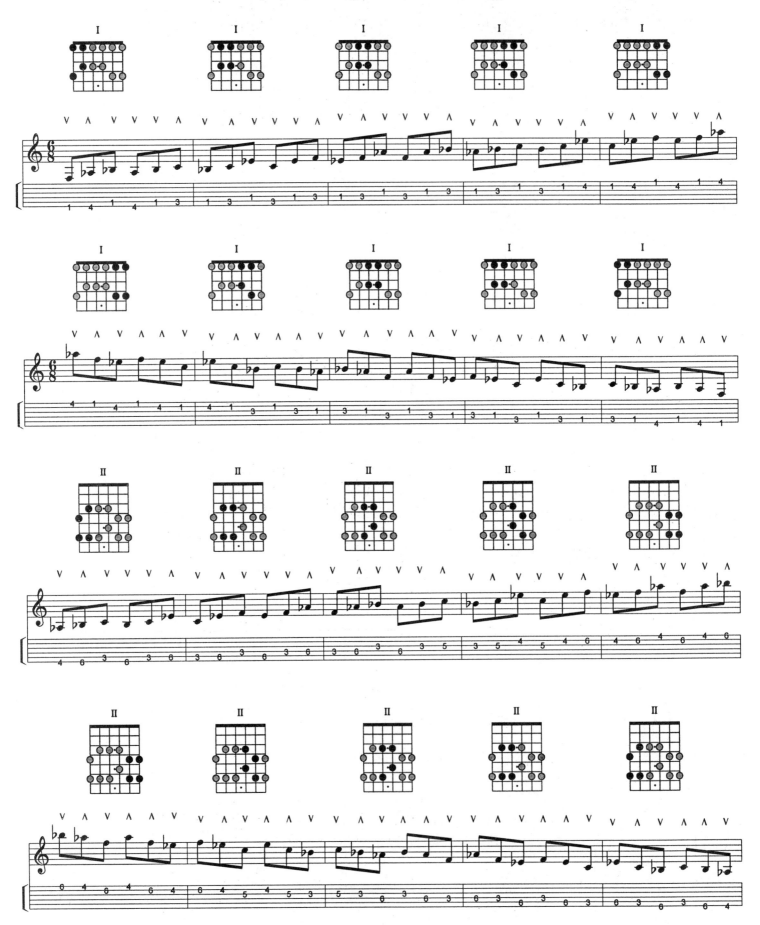

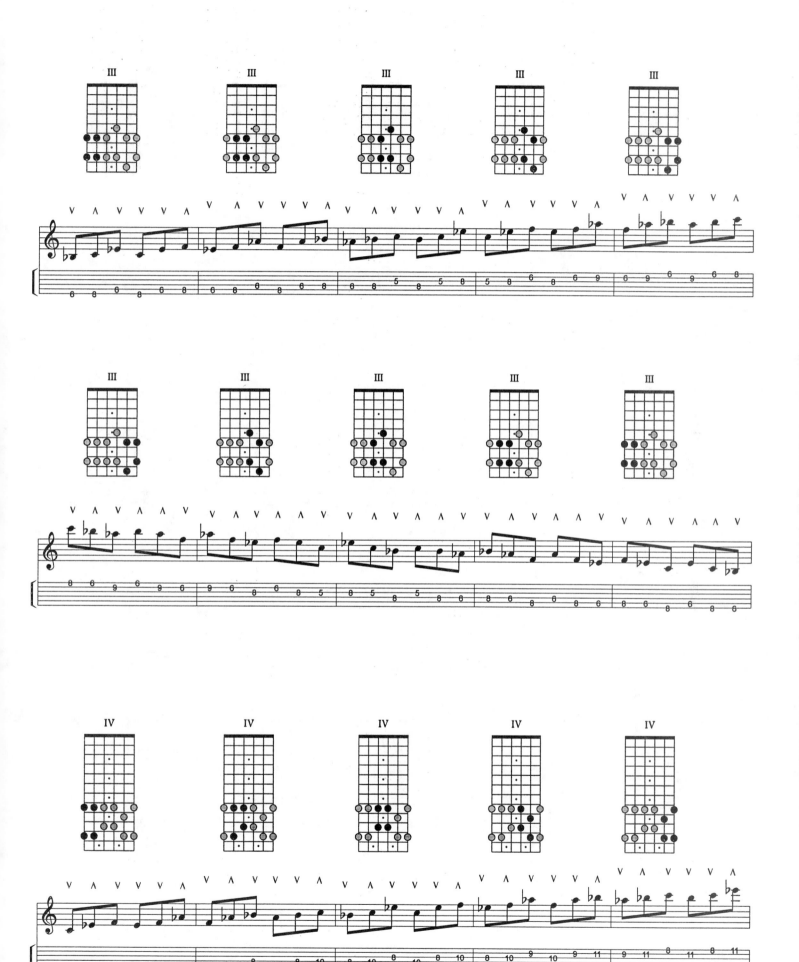

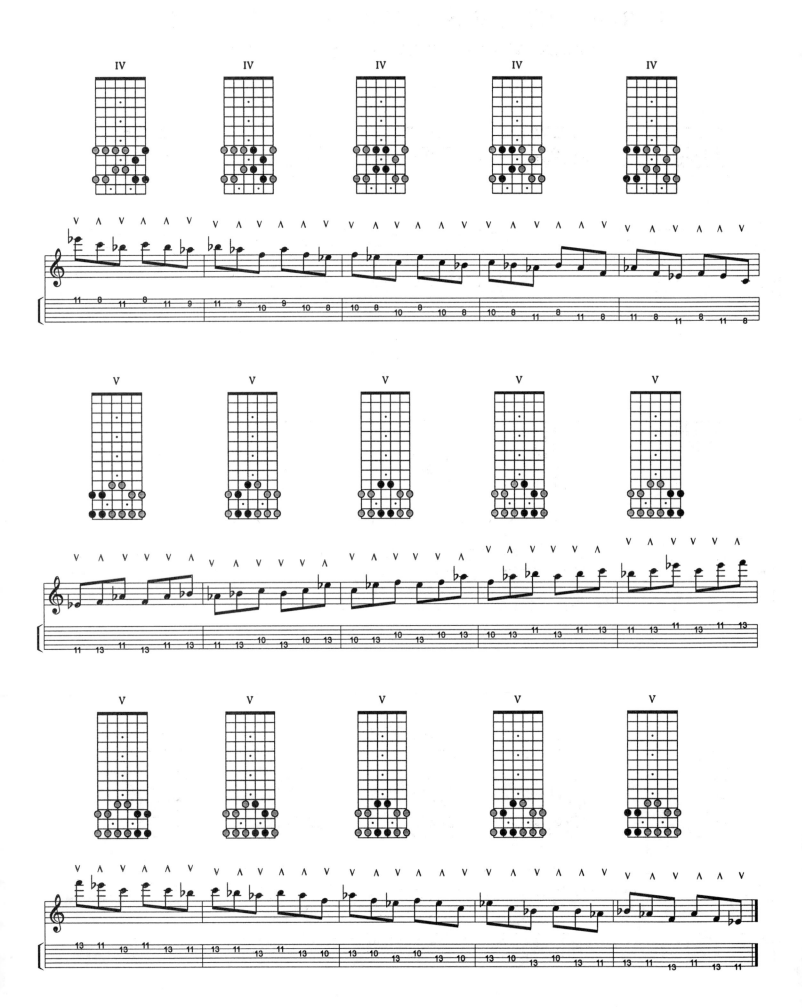

THREE NOTE COILS IN F MINOR PENTATONIC
(ascending & descending - alternating patterns)

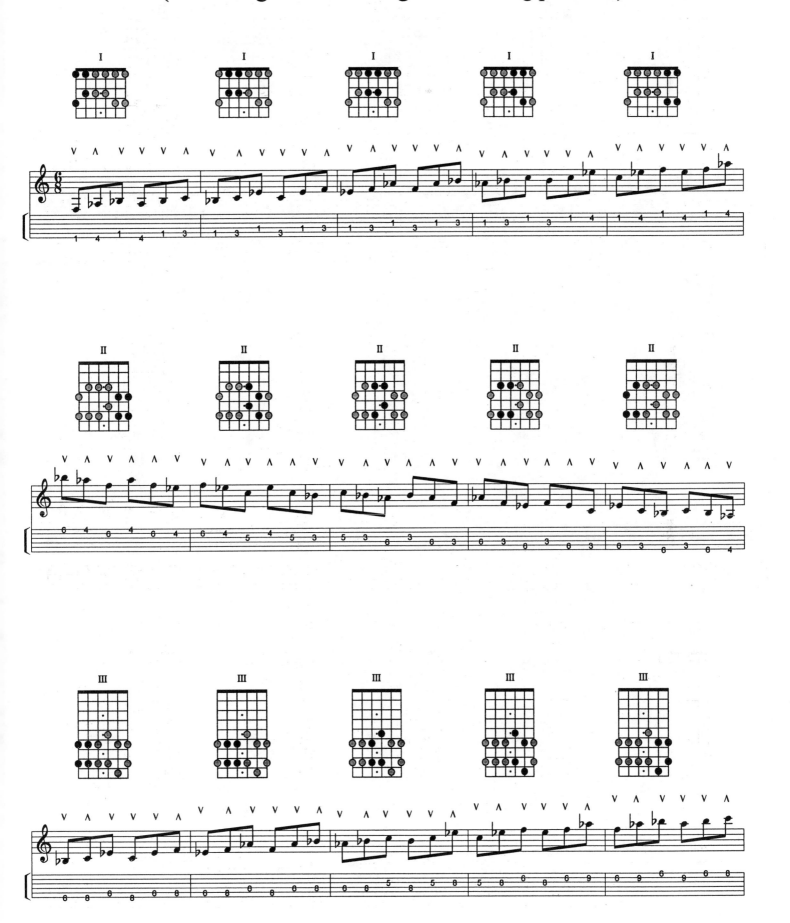

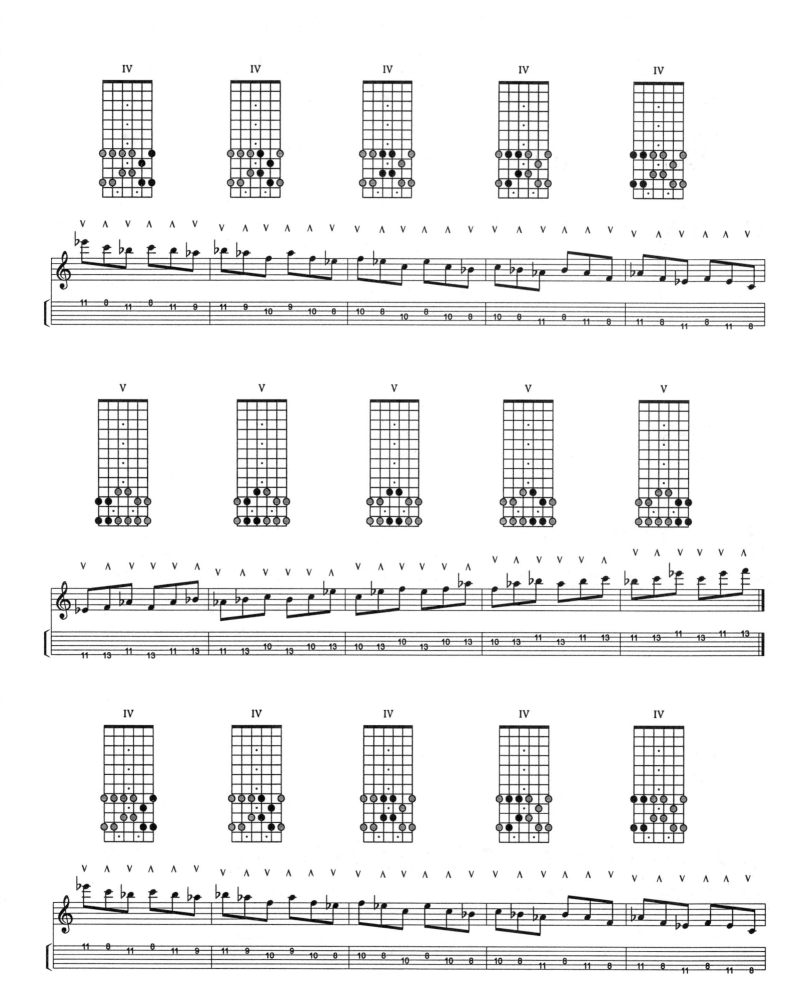

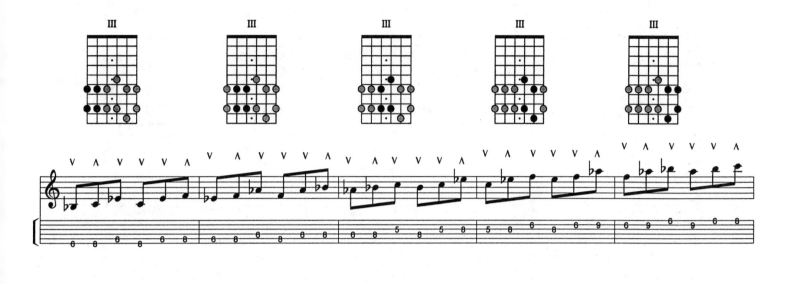

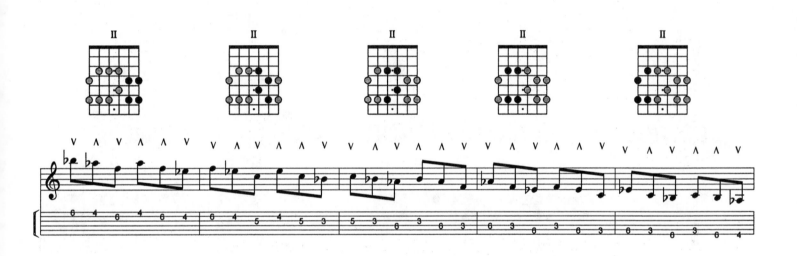

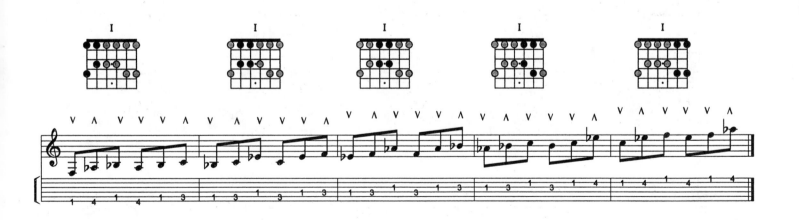

FOUR NOTE COIL ASCENDING PICKING PATTERNS
(for pentatonic)

Now we do the four note coils for the Minor pentatonic. There's the picking patterns now go for it.

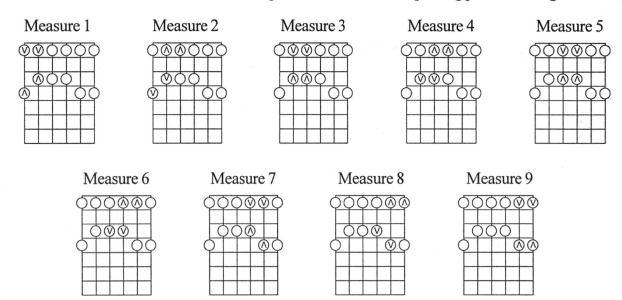

FOUR NOTE COILS IN F MINOR PENTATONIC (ascending)

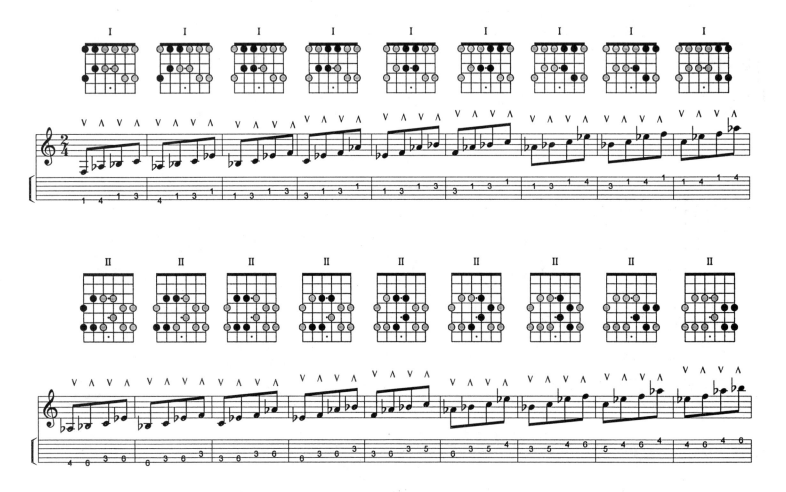

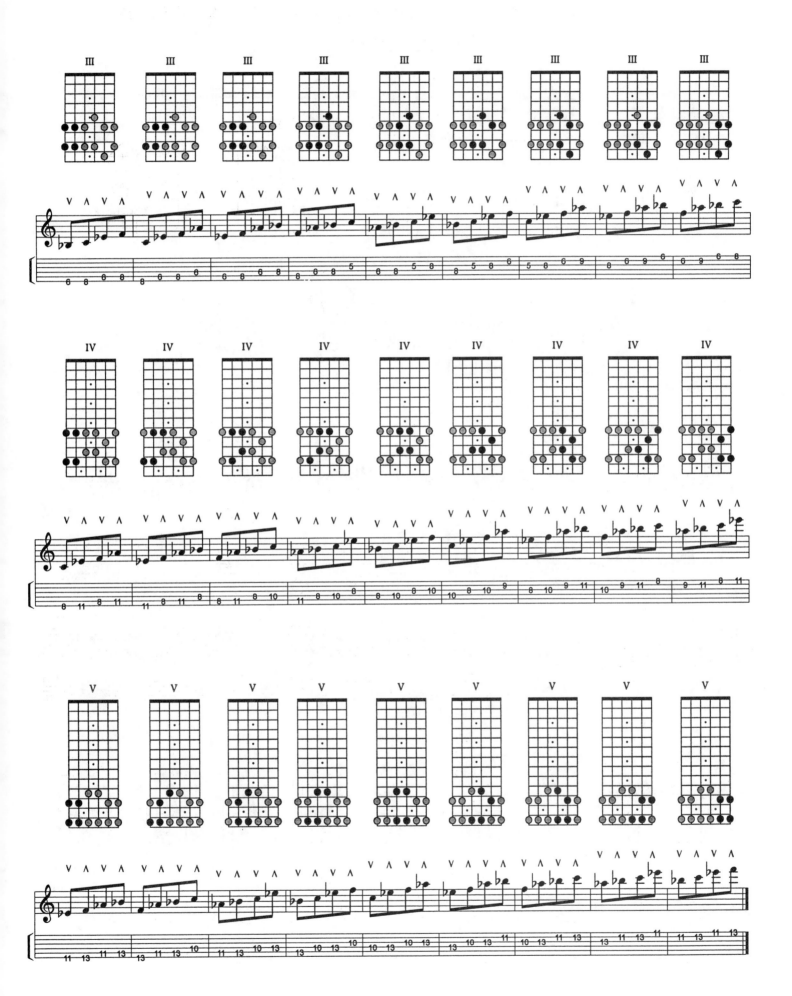

FOUR NOTE COIL DECENDING PICKING PATTERNS
(for pentatonic)

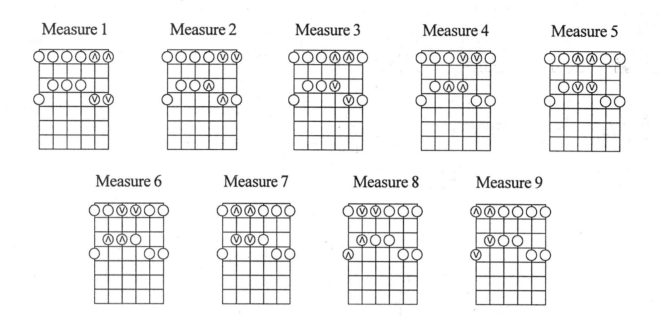

FOUR NOTE COILS IN F MINOR PENTATONIC (descending)

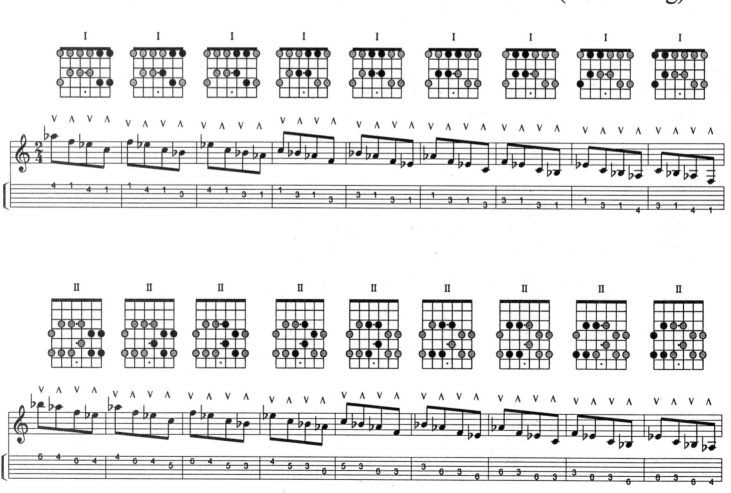

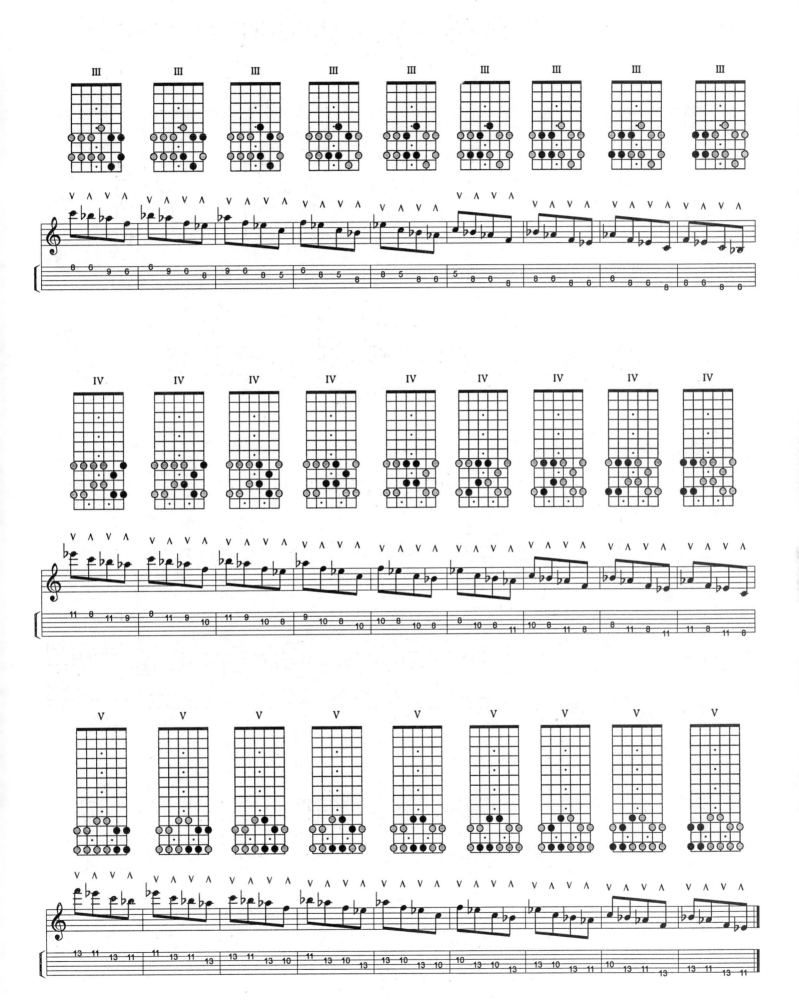

FOUR NOTE COILS IN F MINOR PENTATONIC
(ascending & descending)

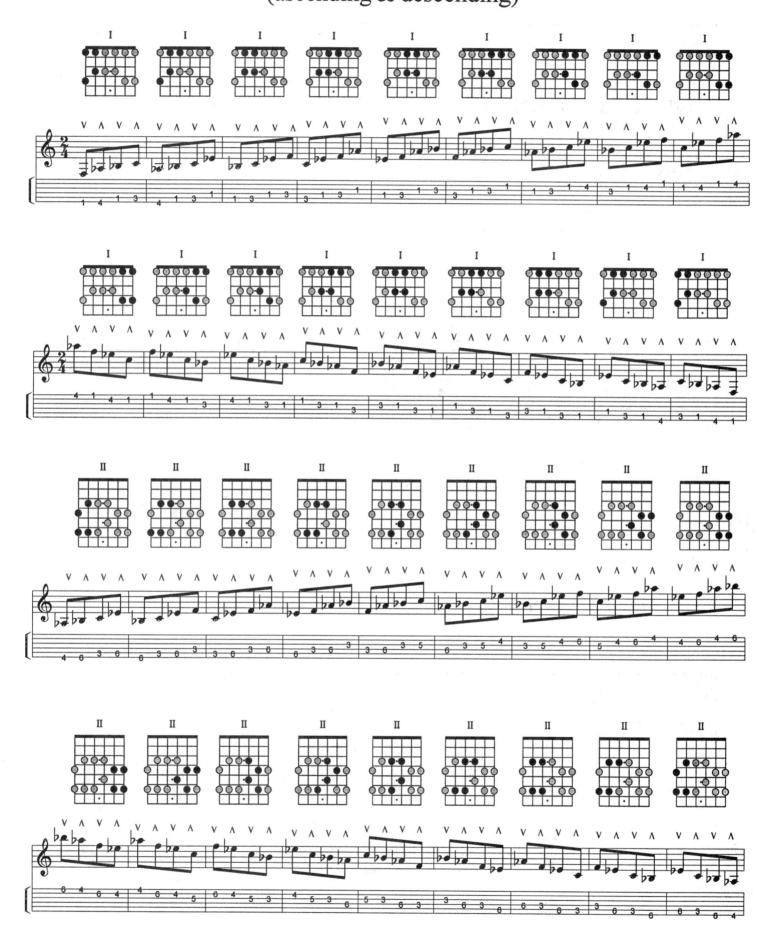

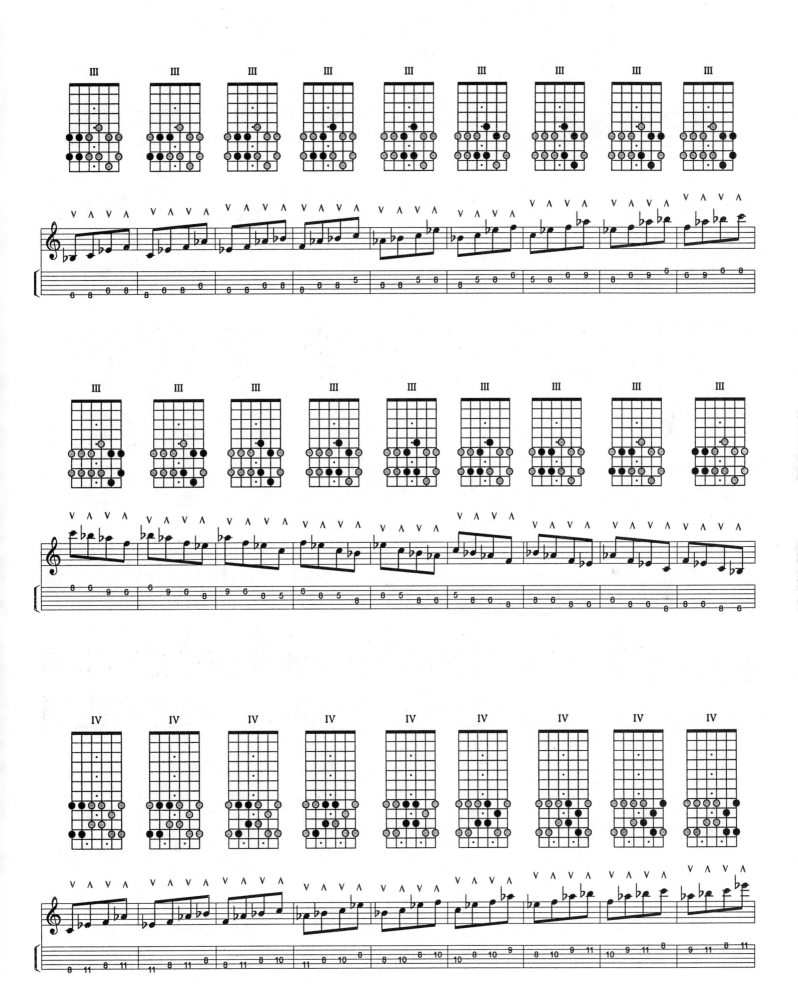

101

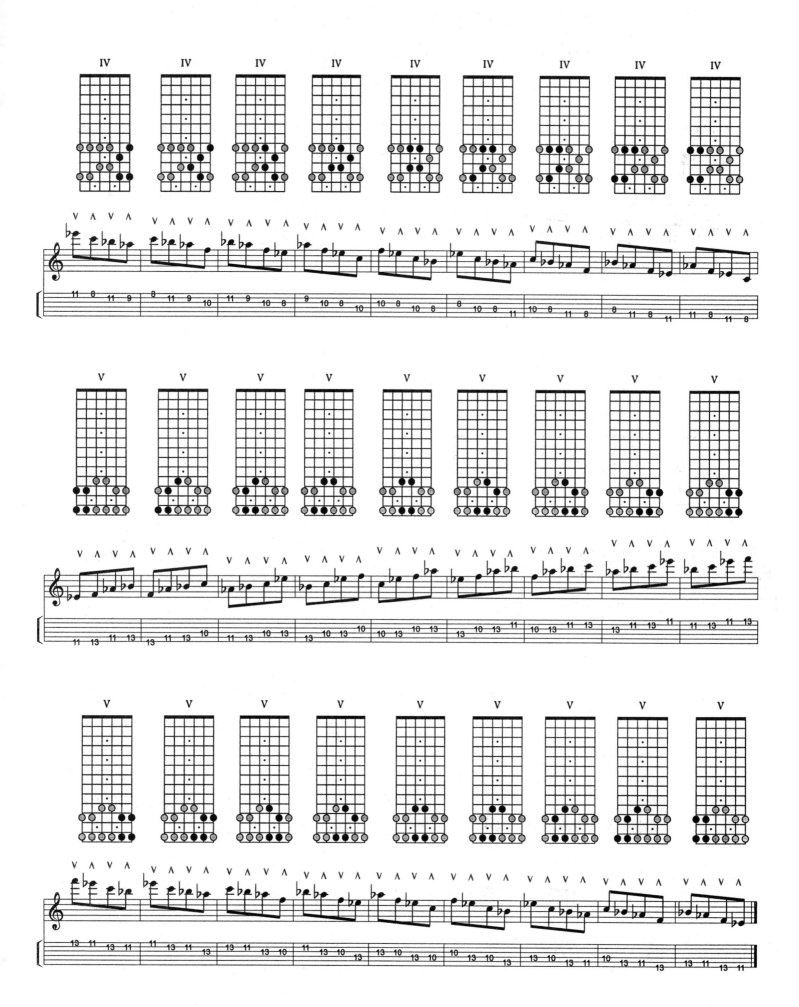

102

FOUR NOTE COILS IN F MINOR PENTATONIC
(ascending & descending - alternating patterns)

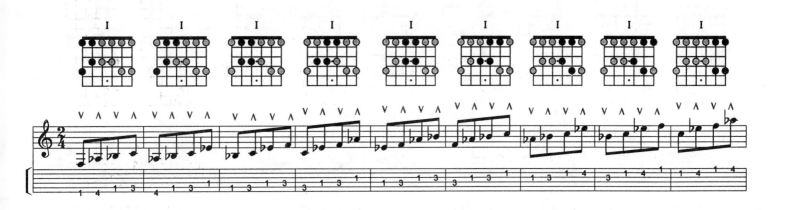

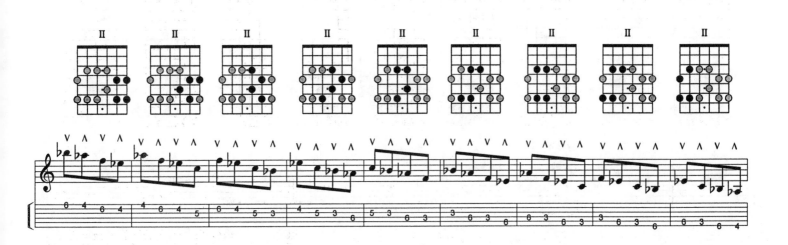

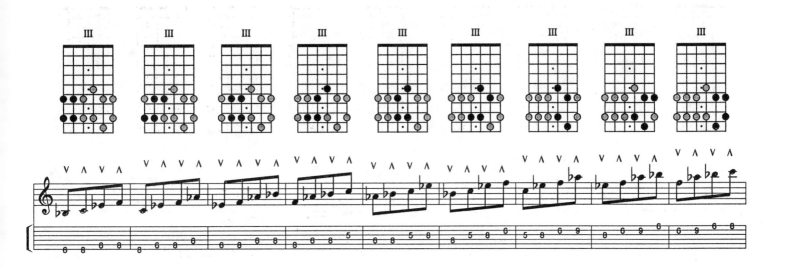

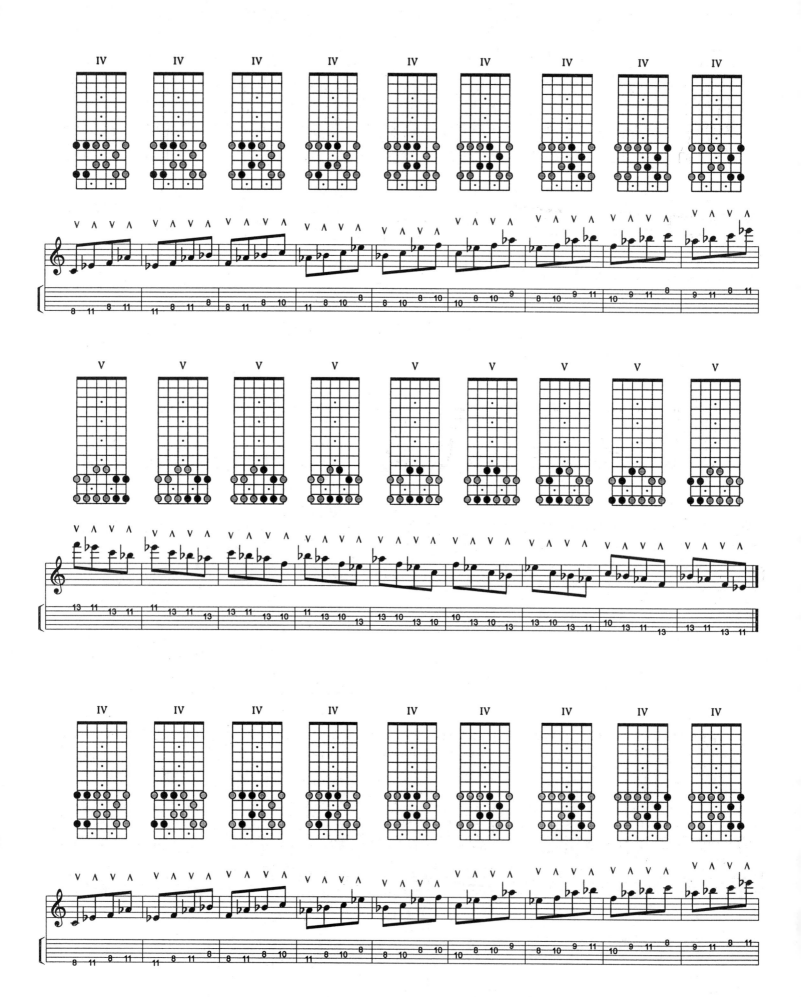

104

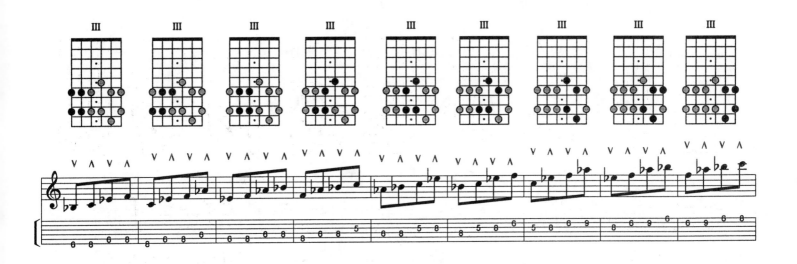

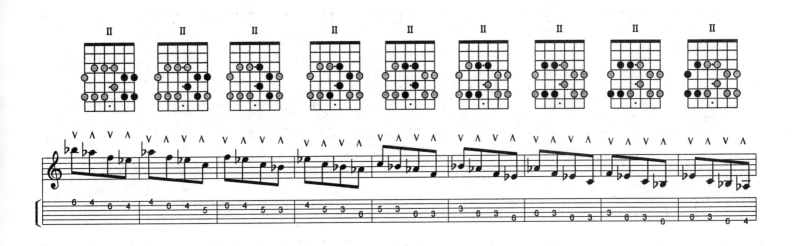

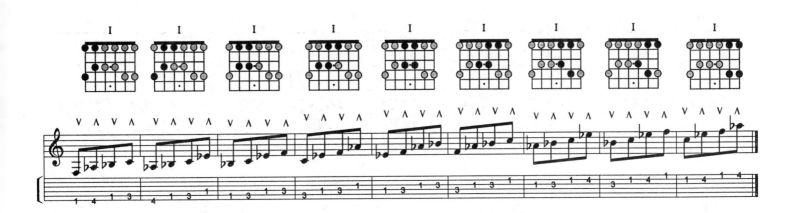

TWO STRING PENTATONIC EXERCISES

These two string exercises are designed to create the dexterity needed to change patterns from any string.

THREE NOTE EXERCISE

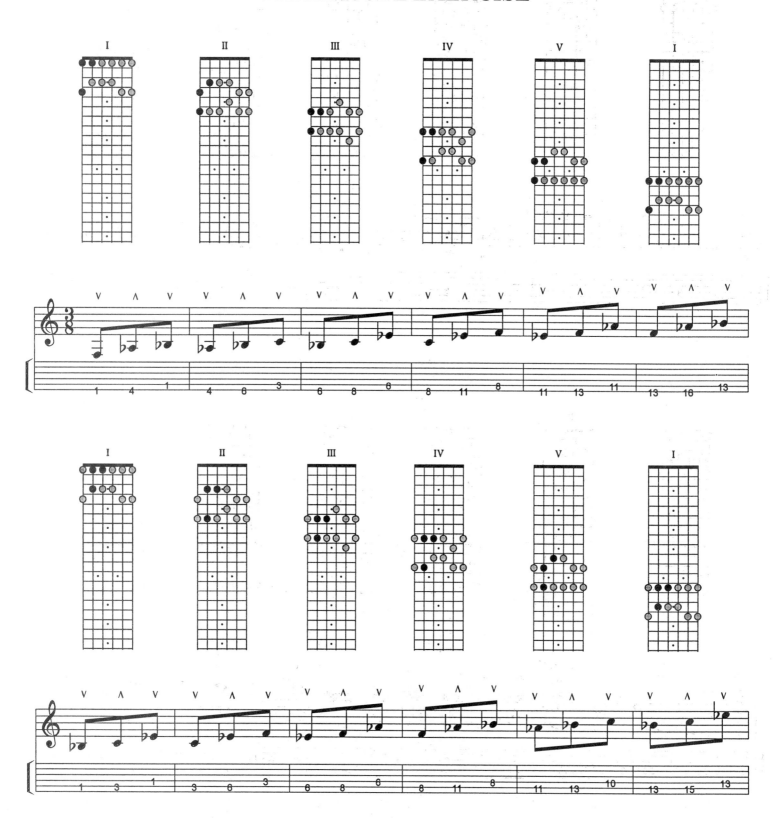

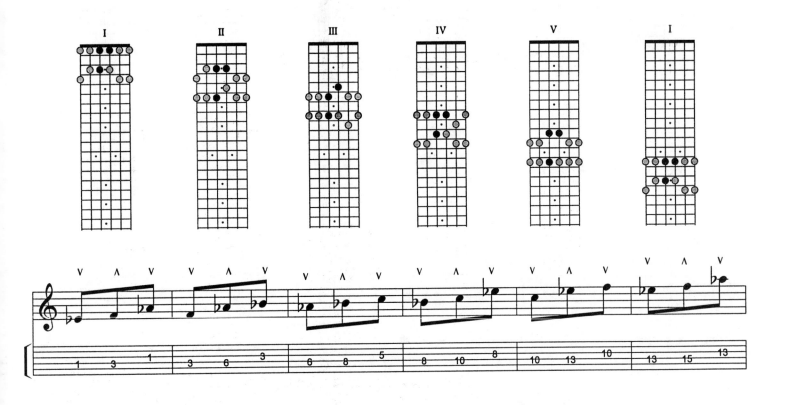

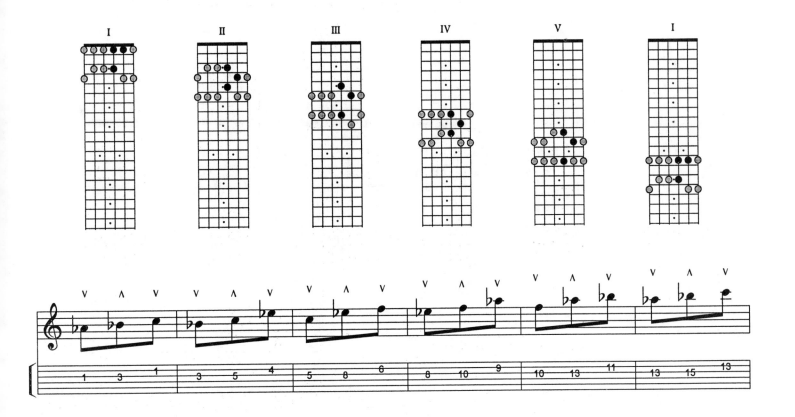

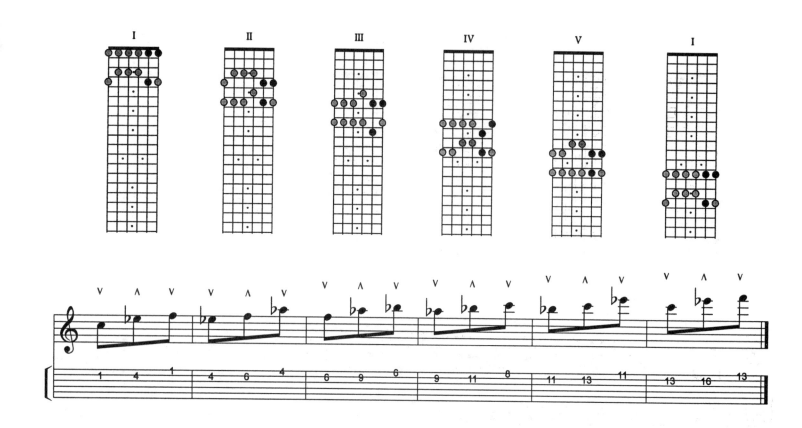

FOUR NOTE EXERCISE

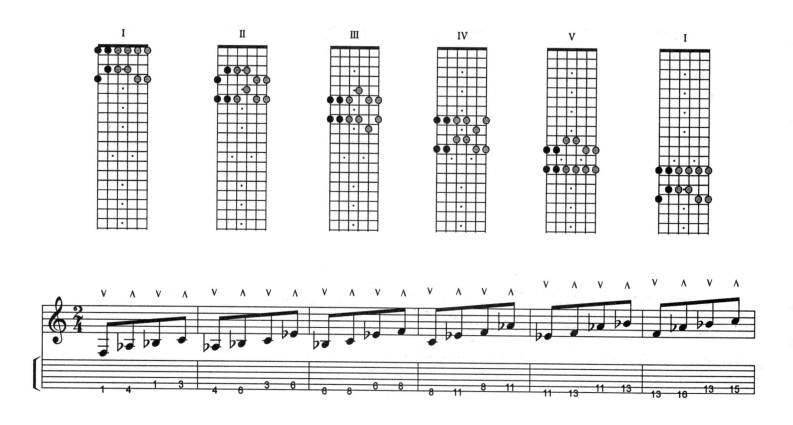

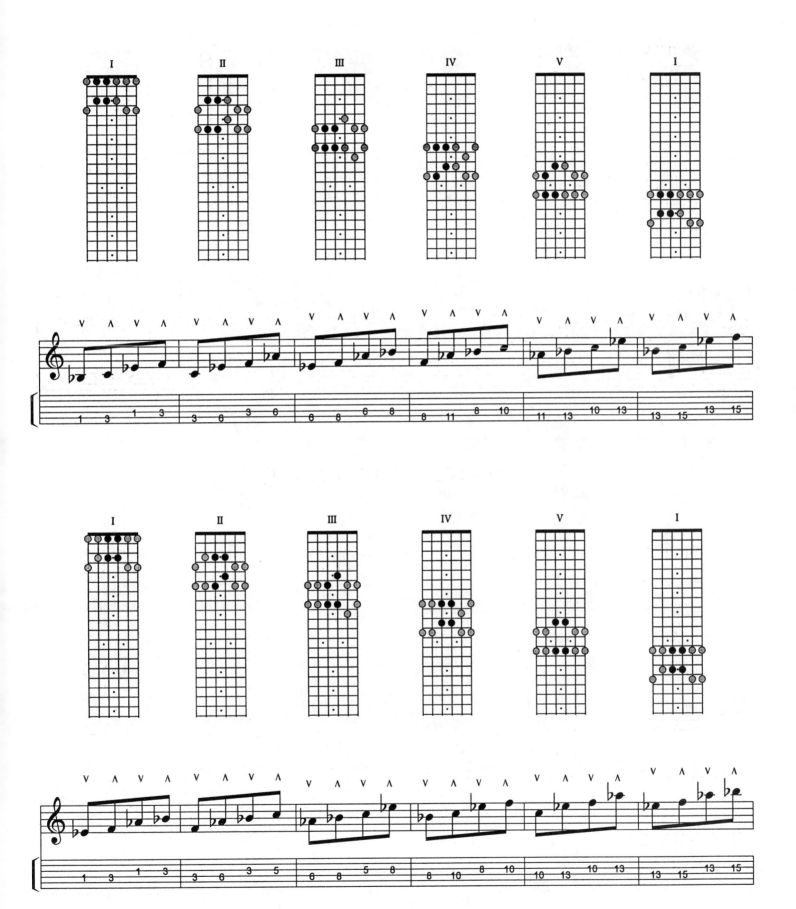

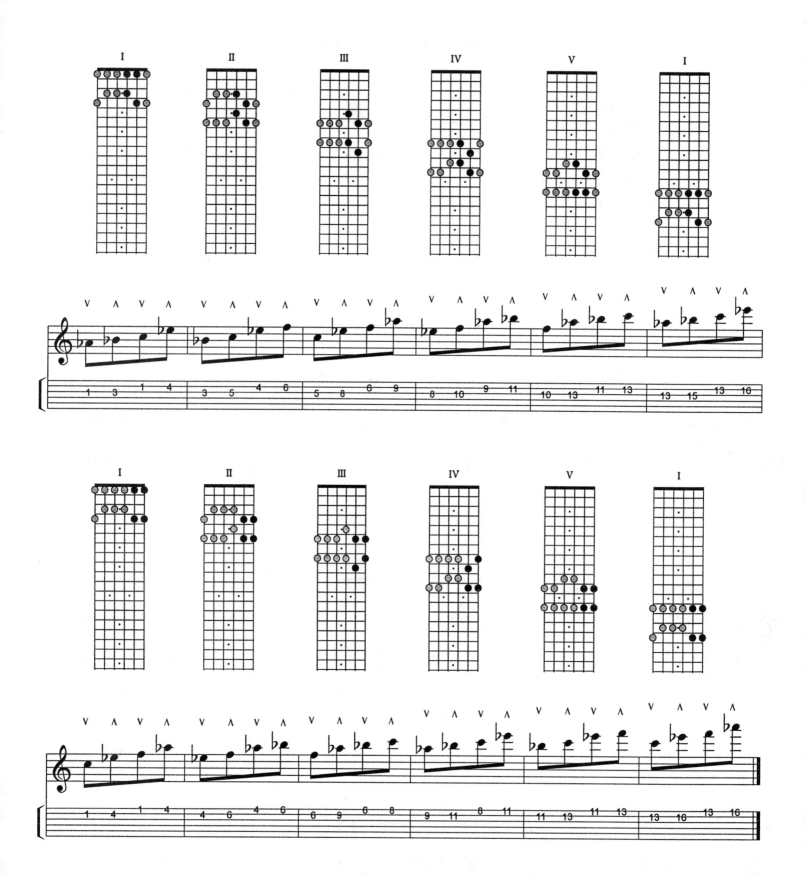

The following pages show the Minor Pentatonic in the other keys. I did not include the enharmonic keys (G♭, C♭, D♭, etc.) because there are no key signatures involved. Just as with the Major scale, all the exercises learned for the F Minor Pentatonic can be applied to the other keys. The picking for the following pages is alternating picking (down, up, down, up, etc.).

F# MINOR PENTATONIC

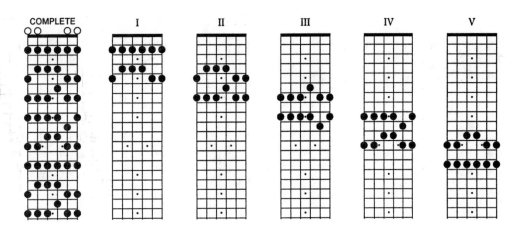

Pattern 1

Pattern 2

Pattern 3

Pattern 4

Pattern 5

G MINOR PENTATONIC

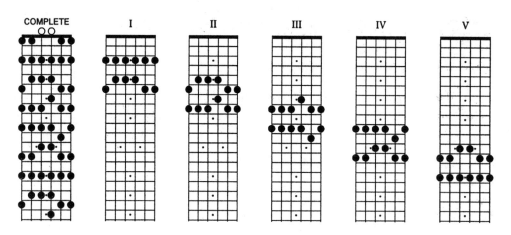

Pattern 1

Pattern 2

Pattern 3

Pattern 4

Pattern 5

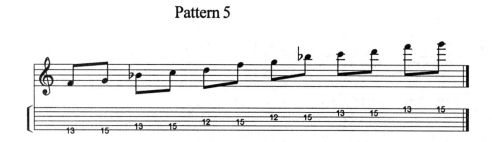

Ab MINOR PENTATONIC

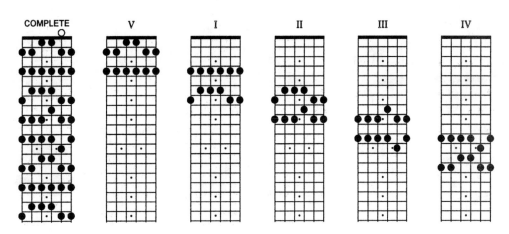

Pattern 5   Pattern 1

Pattern 2   Pattern 3

Pattern 4

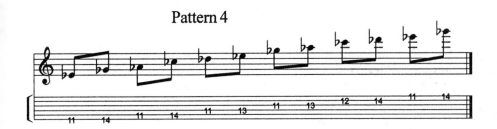

A MINOR PENTATONIC

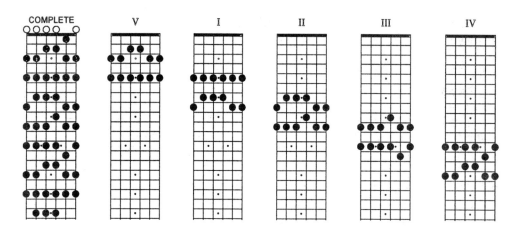

COMPLETE   V   I   II   III   IV

Pattern 5   Pattern 1

Pattern 2   Pattern 3

Pattern 4

Bb MINOR PENTATONIC

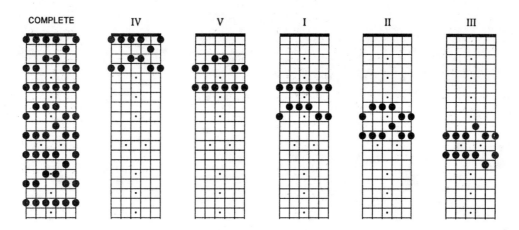

Pattern 4   Pattern 5

Pattern 1   Pattern 2

Pattern 3

B MINOR PENTATONIC

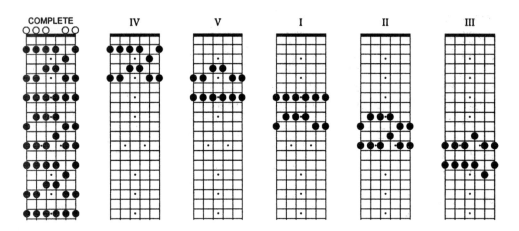

Pattern 4   ### Pattern 5

Pattern 1   ### Pattern 2

Pattern 3

C MINOR PENTATONIC

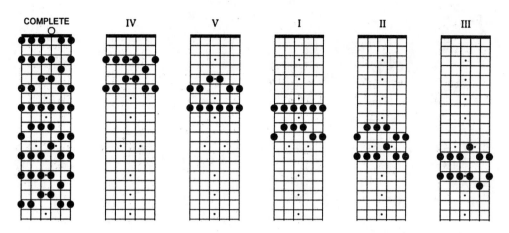

Pattern 4   Pattern 5

Pattern 1   Pattern 2

Pattern 3

C# MINOR PENTATONIC

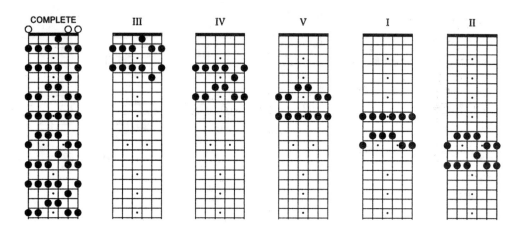

Pattern 3   Pattern 4

Pattern 5   Pattern 1

Pattern 2

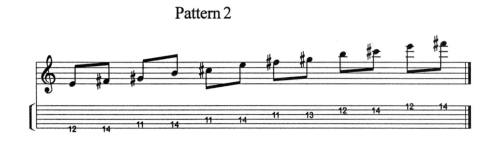

D MINOR PENTATONIC

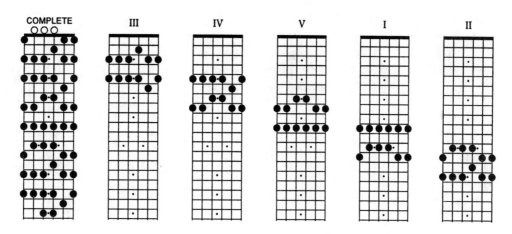

COMPLETE   III   IV   V   I   II

Pattern 3   Pattern 4

Pattern 5   Pattern 1

Pattern 2

Eb MINOR PENTATONIC

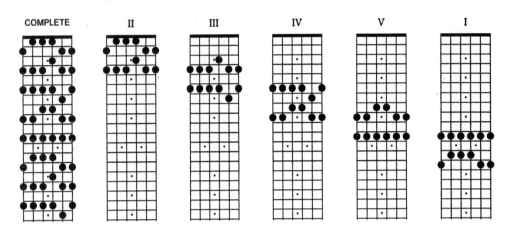

COMPLETE   II   III   IV   V   I

Pattern 2   Pattern 3

Pattern 4   Pattern 5

Pattern 1

E MINOR PENTATONIC

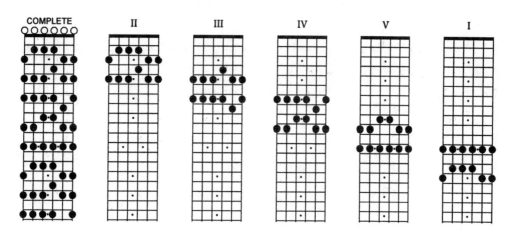

Pattern 2   Pattern 3

Pattern 4   Pattern 5

Pattern 1

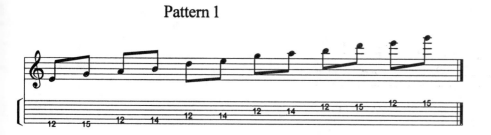

PART THREE

CHORD RUN EXERCISES

F MAJOR RUN

FINGERING

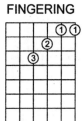

This section deals with creating exercises out of chords and or chord runs. We'll start off with a voicing for a Major chord that you should be quite familiar with. We start at the F position on the first fret and move our way up and then descend again. Pay attention to the picking in this. The picking is simple but takes time for smoothness and continuity.

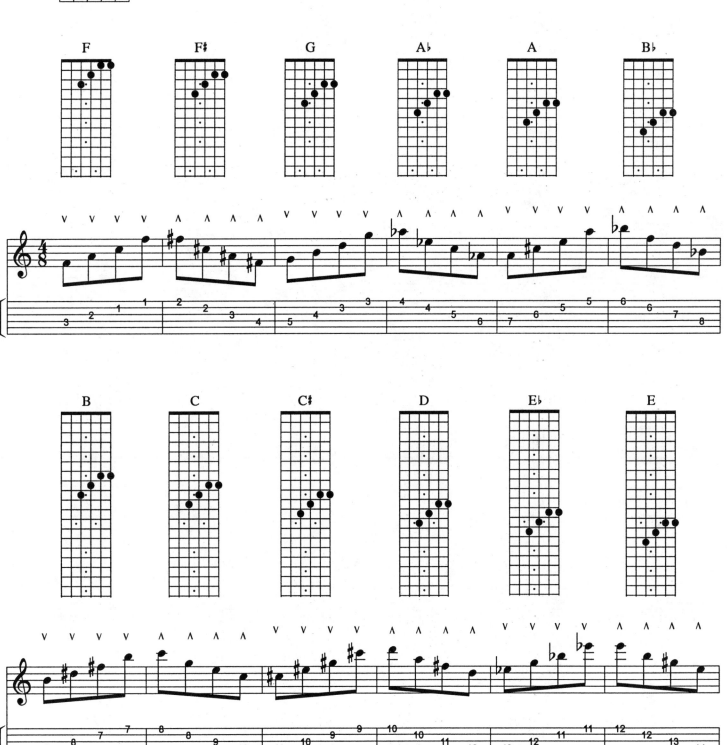

125

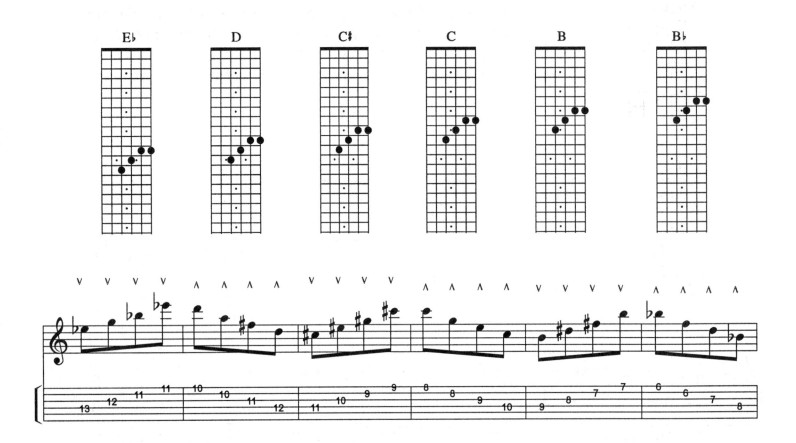

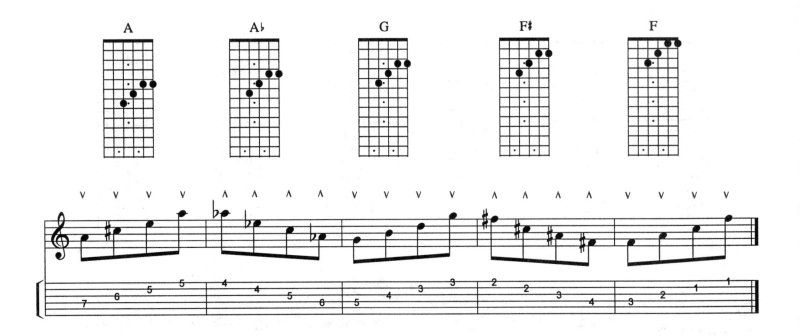

C# MAJOR RUN

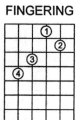

This next one is the same as the last one except we are using a different voicing. Well it is actually the same voicing played on the center four strings. We start at the C# position. The picking is the same as the last exercise.

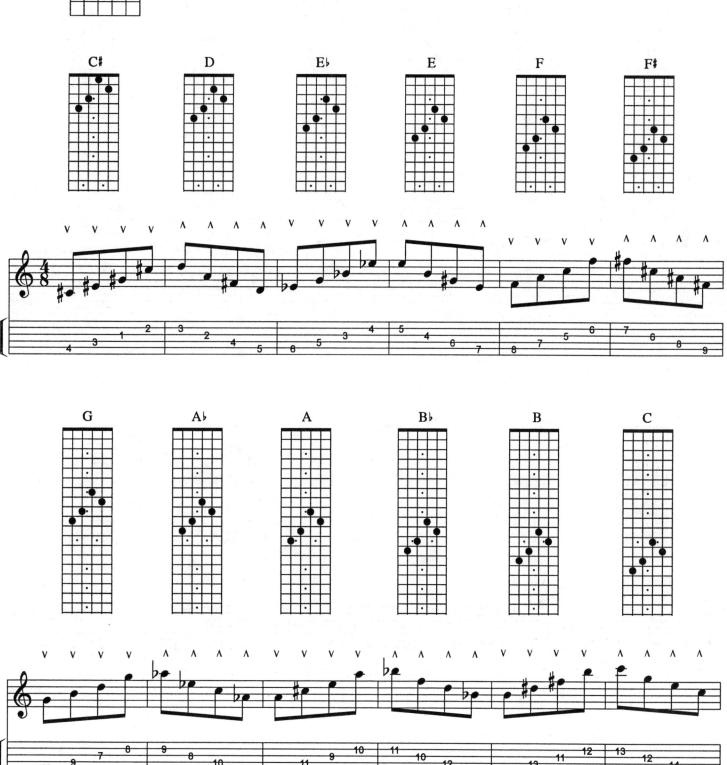

127

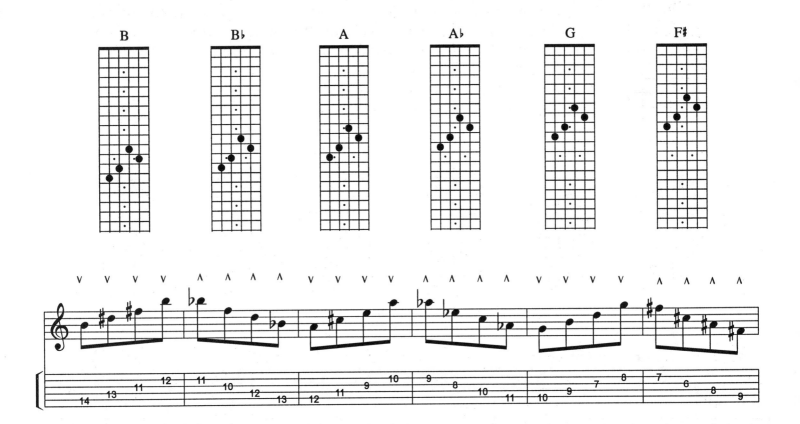

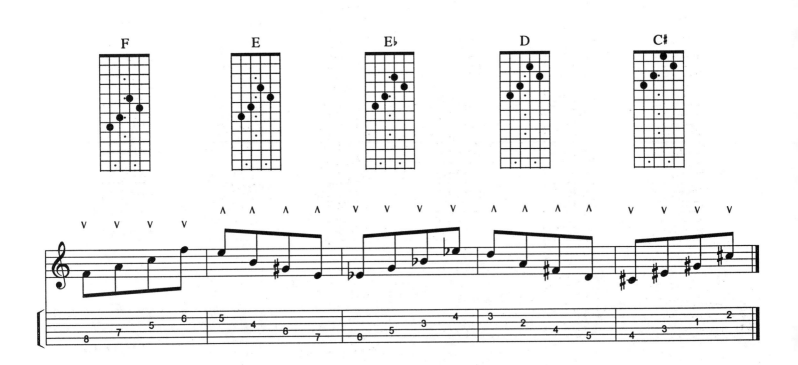

MINOR 7TH RUN #1

FINGERING

This next exercise uses a Minor 7th run. It's a run because we break up the notes of the Minor 7th chord. We start at the G♯ position and work our way up then descend. Observe the picking pattern. This is a good one for developing sweep "bursts".

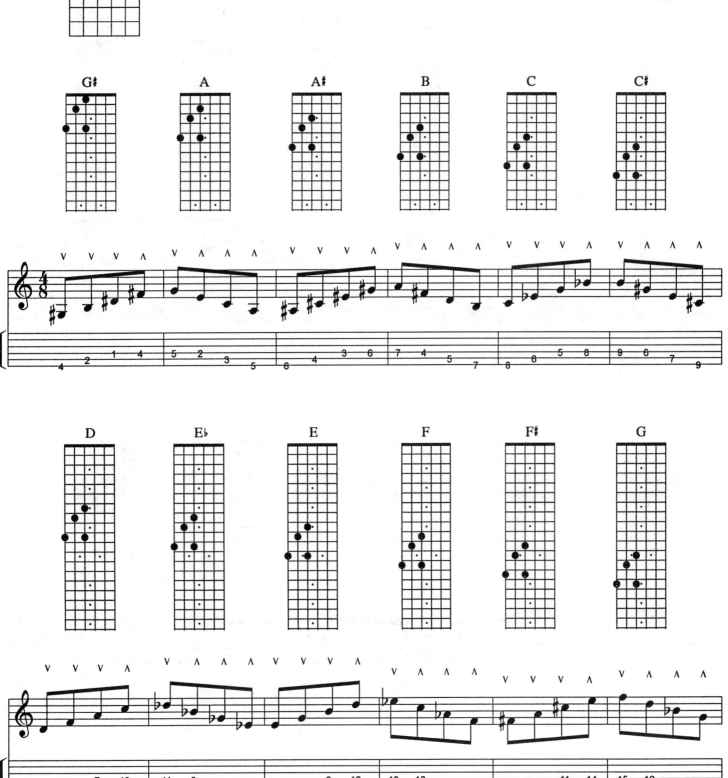

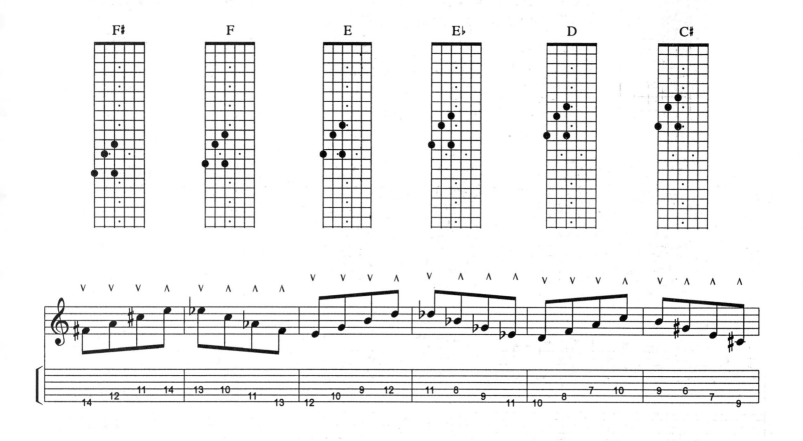

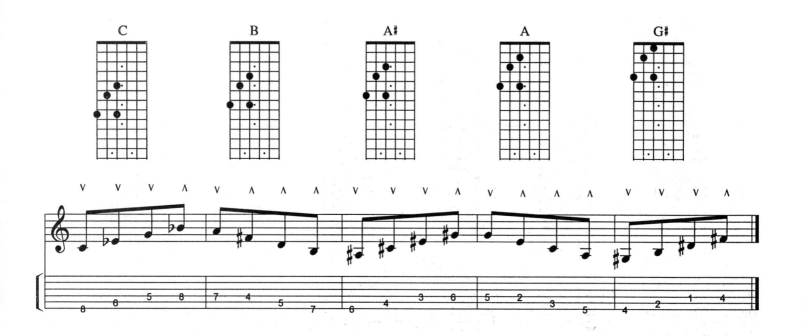

MINOR 7TH RUN #2

FINGERING

This is the same as Minor 7th #1 except we have moved to the next three strings. Same picking pattern.

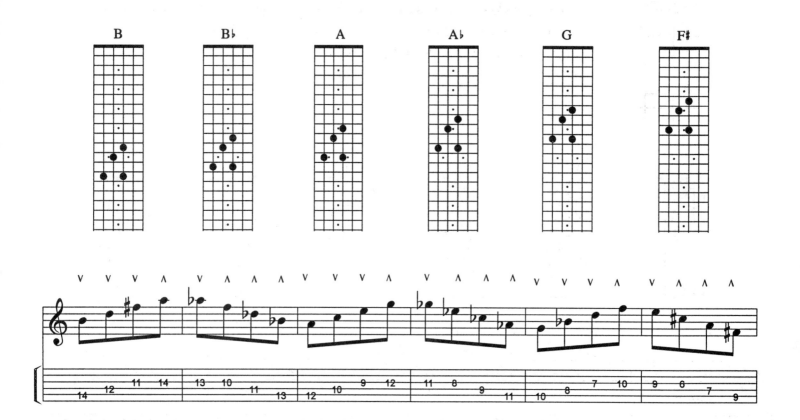

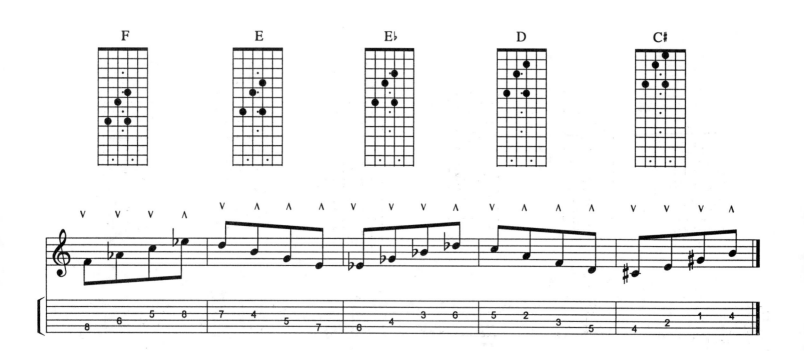

MINOR 7TH RUN #3

FINGERING

This is the same as Minor 7th #1 & #2 except we have moved to the next three strings. Note the pattern looks different because of the tuning between the 2nd and 3rd string. Same picking pattern.

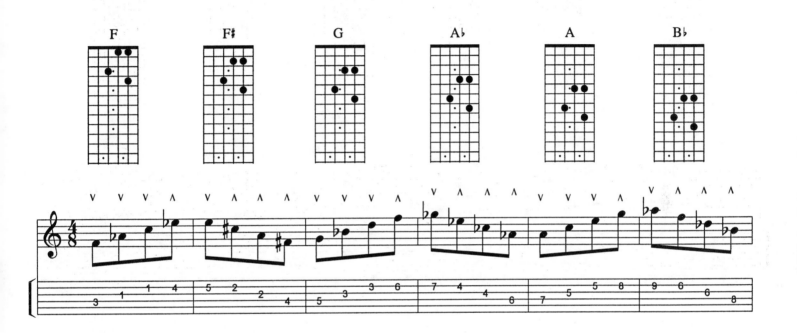

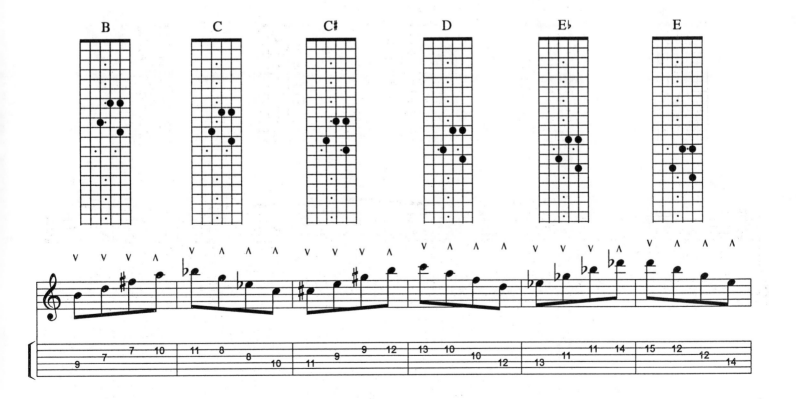

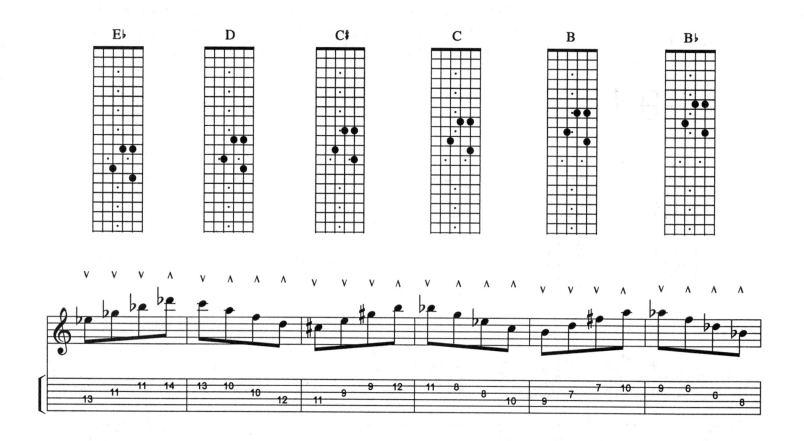

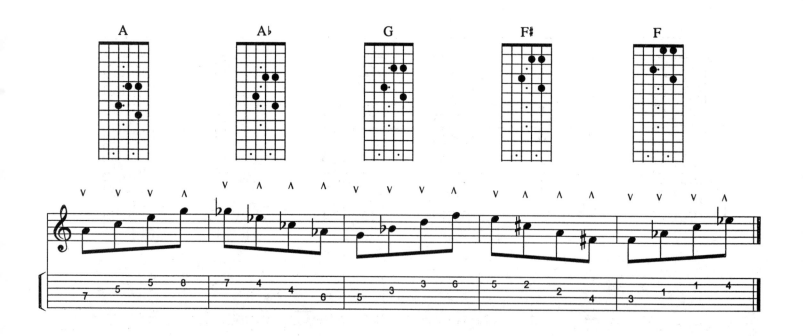

MINOR 7TH RUN #4

FINGERING

This is the same as Minor 7th #1, #2 & #3 except we have moved to the next three strings. Note the pattern looks different again because of the tuning between the 2nd and 3rd string. Same picking pattern.

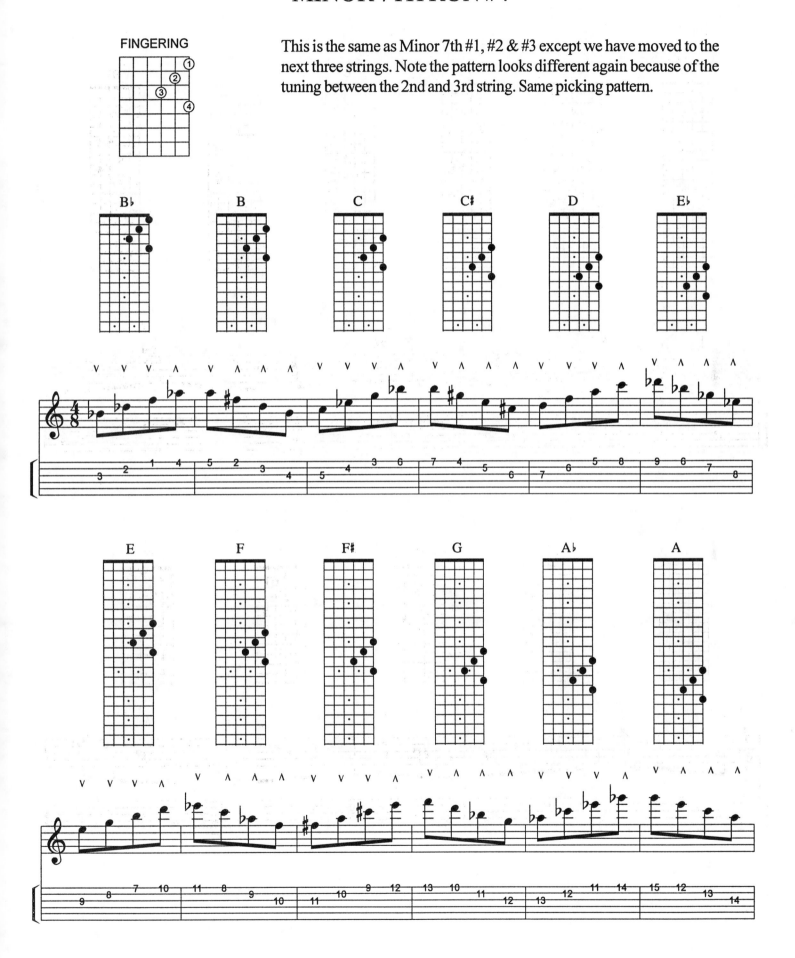

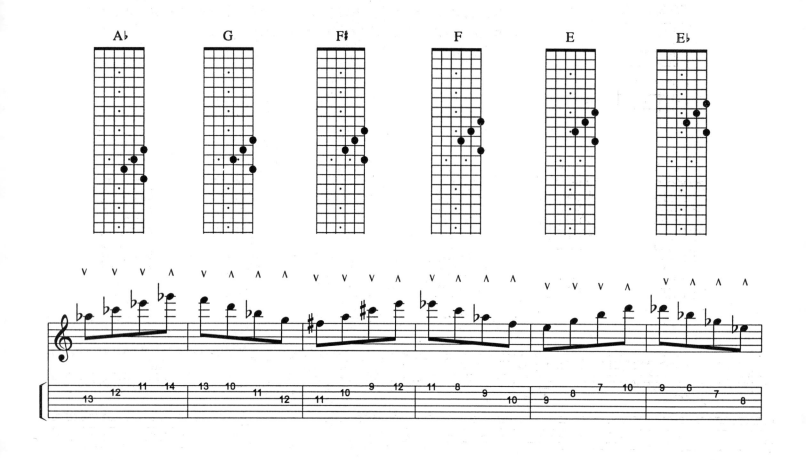

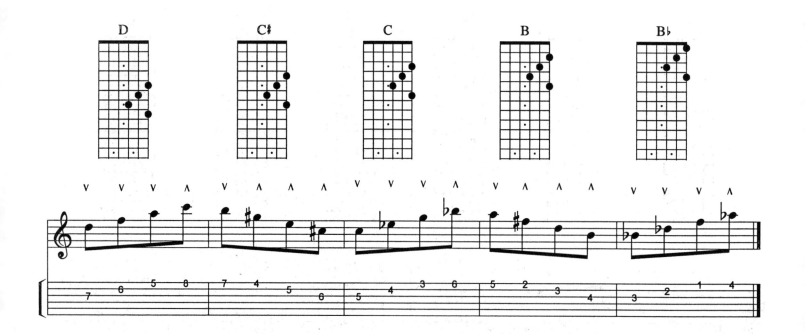

MINOR 7TH RUN #5

FINGERING

Minor 7th run #5 changes slightly requiring a different picking pattern. It contains all the tones of the Minor 7th chord 1, ♭3, 5, ♭7.

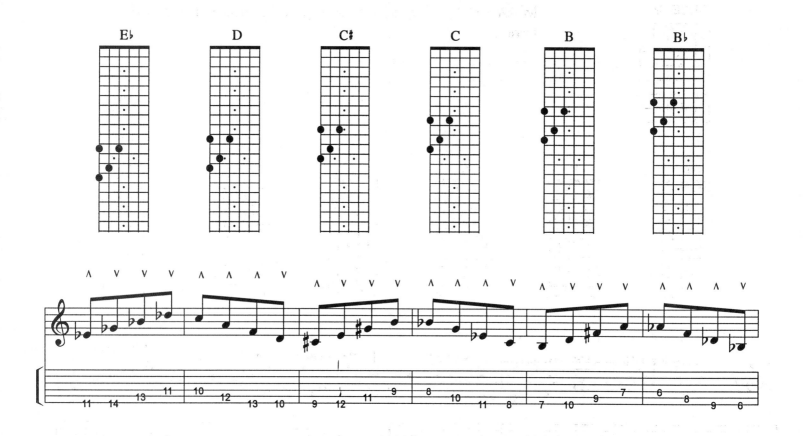

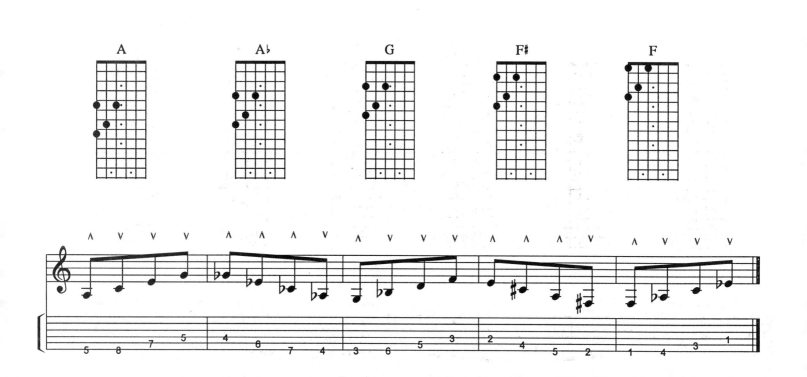

MINOR 7TH RUN #6

FINGERING

Minor 7th run #6 is the same as #5 just moved over to the next set of strings.

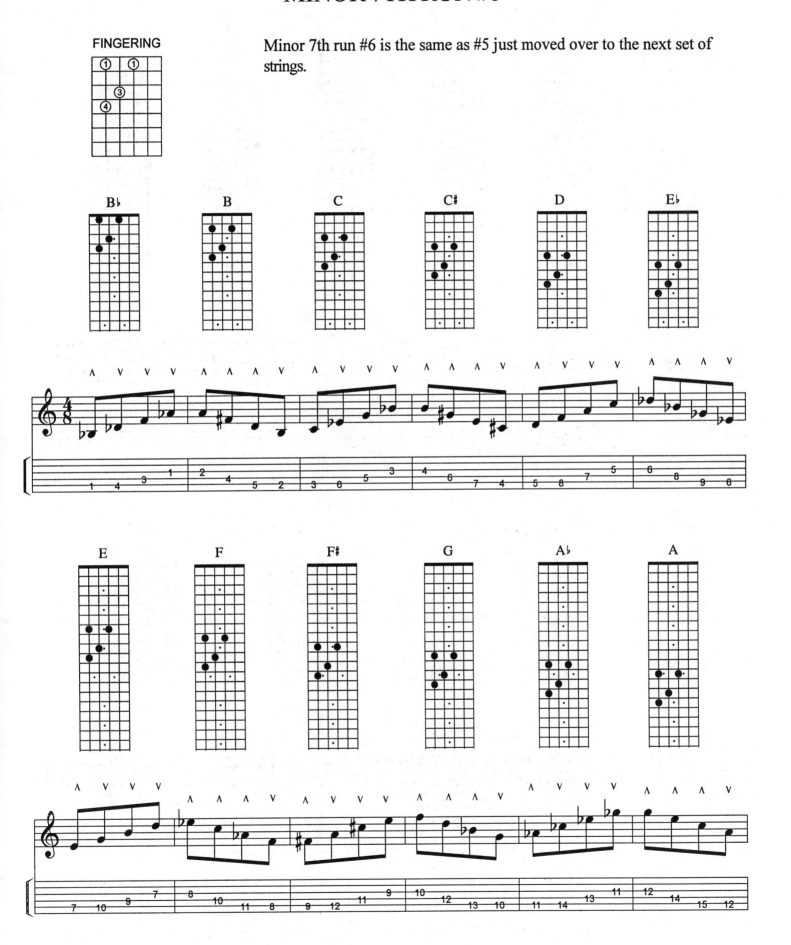

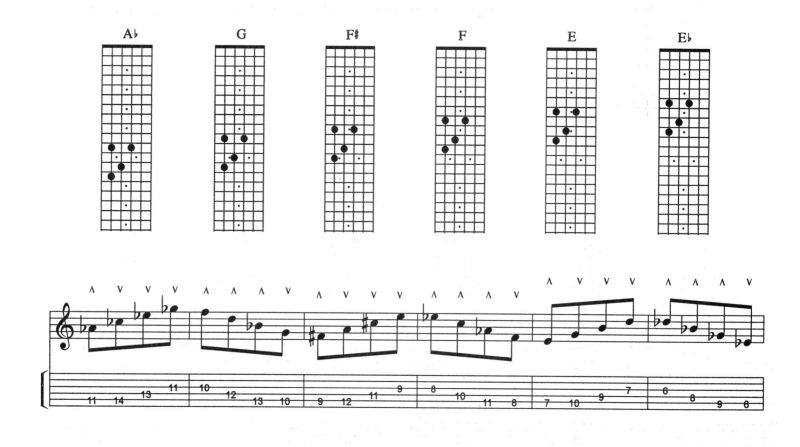

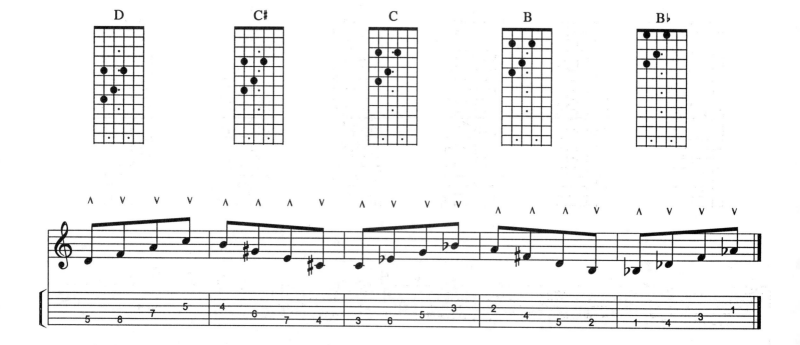

MINOR 7TH RUN #7

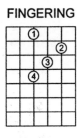

Minor 7th run #7 is the same as #5 & #6 just moved over to the next set of strings.

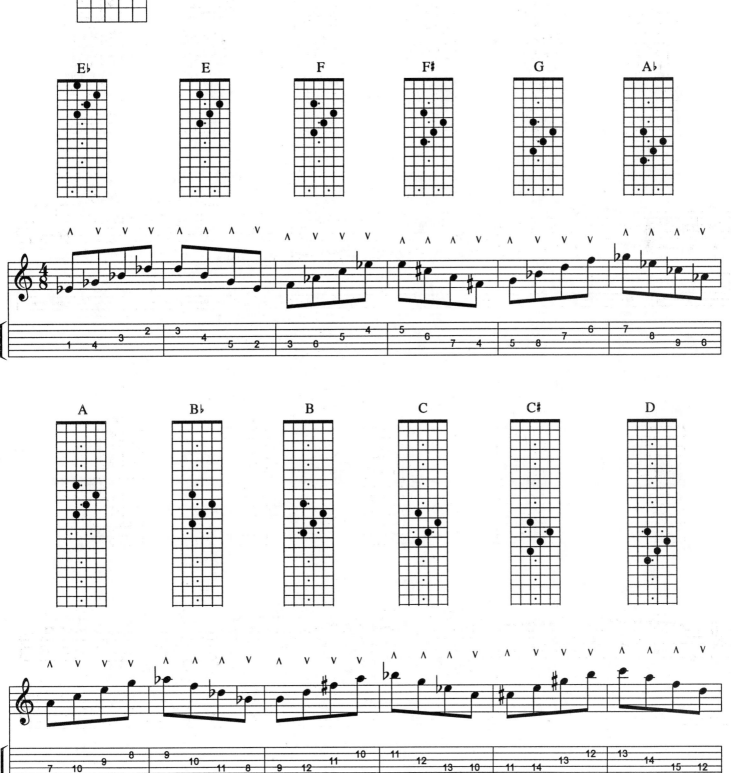

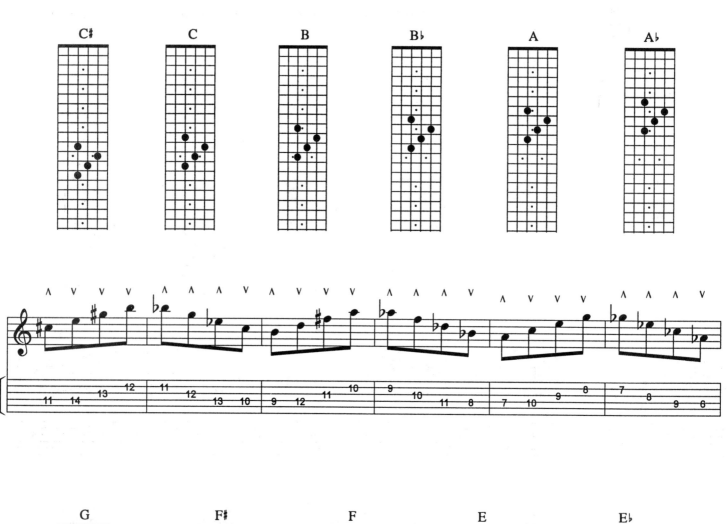

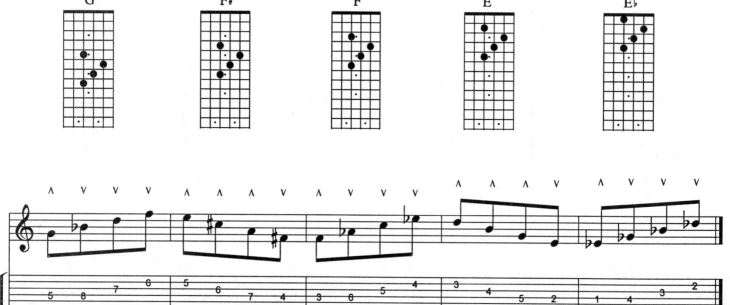

MINOR 7TH RUN #8

FINGERING

Minor 7th run #8 is the same as #5, #6 & #7 just moved over to the next set of strings.

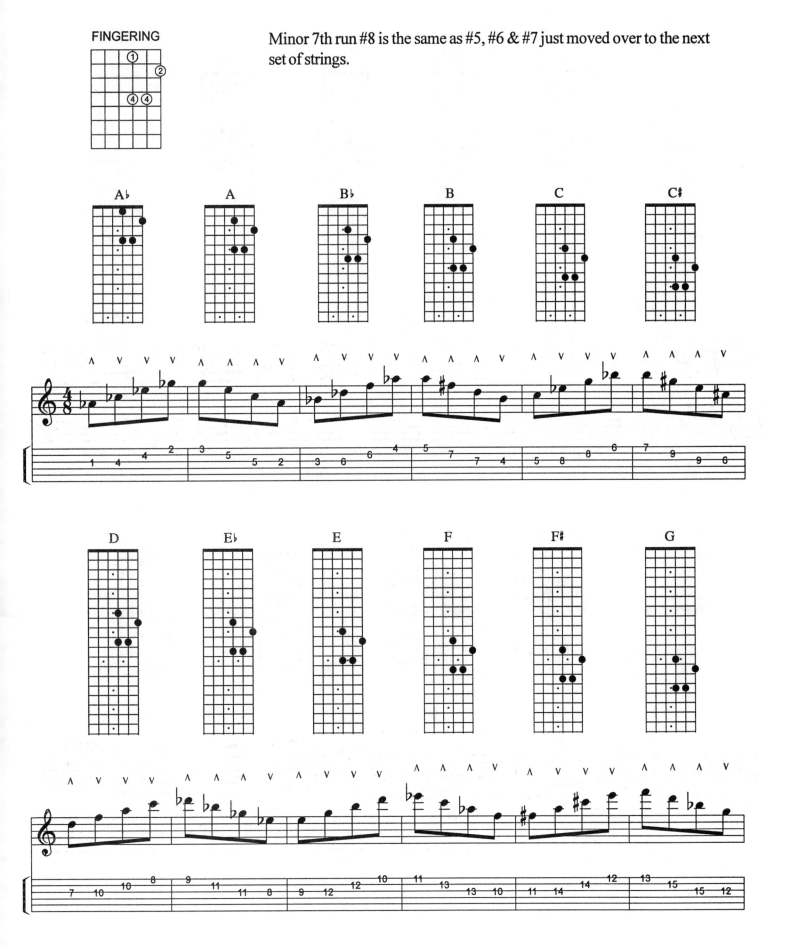

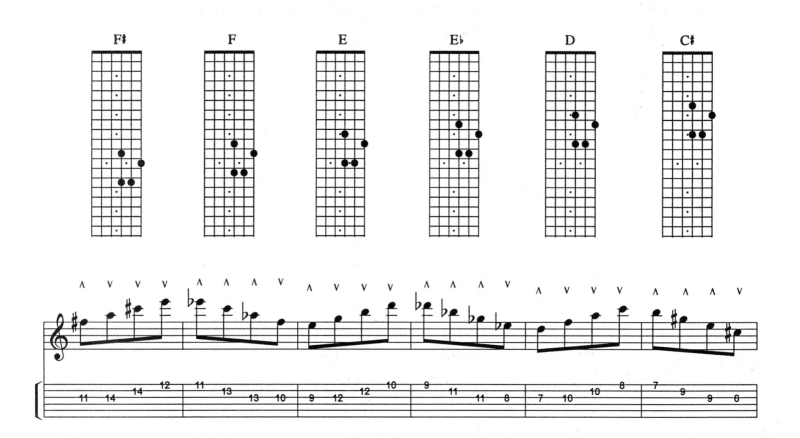

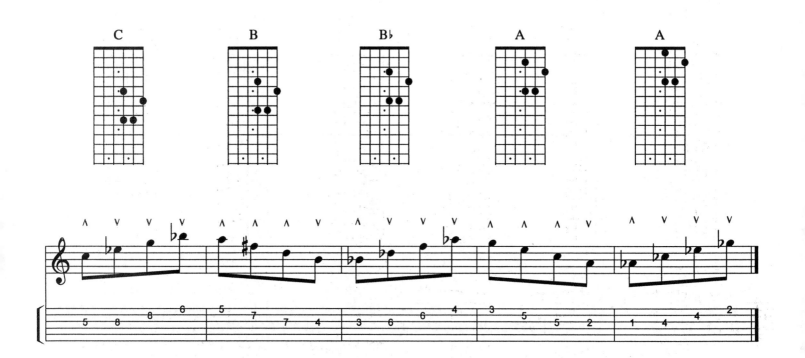

DOMINANT 7TH RUN #1

FINGERING

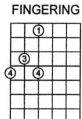

This is the same as Minor 7th exercise #1 except it is using a Dominant 7th run.
The picking is the same too.

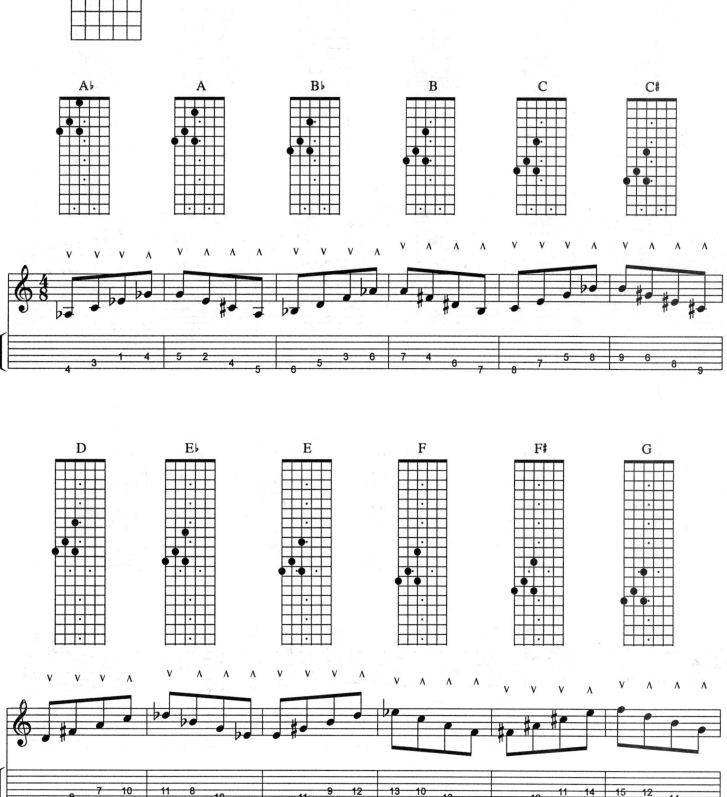

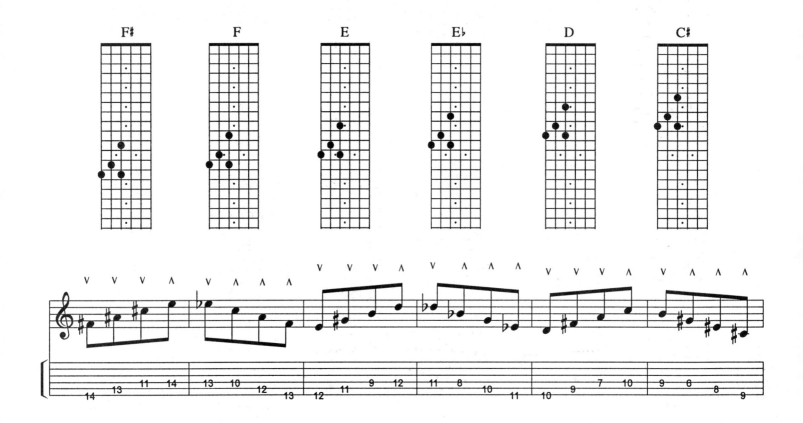

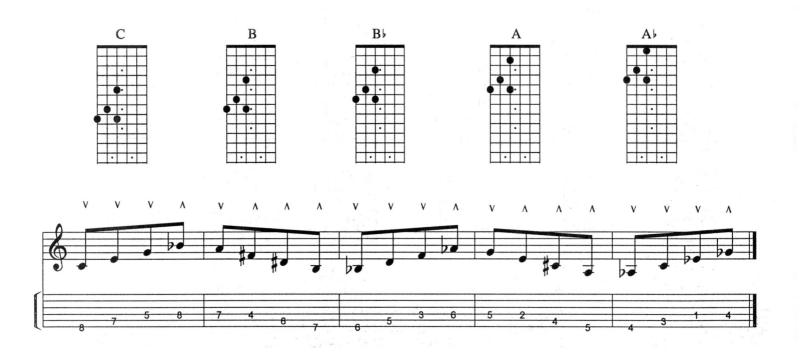

DOMINANT 7TH RUN #2

FINGERING

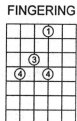

This is the same as Minor 7th exercise #2 except it is using a Dominant 7th run. The picking is the same too.

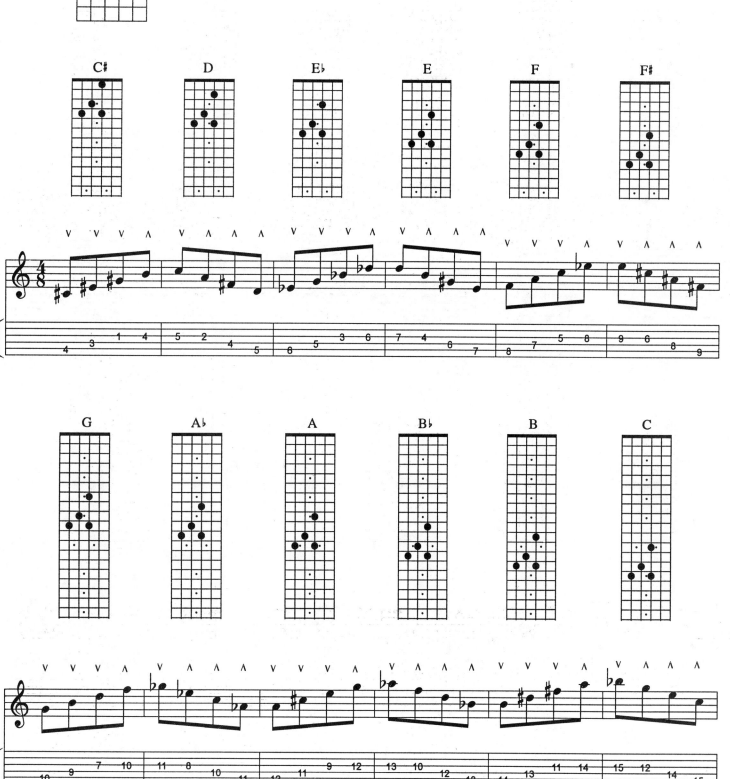

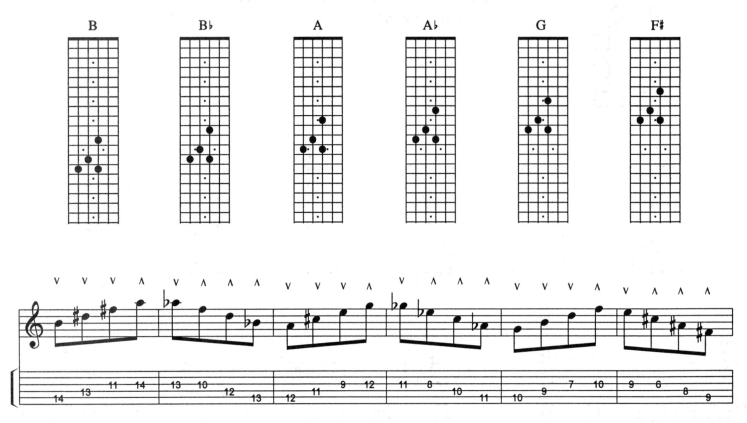

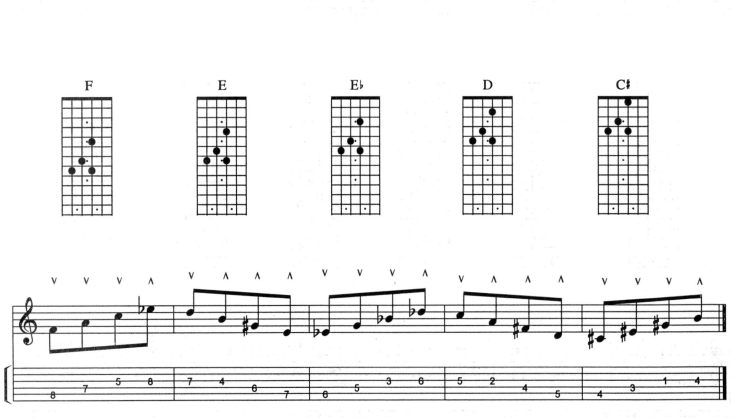

DOMINANT 7TH RUN #3

FINGERING

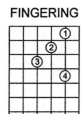

This is the same as Minor 7th exercise #3 except it is using a Dominant 7th run.
The picking is the same too.

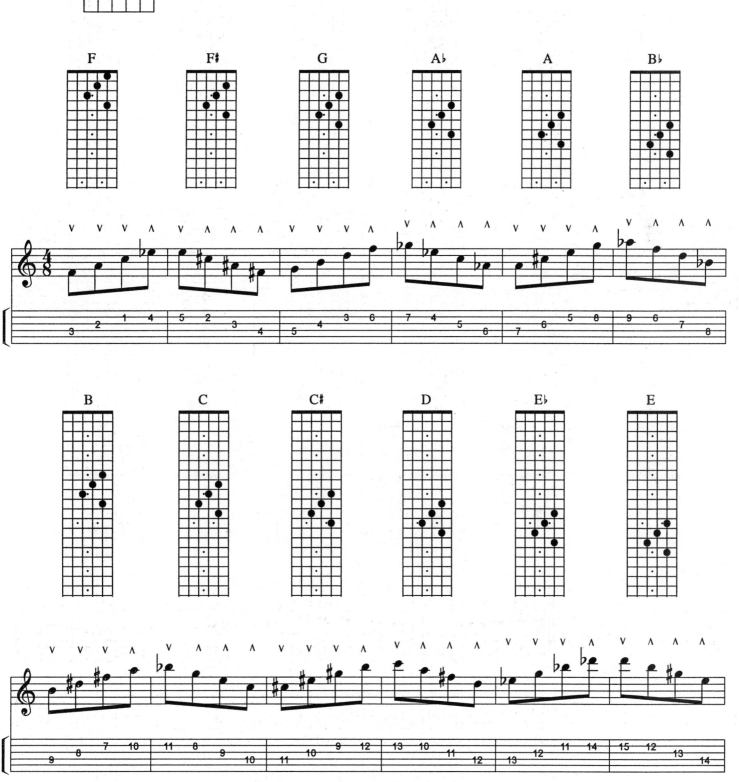

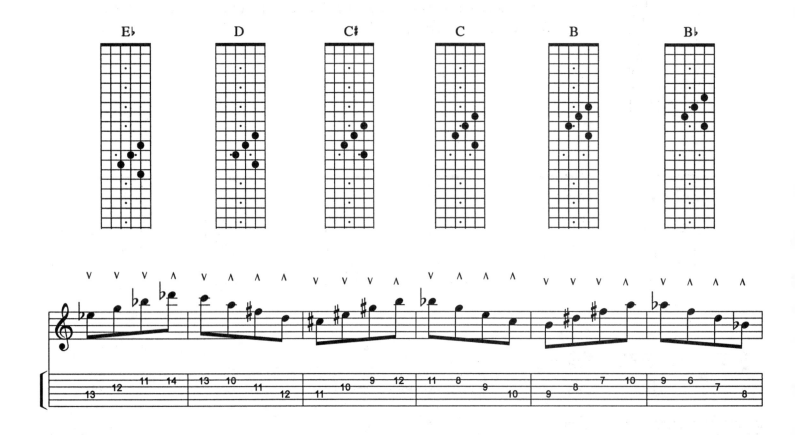

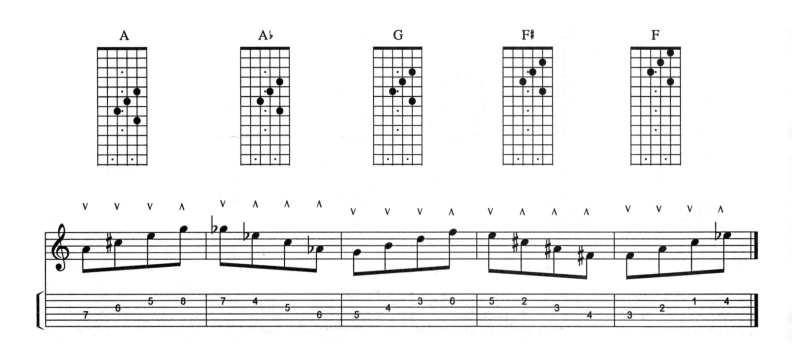

DOMINANT 7TH RUN #4

FINGERING

This is the same as Minor 7th exercise #4 except it is using a Dominant 7th run. The picking is the same too.

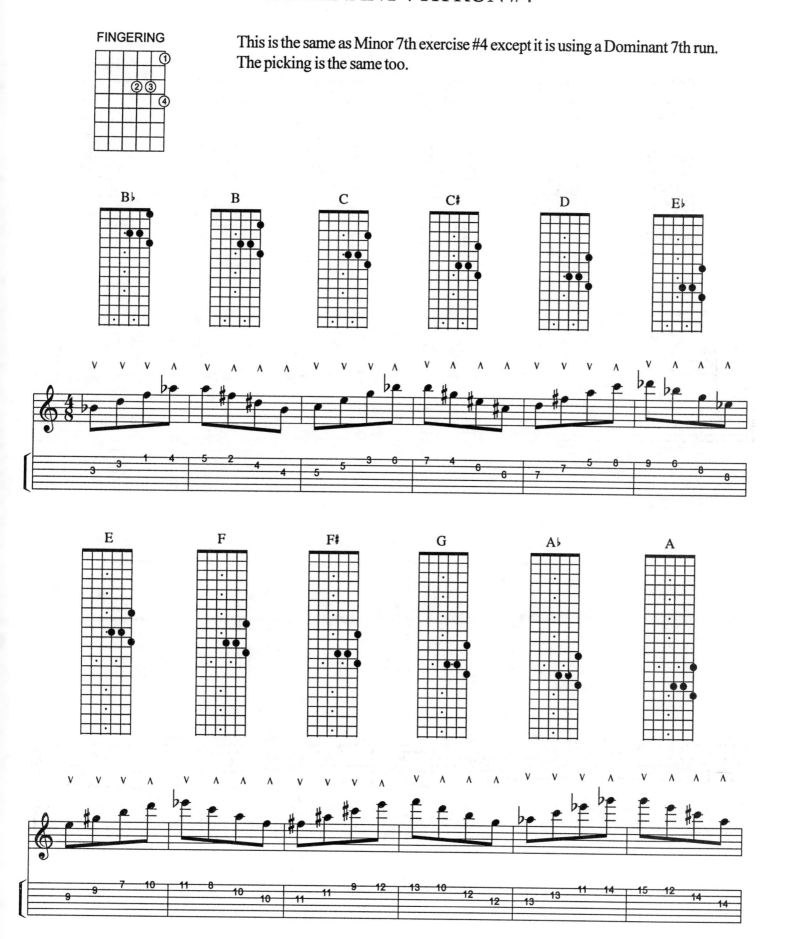

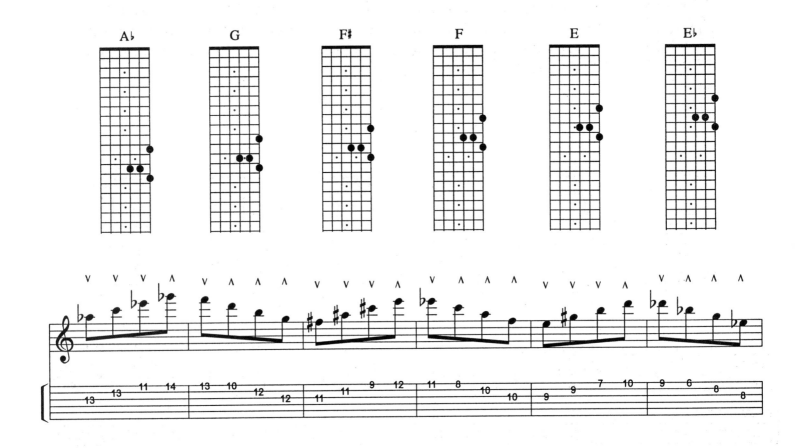

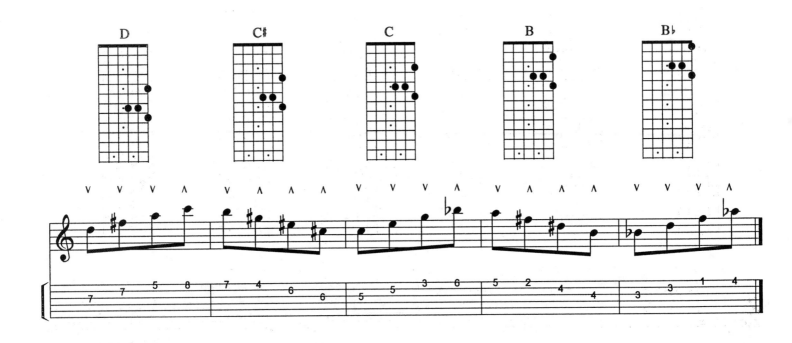

DOMINANT 7TH RUN #5

FINGERING

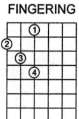

Dominant 7th run # 5 is an example of a rootless run. The ♭7 tone is doubled up with its octave. (If you don't understand the theory of the tones I suggest you get the **Guitar Grimoire - Scales & Modes** book and video). The picking is the same as Dominant 7th runs #1 thru #4.

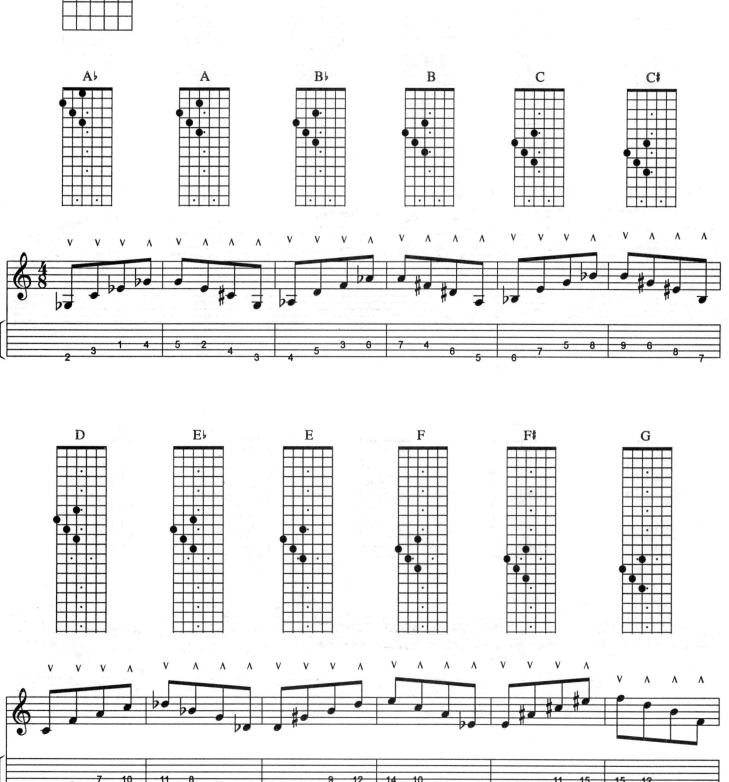

153

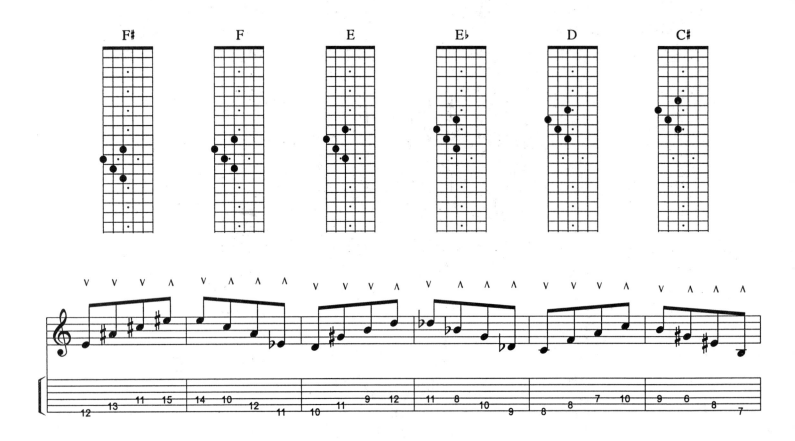

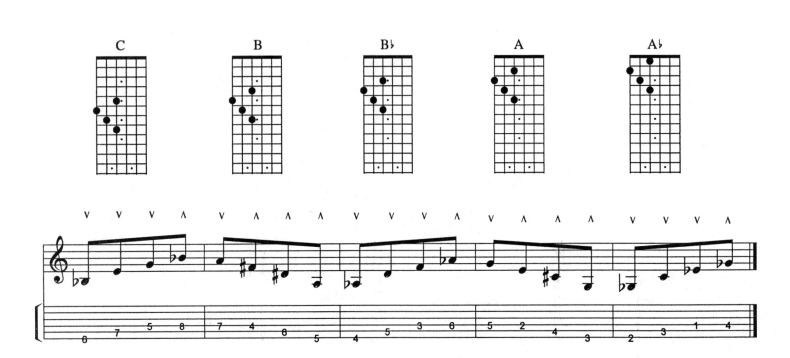

DOMINANT 7TH RUN #6

FINGERING

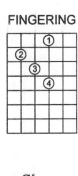

Dominant 7th run # 6 is the same as # 5 just moved over to the next strings.
The picking is the same.

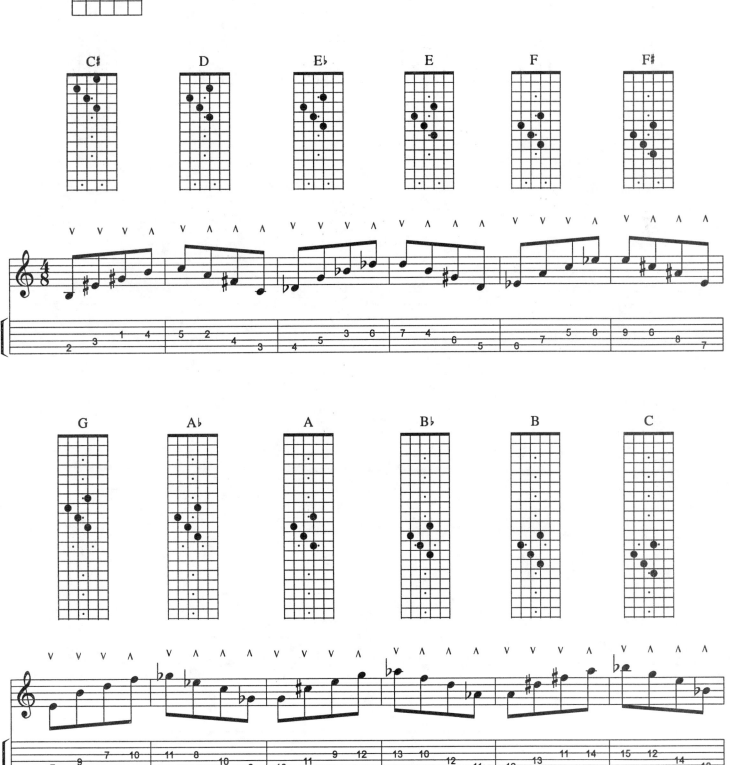

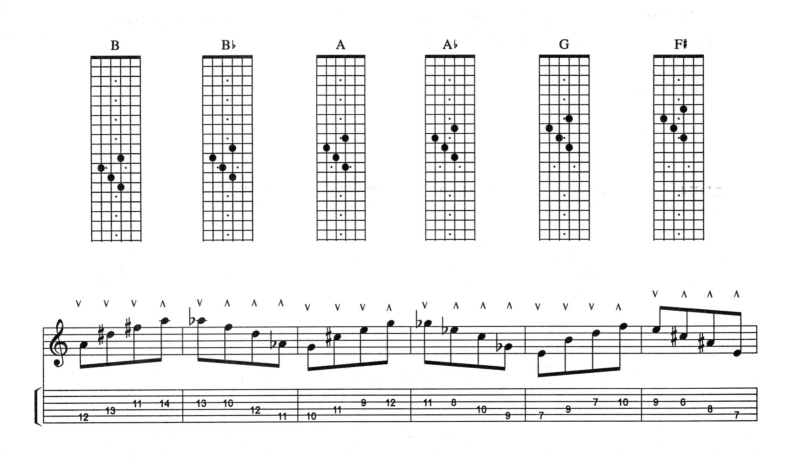

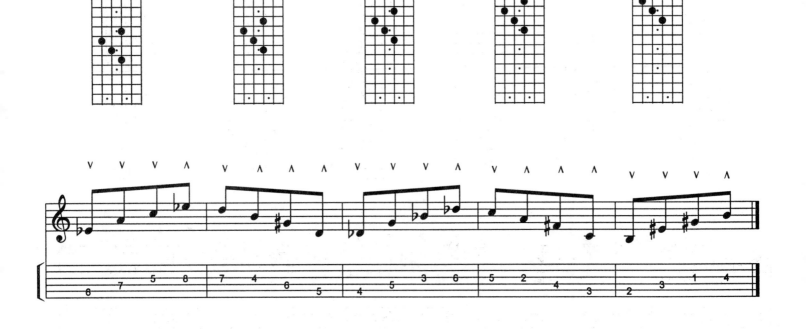

156

DOMINANT 7TH RUN #7

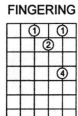

FINGERING

Dominant 7th run # 7 is the same as # 5 & #6 just moved over to the next strings. The picking is the same.

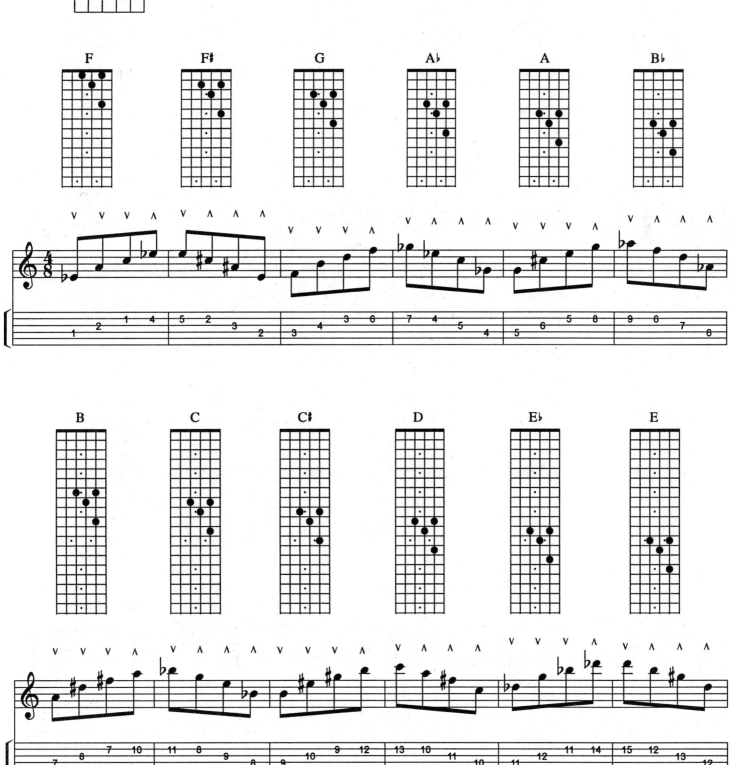

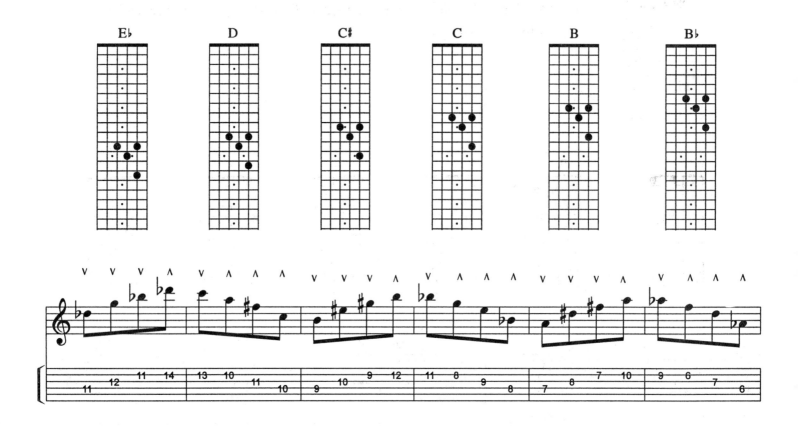

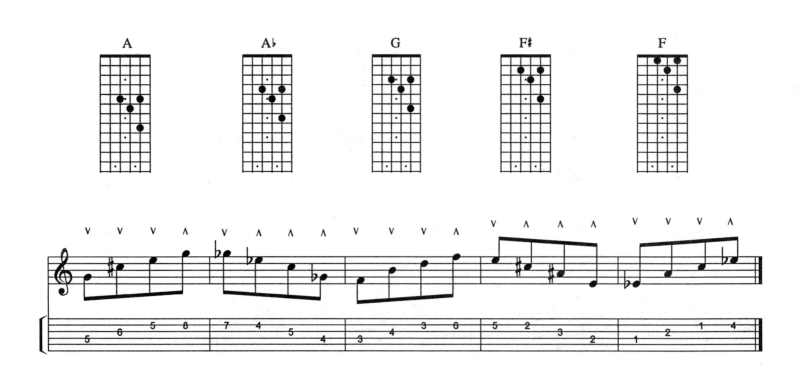

DOMINANT 7TH RUN #8

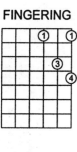

FINGERING

Dominant 7th run # 8 is the same as # 5, #6 & #7 just moved over to the next strings. The picking is the same.

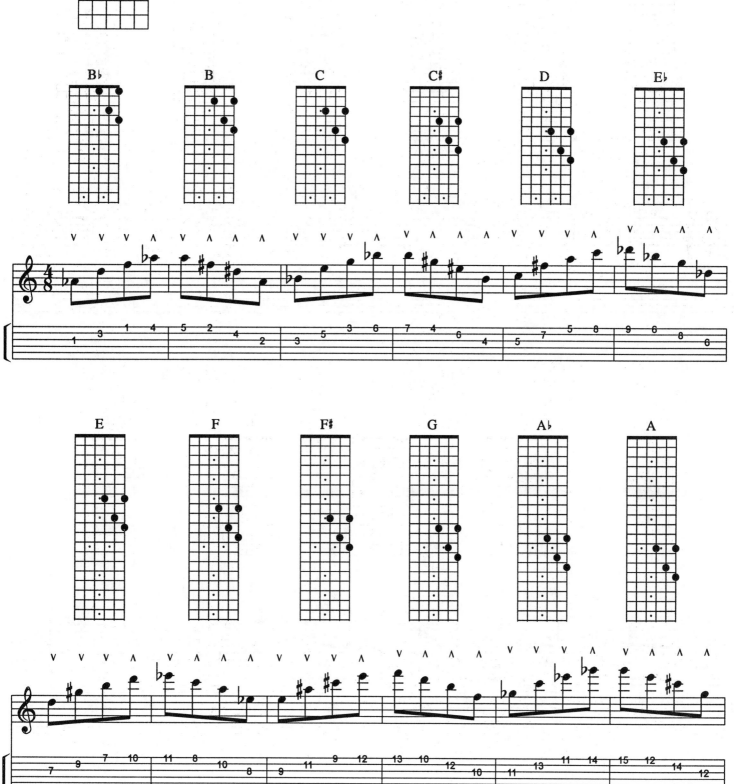

159

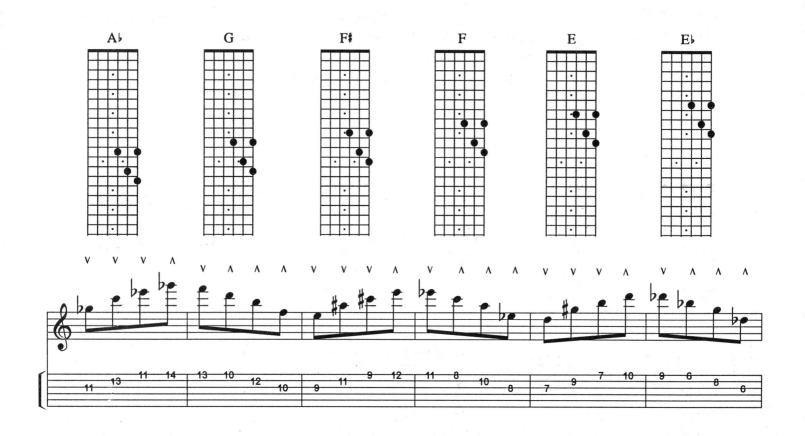

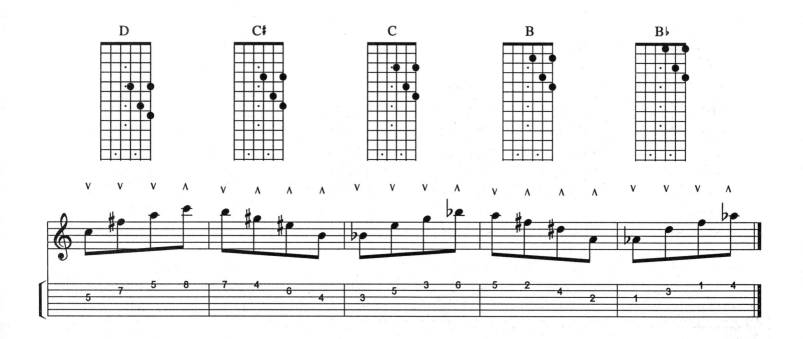

DOMINANT 9TH RUN #1

FINGERING

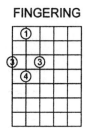

Dominant 9th run #1 is another example of a rootless run. It contains all the other tones of the Dominant 9th chord 3, 5, ♭7,9. Pay attention to the picking pattern in this one. This is an excellent excercise for mixing economy picking (or sweep picking) with regular picking.

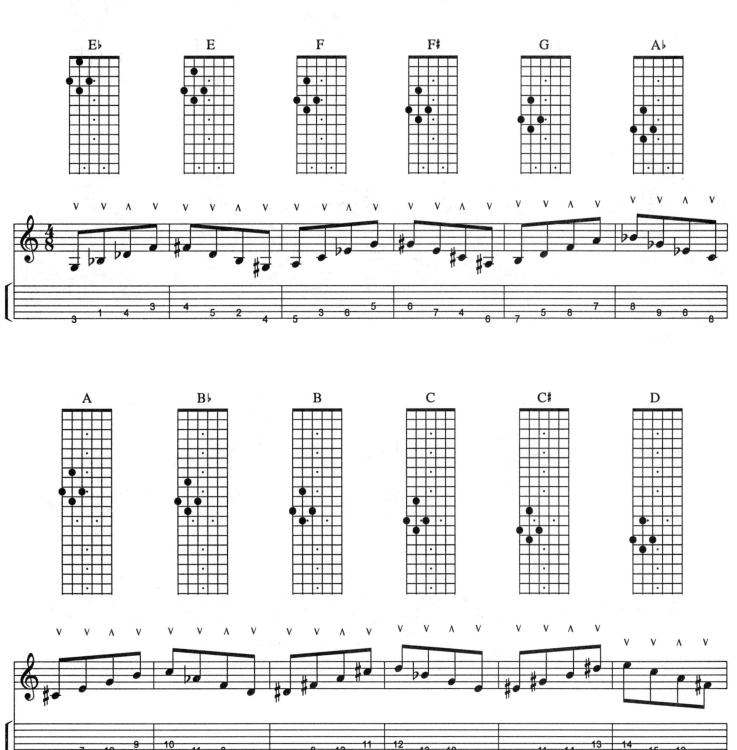

161

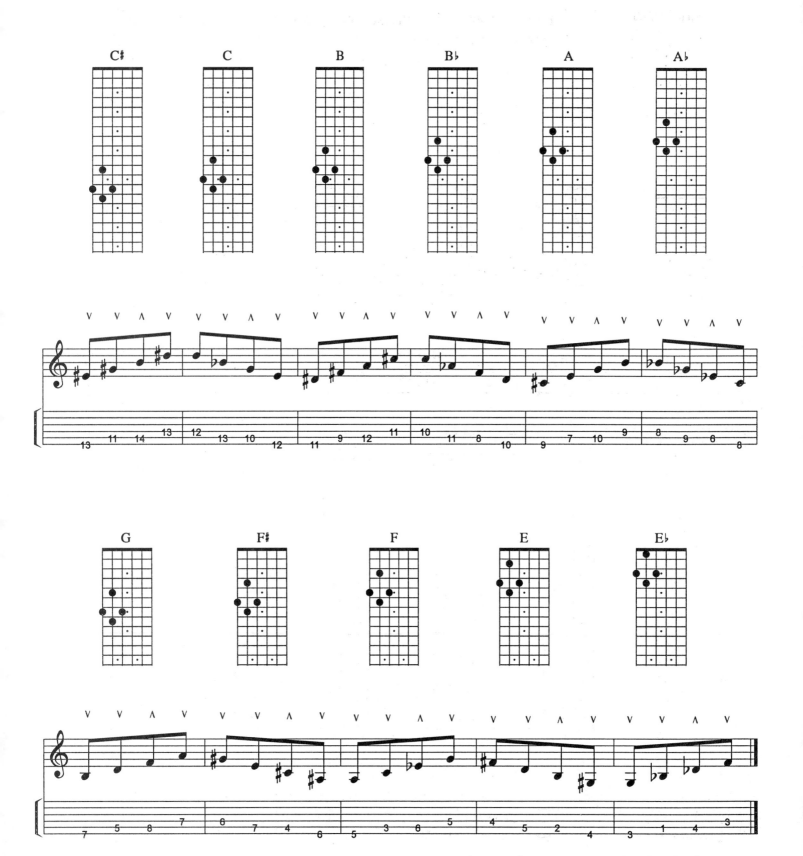

DOMINANT 9TH RUN #2

FINGERING

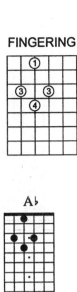

Dominant 9th run #2 is the same as #1 just moved over to the next strings. The picking is the same too.

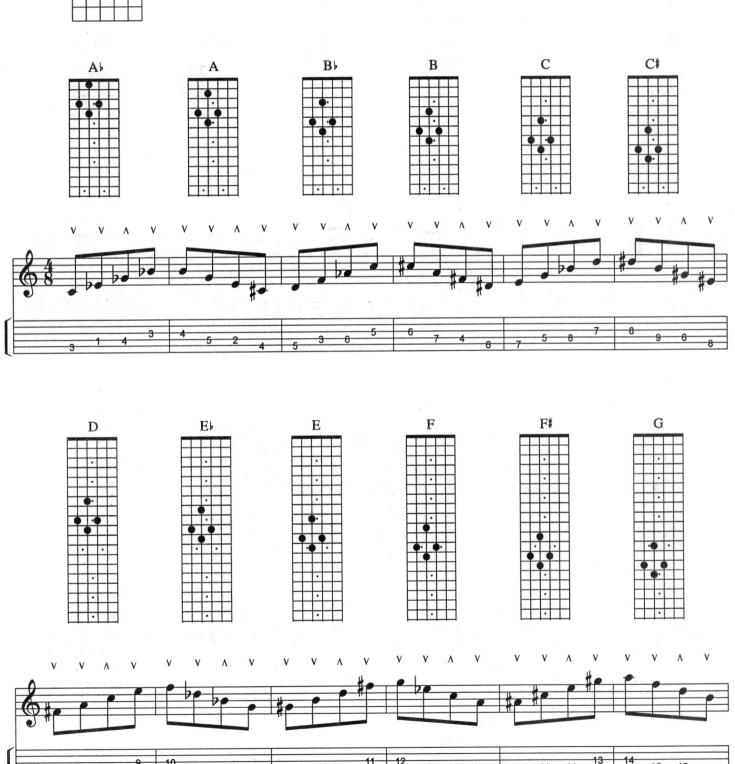

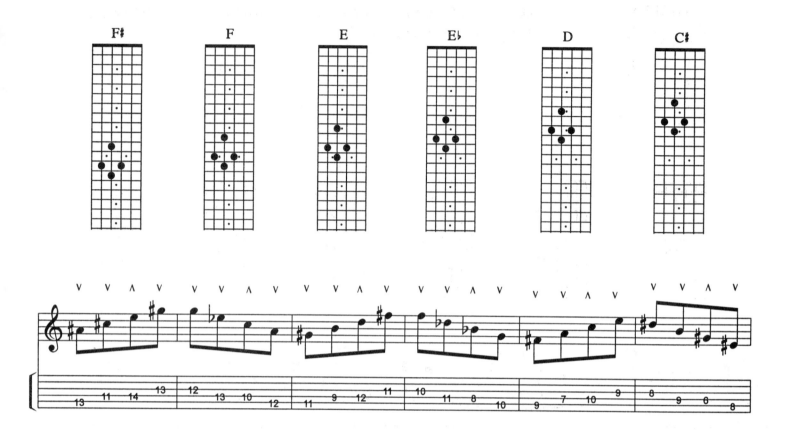

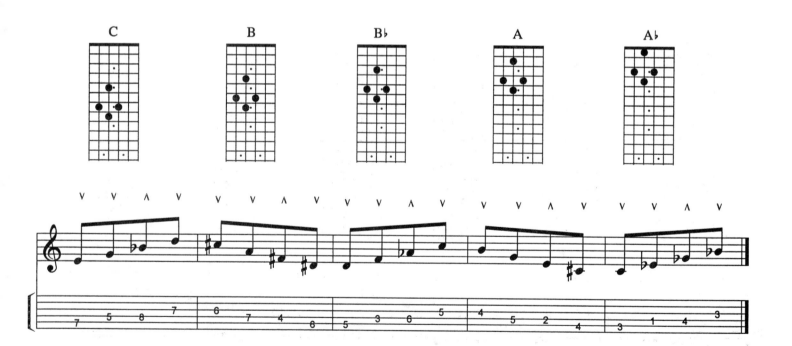

DOMINANT 9TH RUN #3

Dominant 9th run #3 is the same as #2 just moved over to the next strings.
The picking is the same too.

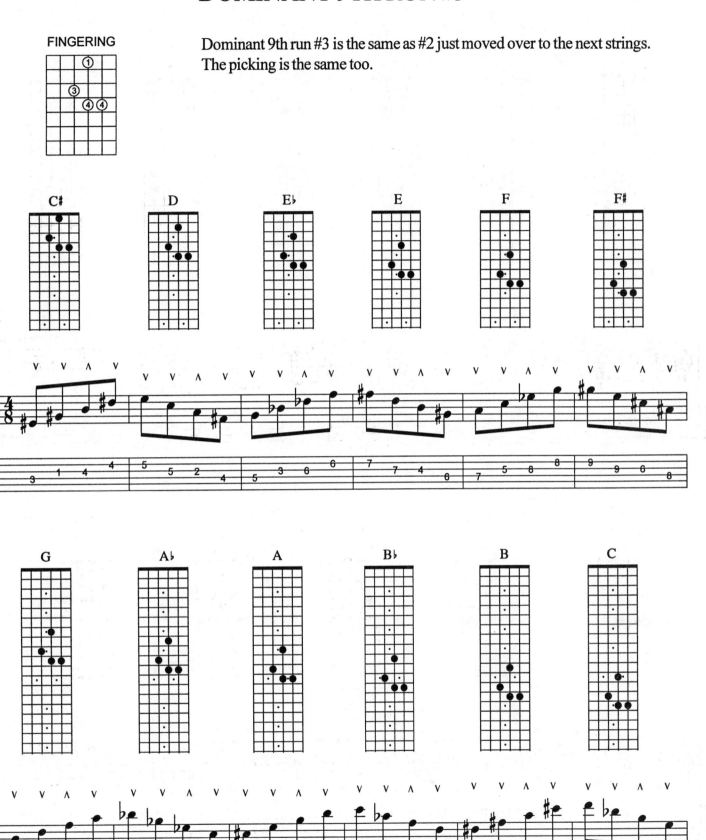

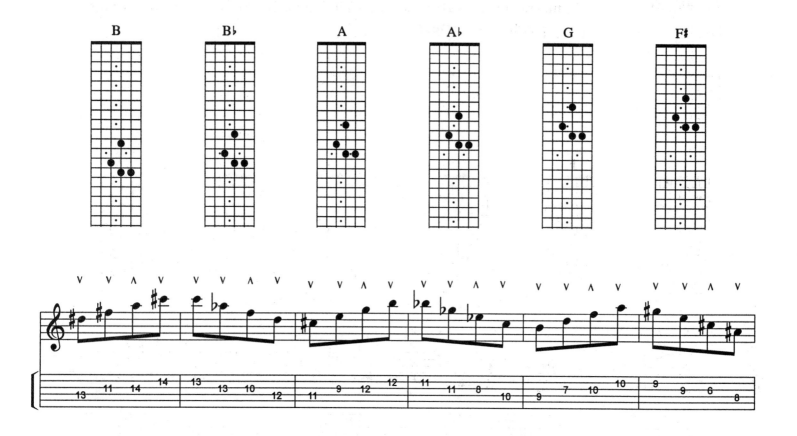
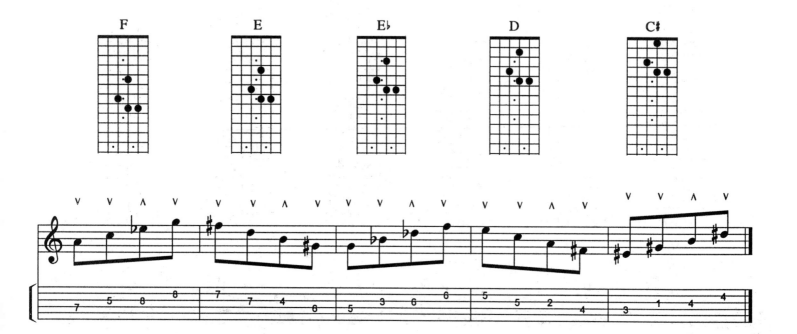

DOMINANT 9TH RUN #4

FINGERING

Dominant 9th run #4 is the same as #3 just moved over to the next strings. The picking is the same too.

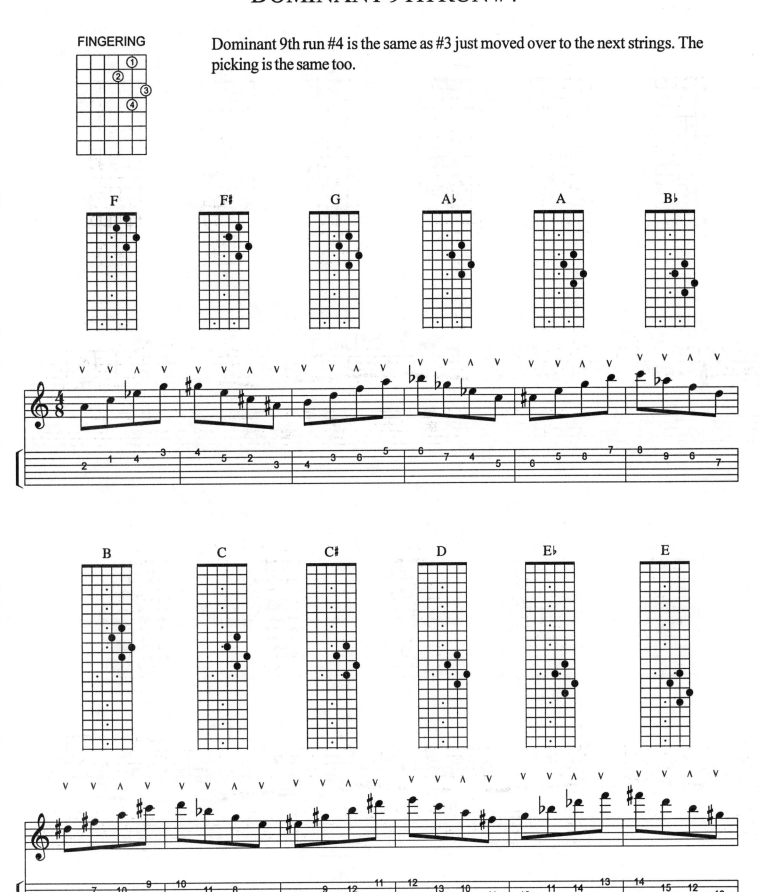

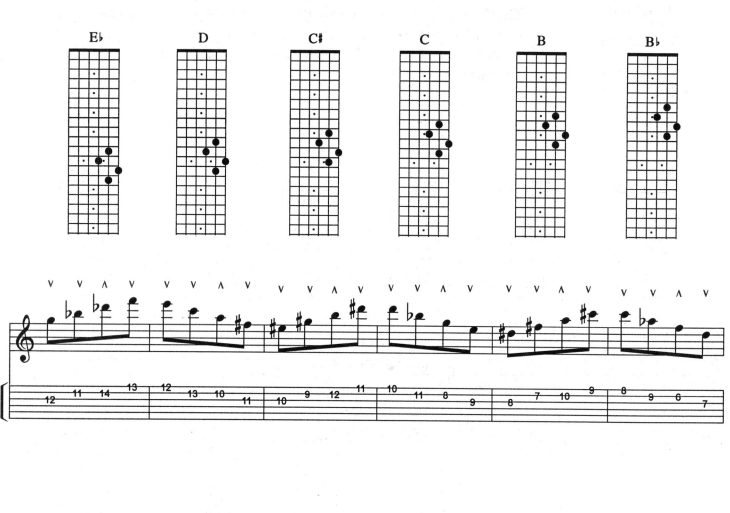

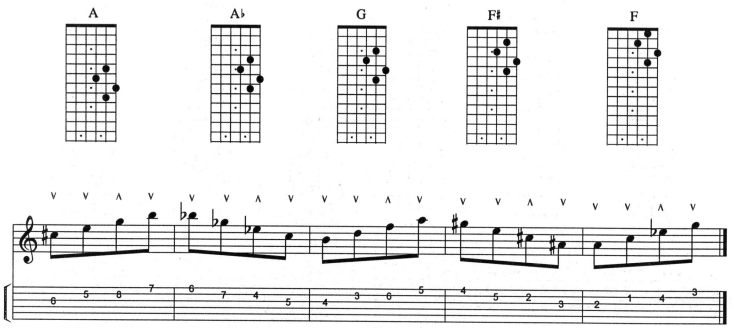

DIMINISHED 7TH RUN #1

FINGERING

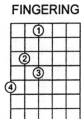

The Diminished 7th run #1 contains all the tones of the Diminished 7th chord 1, ♭3, ♭5, ♯7 with the root on top. The picking pattern is the same as Minor 7th runs #1 thru #4 and Dominant 7th runs #1 thru #4. The extra little stretch of this run is good for the left hand.

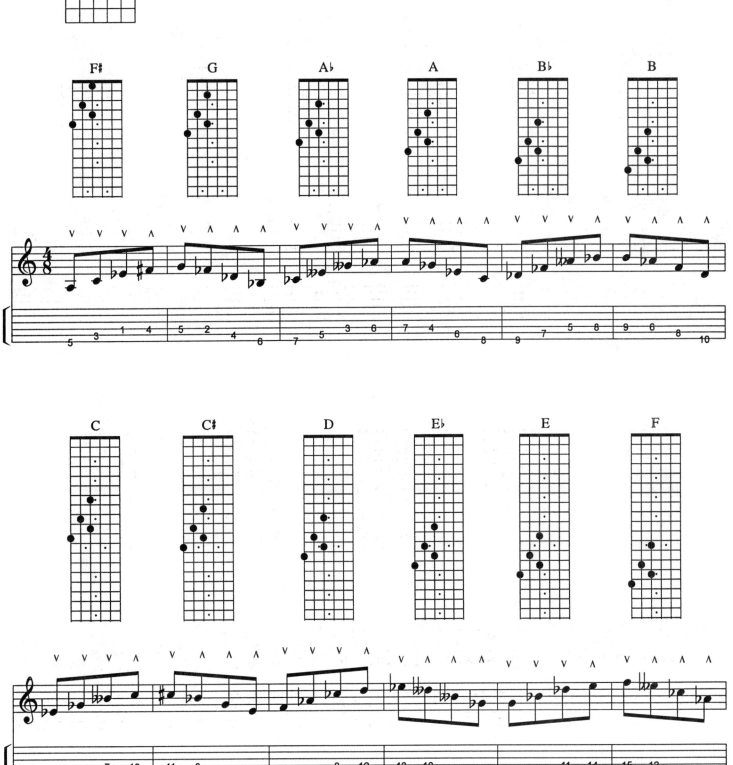

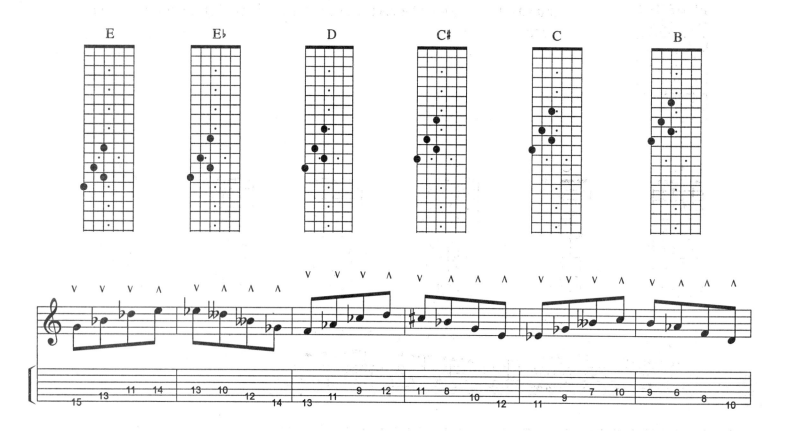
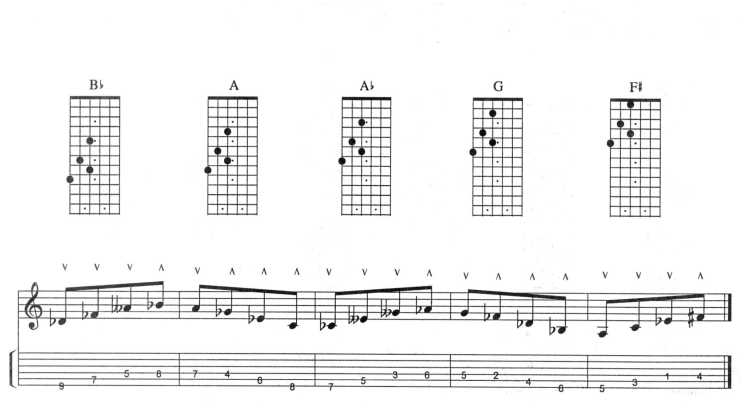

DIMINISHED 7TH RUN #2

FINGERING

Diminished 7th run #2 is the same as #1 just moved over to the next strings. The picking is the same too.

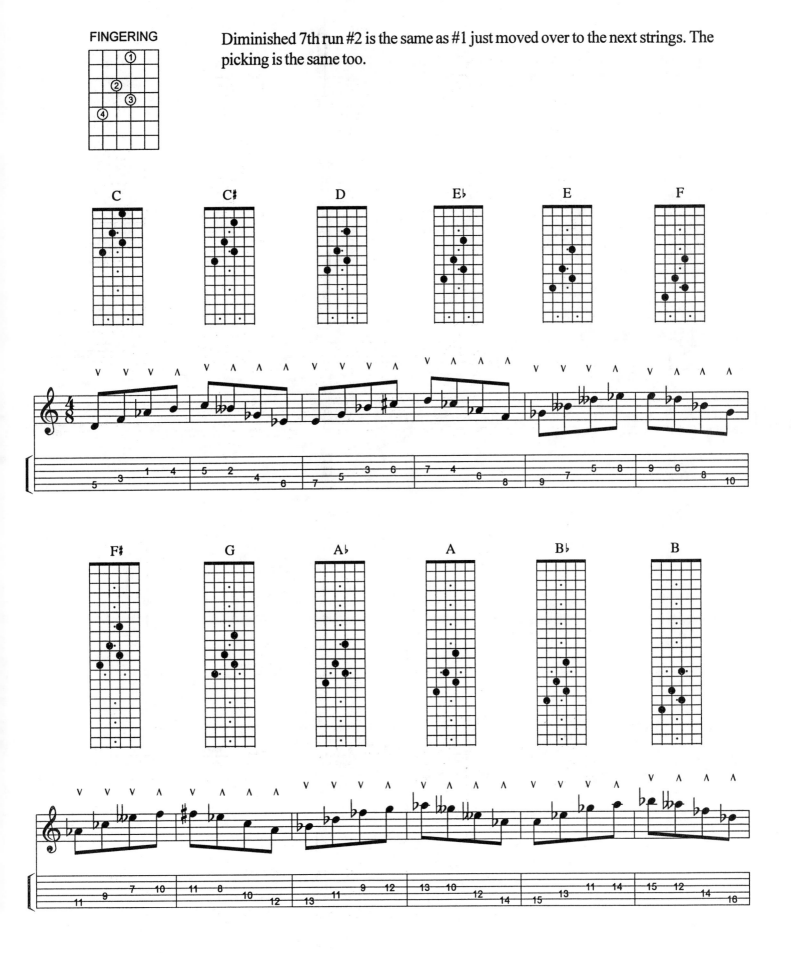

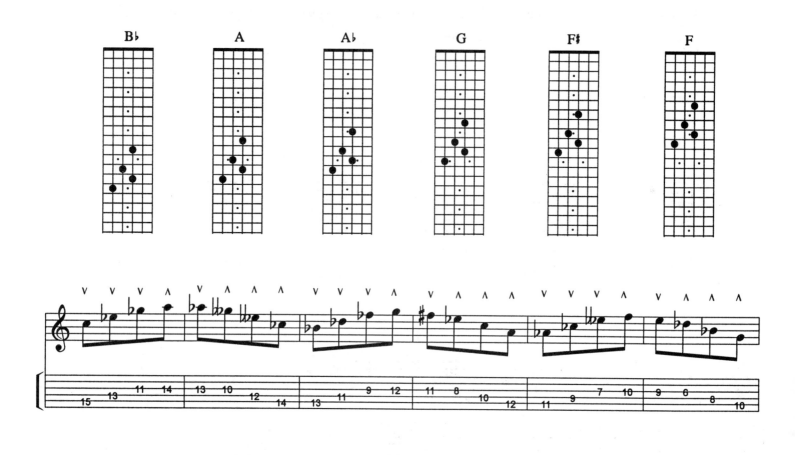

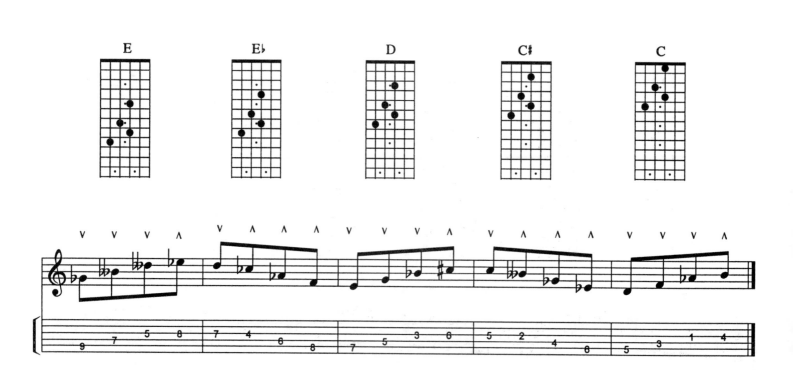

DIMINISHED 7TH RUN #3

FINGERING

Diminished 7th run #3 is the same as #2 just moved over to the next strings. The picking is the same too.

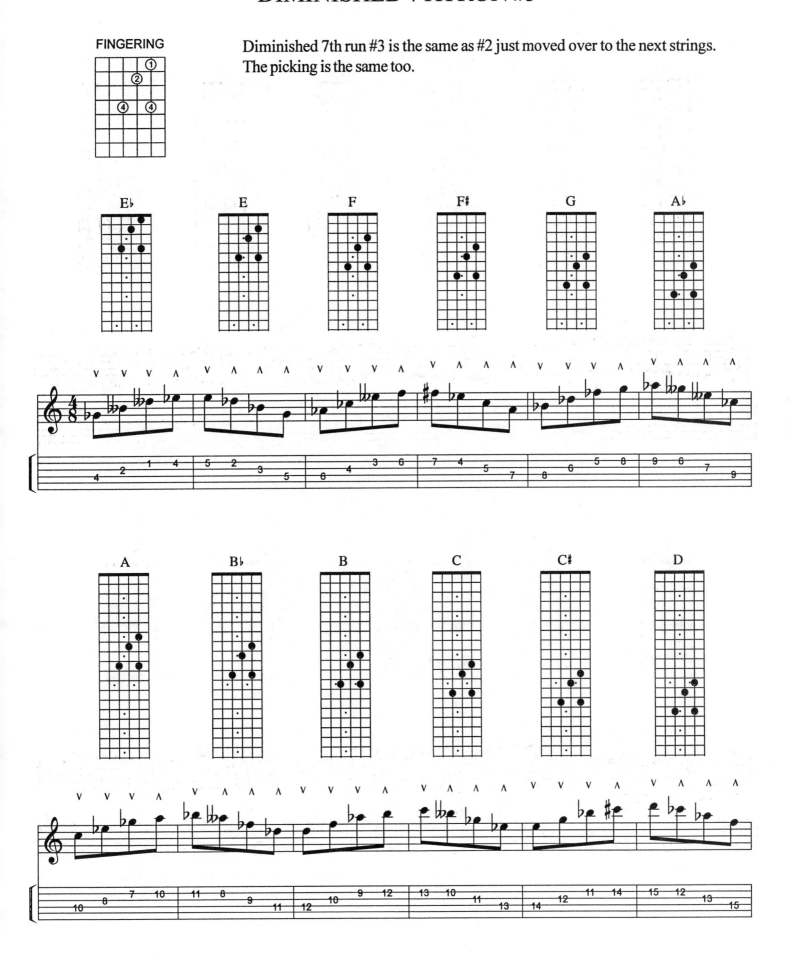

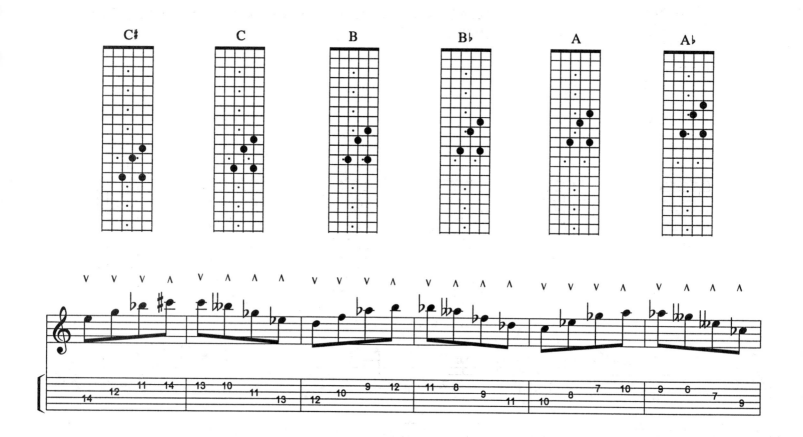

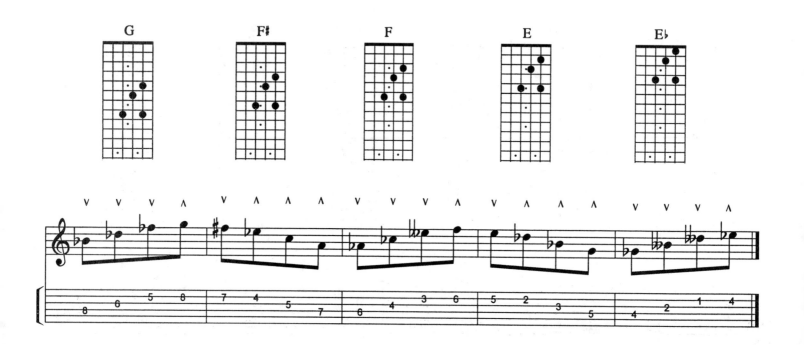

DIMINISHED 7TH RUN #4

FINGERING

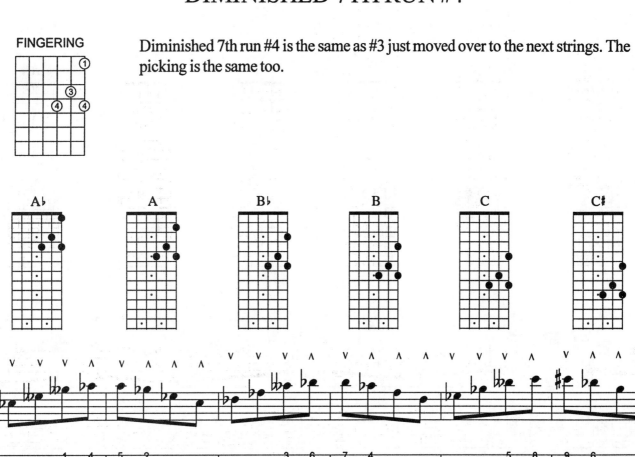

Diminished 7th run #4 is the same as #3 just moved over to the next strings. The picking is the same too.

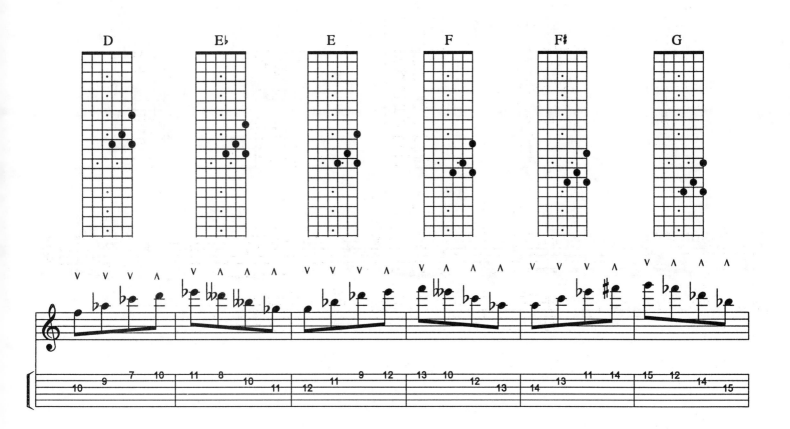

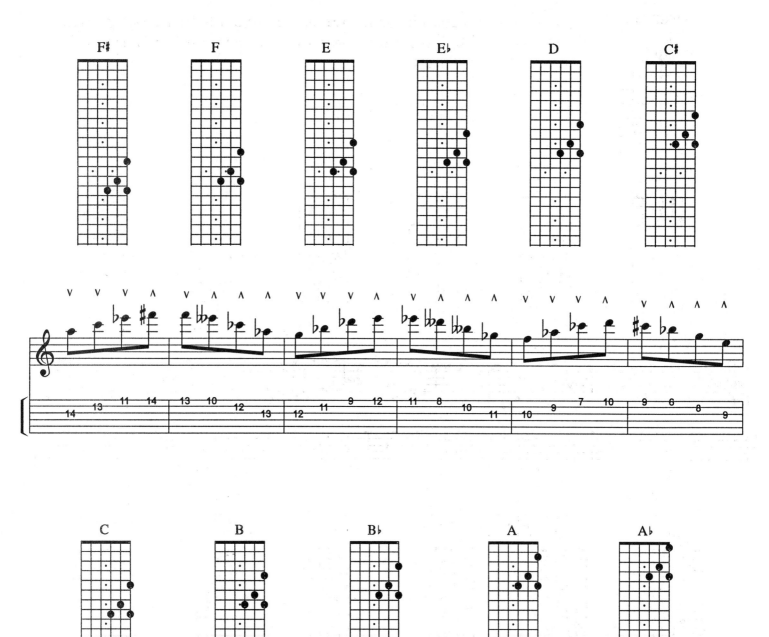

176

DIMINISHED 7TH RUN #5

FINGERING

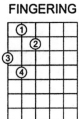

The Diminished 7th run #5 contains all the tones of the Diminished 7th chord 1, ♭3 ,♭5, ♯7 with the root on the bottom. The picking pattern is the same as Dominant 9th run #1.

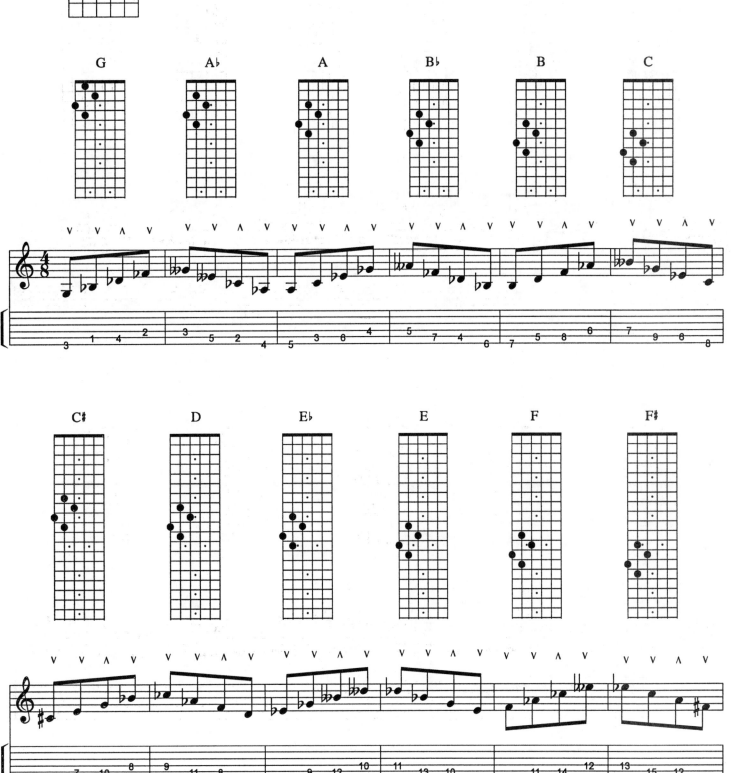

177

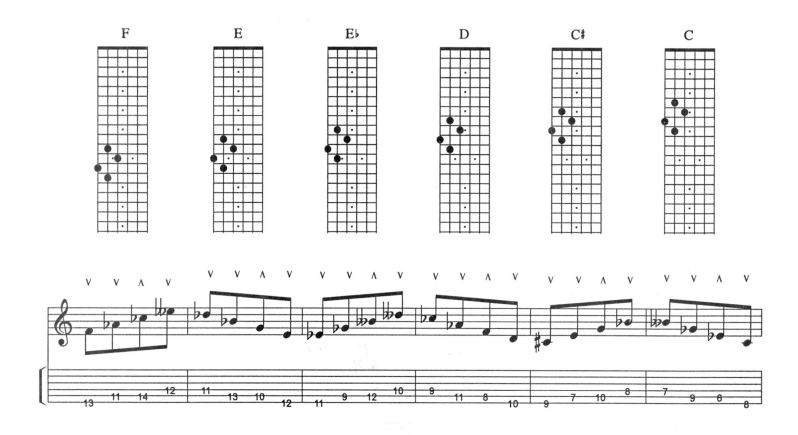

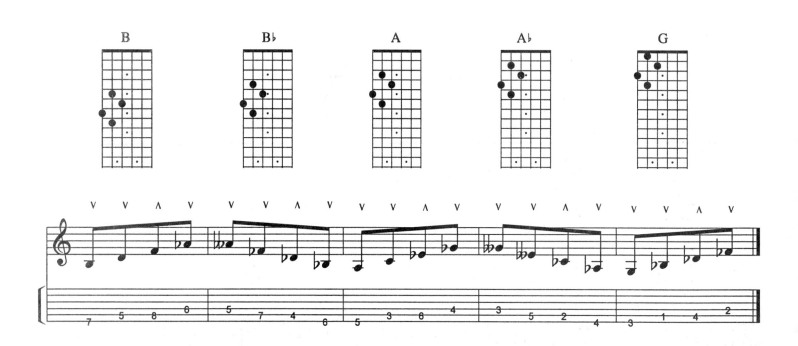

DIMINISHED 7TH RUN #6

FINGERING

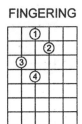

Diminished 7th run #6 is the same as #5 just moved over to the next strings. The picking is the same too.

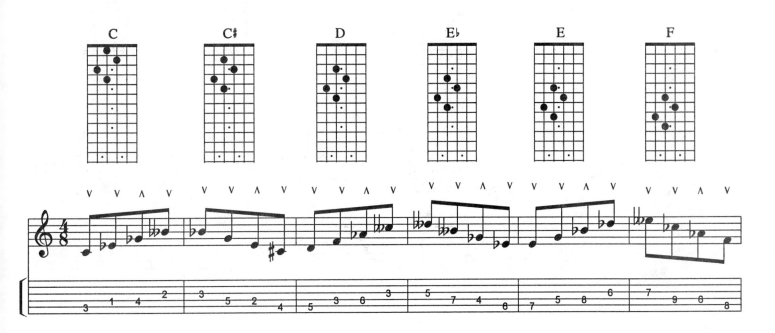

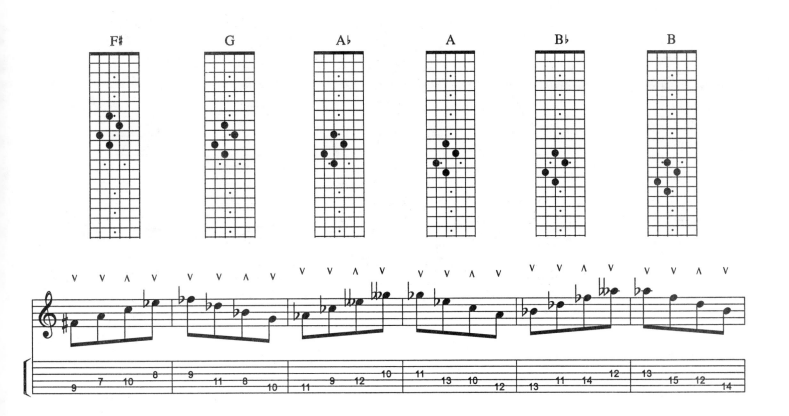

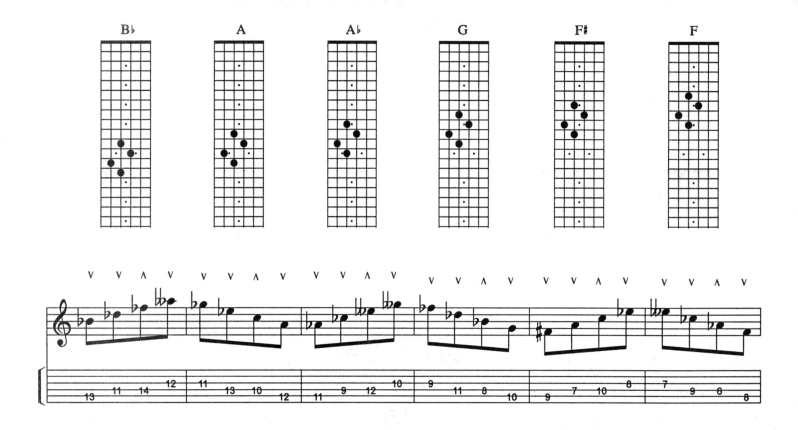

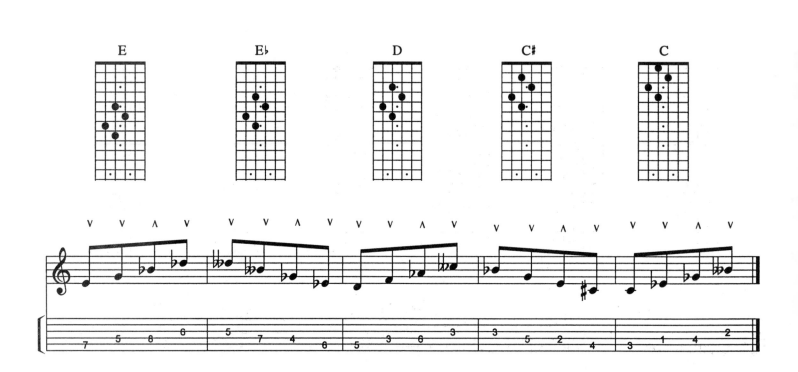

DIMINISHED 7TH RUN #7

FINGERING

Diminished 7th run #7 is the same as #6 just moved over to the next strings. The picking is the same too.

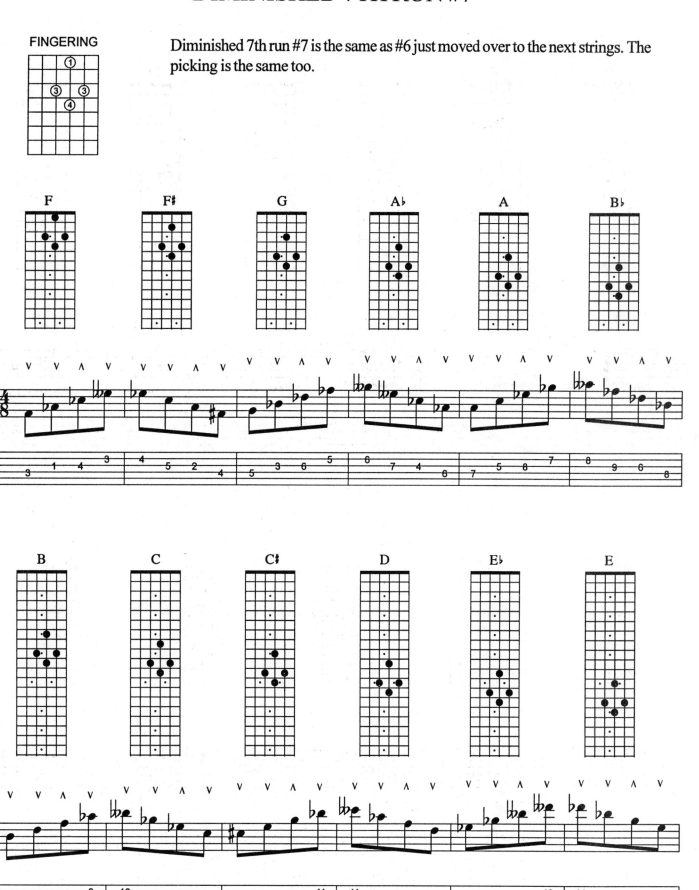

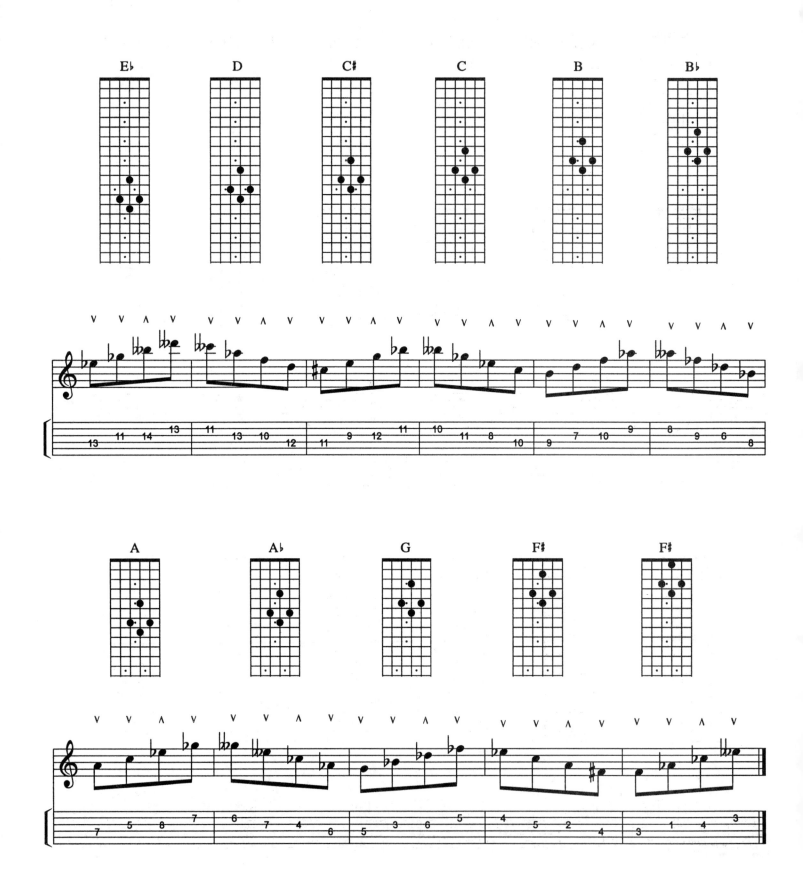

DIMINISHED 7TH RUN #8

FINGERING

Diminished 7th run #8 is the same as #7 just moved over to the next strings. The picking is the same too.

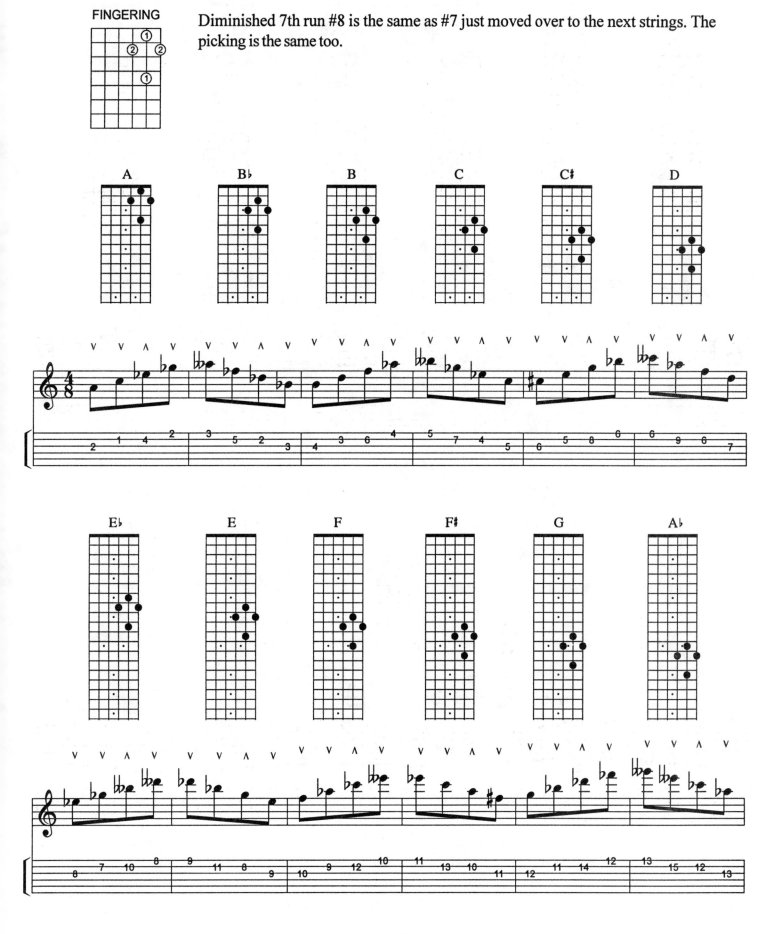

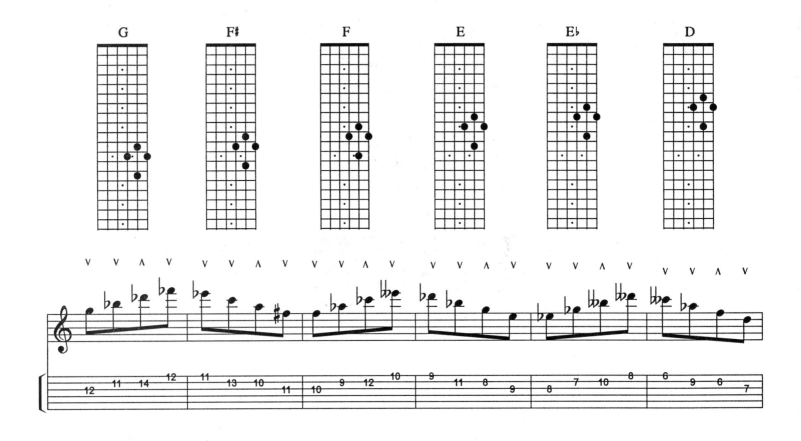

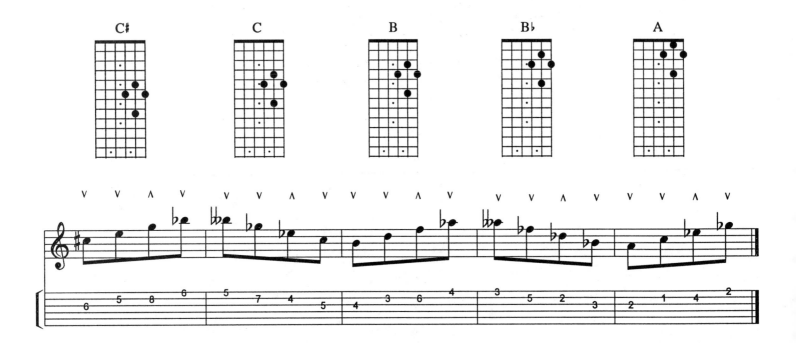

These are just a few of countless possibilities for creating chord run exercises. There should be more than enough here to give you a sufficient start for creating your own exercises. You can even create long complex ones.

PART FOUR

CHROMATIC EXERCISES

THE CHROMATIC EXERCISES

Up to this point all the exercises have dealt with scale or chord runs which can be used in your soloing or improvisations. This next section is called the Chromatic Exercises. They are not designed for their aesthetic value. They don't sound very good and you probably can't use them in your solos except as an effect which can work out quite nice if not over used. They are strictly for exercise.

Well, a true chromatic exercise would contain all 12 half steps as demonstrated below. You could play that by shifting the little finger. But that's not the point.

These exercices only use four fingers per string which means there would be some missing notes.

So we can deduce that these are not true chromatic exercises. Therefore, what do we call these things? Dexterity exercises? Picking exercises? You see the predicament. So because they have a bunch of chromatic notes hence for the sake of simplicity they are called chromatic exercises.

Enough of my musical nit pickings. These are some of my favorite "chromatic" exercises. They are great for picking and dexterity. The fretboard above the measure gives a quickie view of which notes are played. The notation and the tab tells you what order to play the note. And the tab also corresponds to what fingers you use. The picking is alternating (down, up, down, up) for each exercise. The exercises are not in any special order and are numbered for reference and can be learned and practiced out of sequence, so have fun.

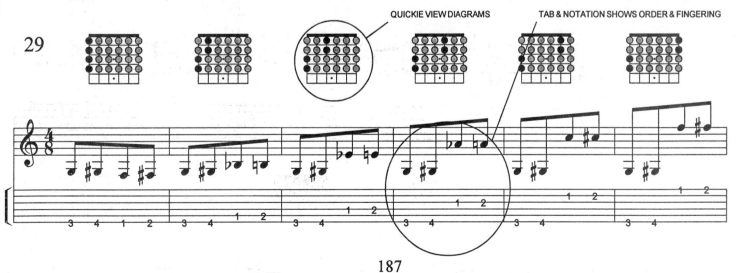

29

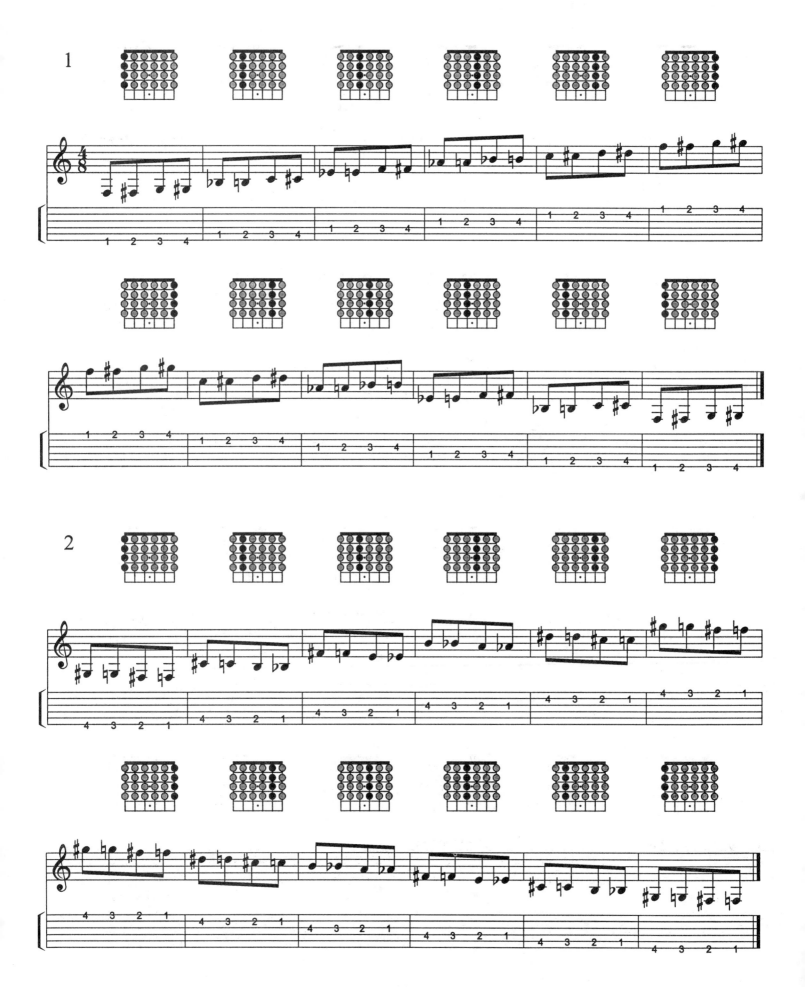

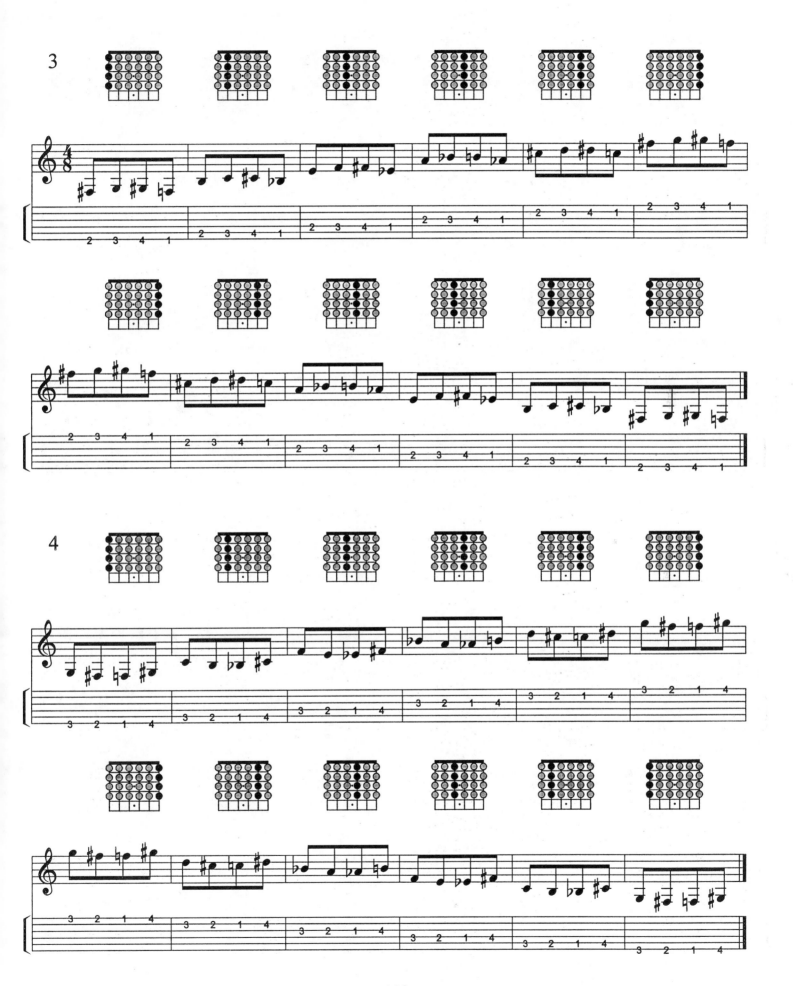

189

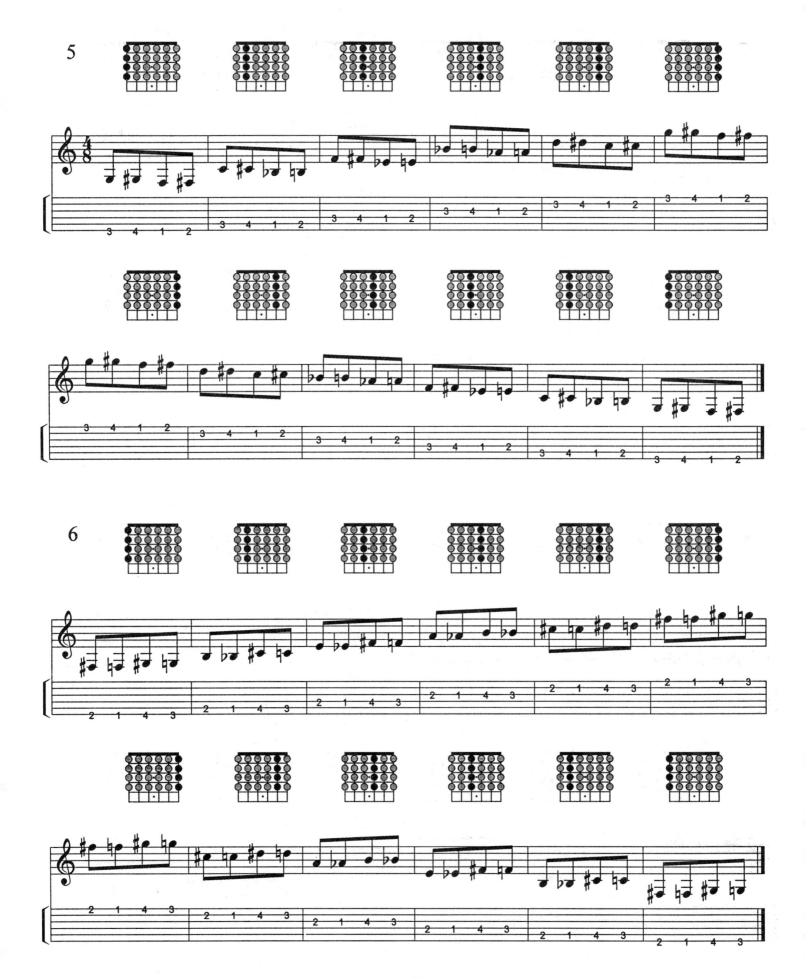

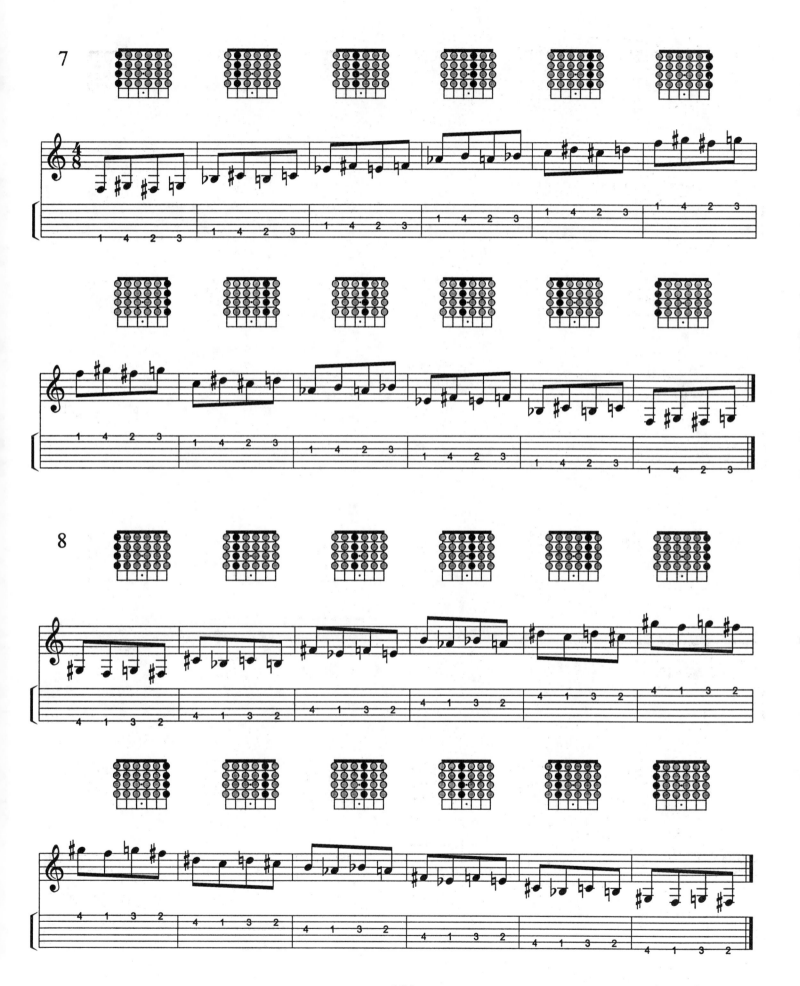

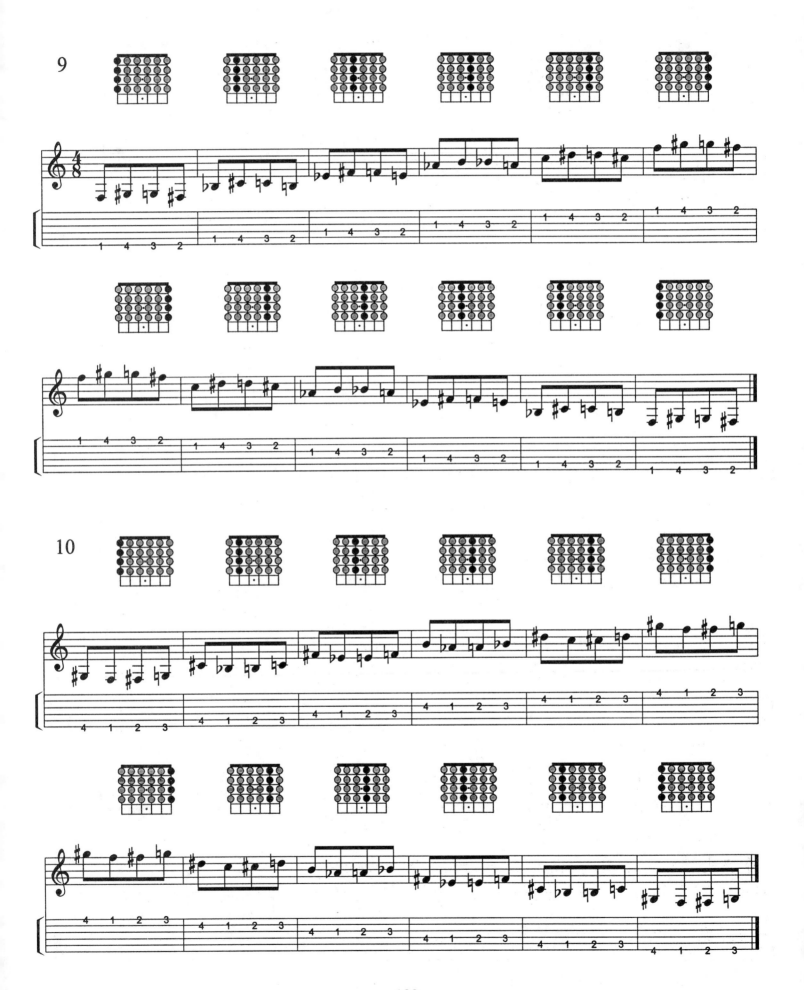

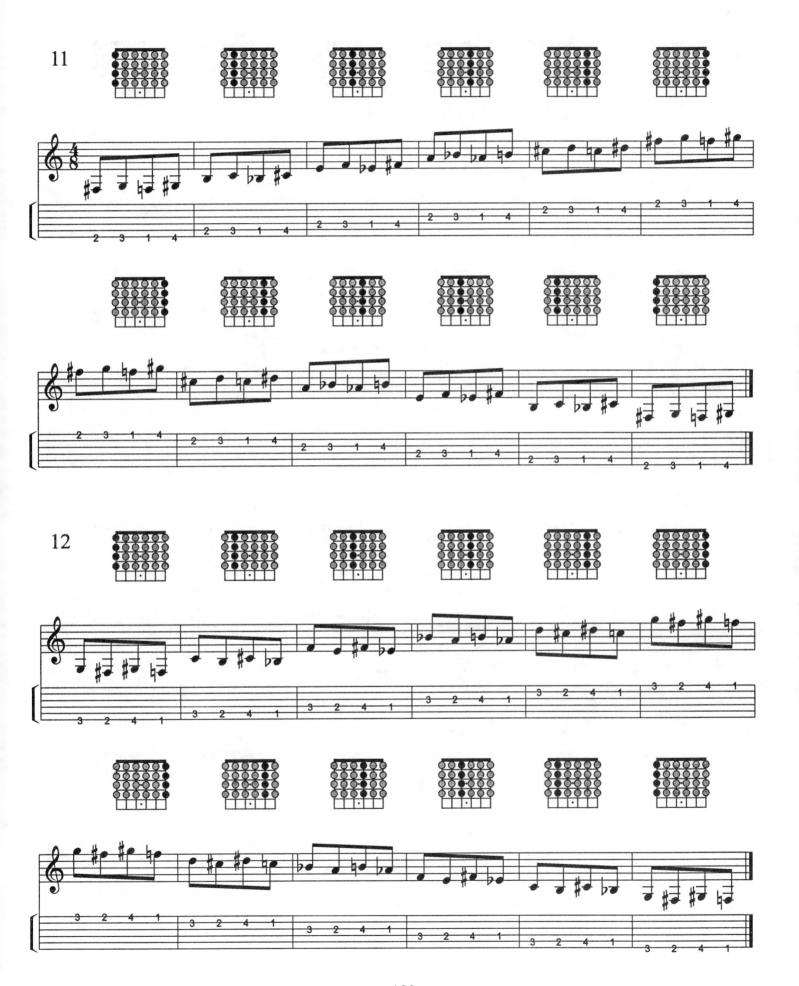

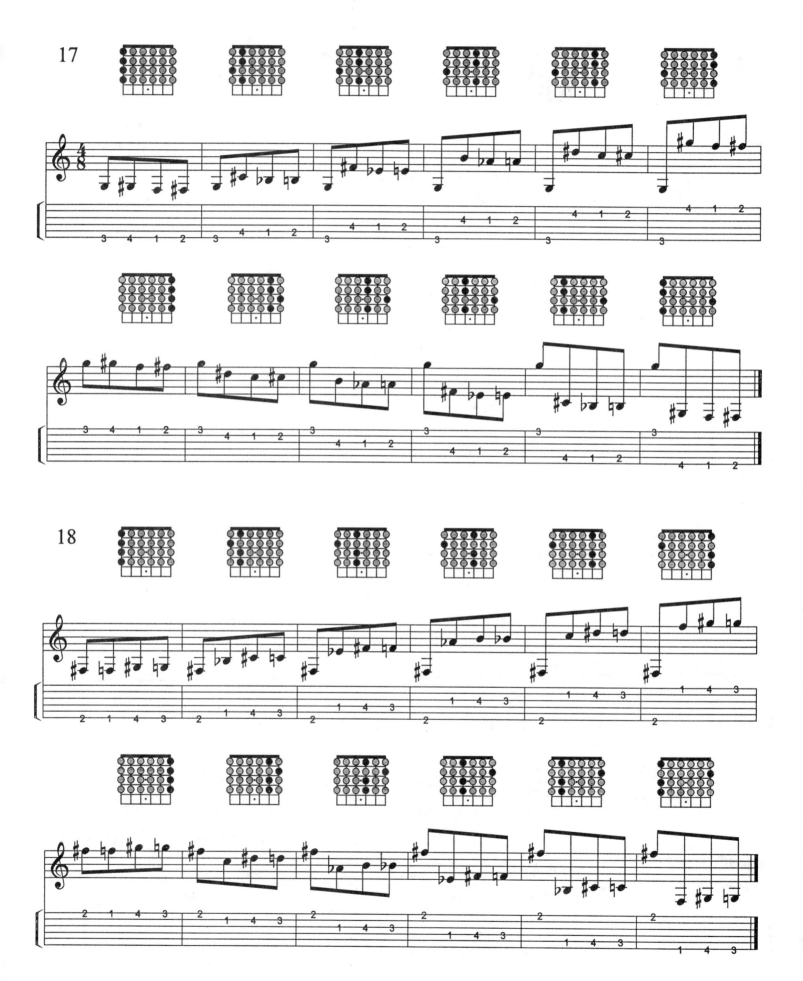

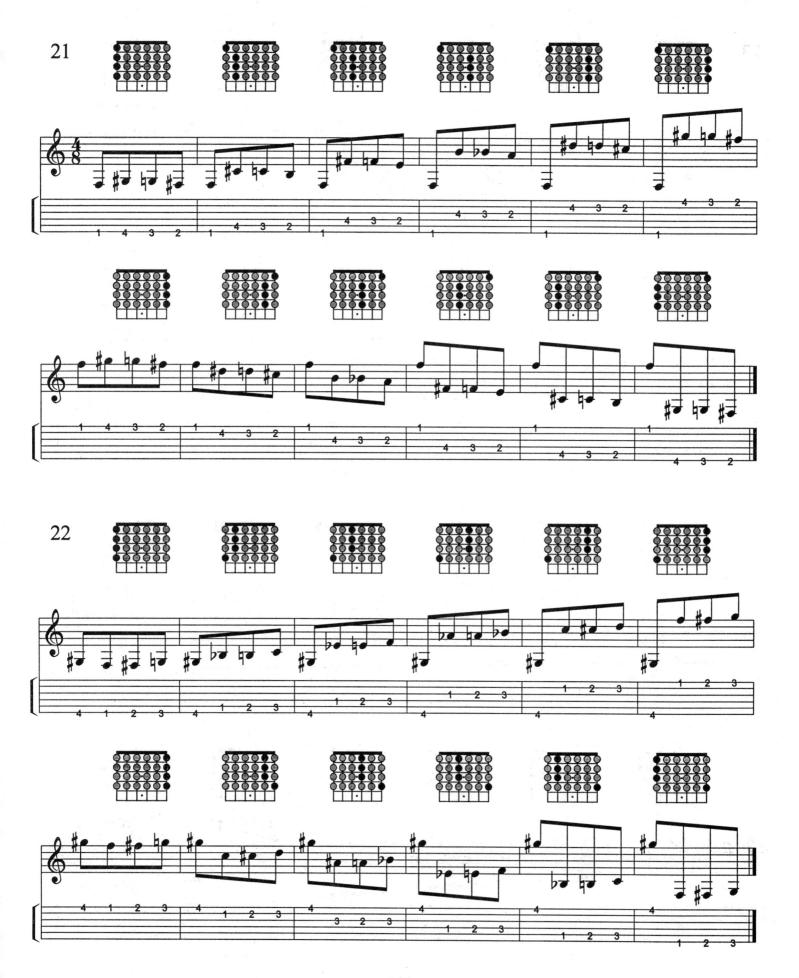

198

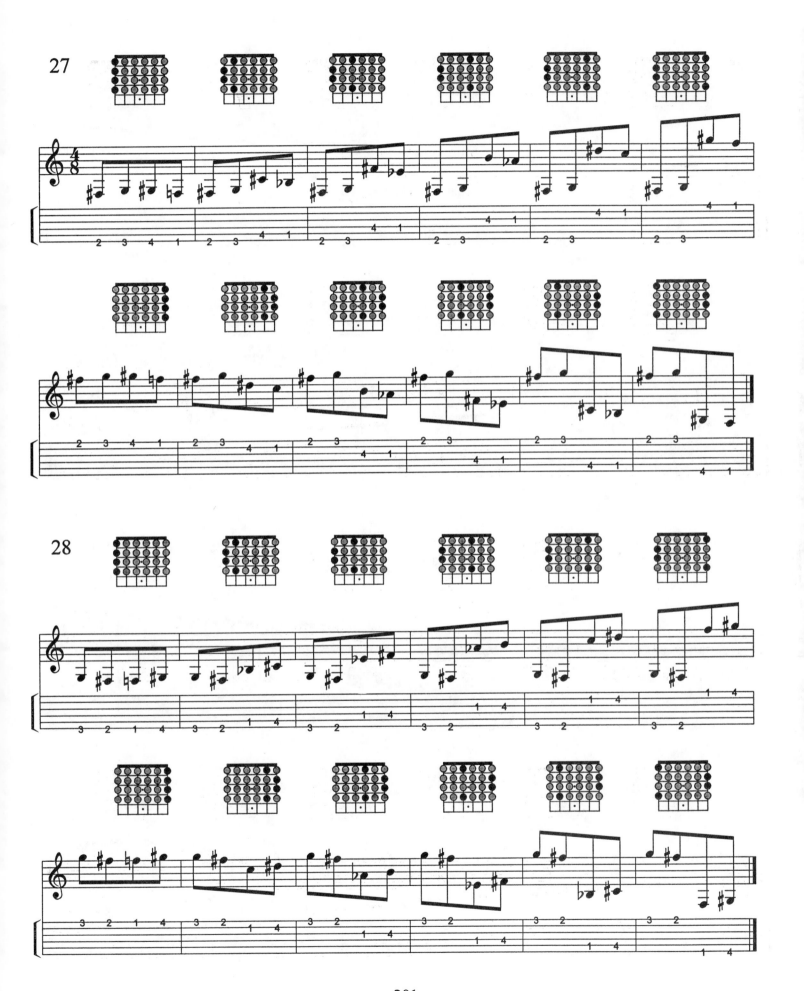

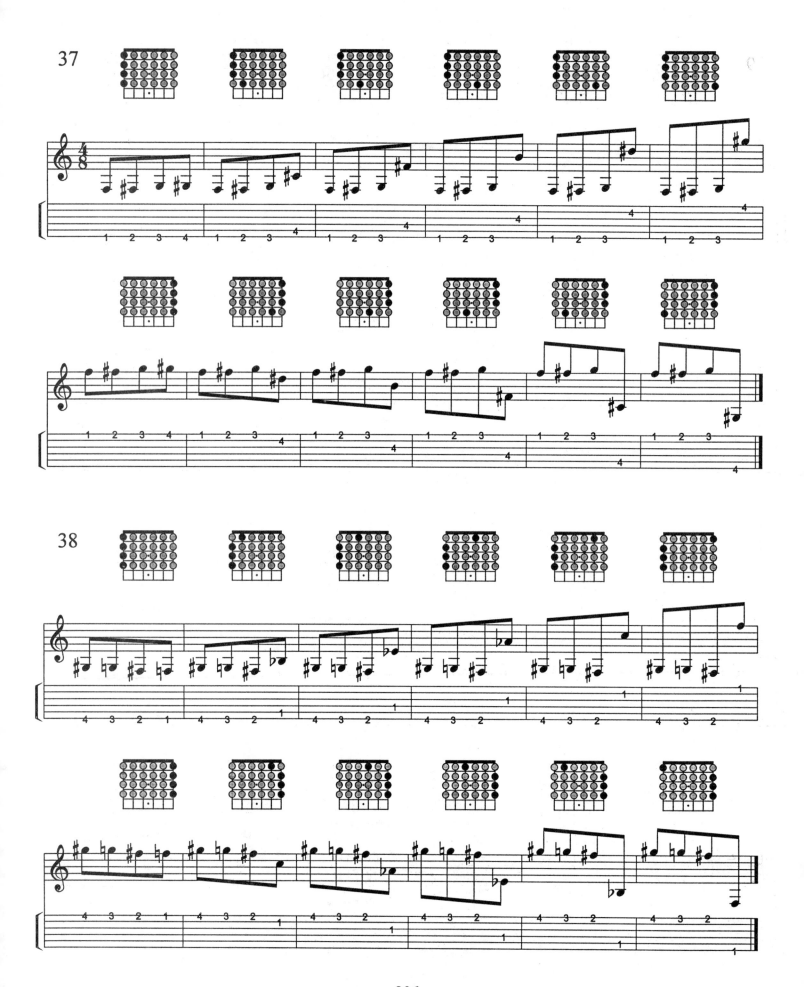

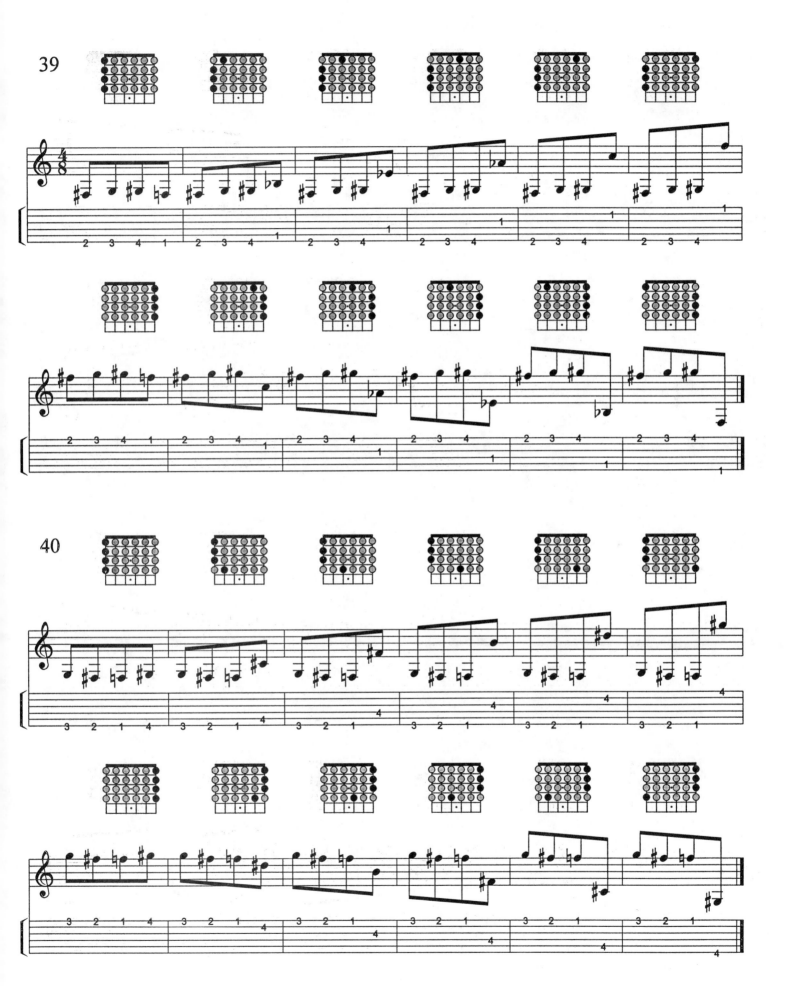

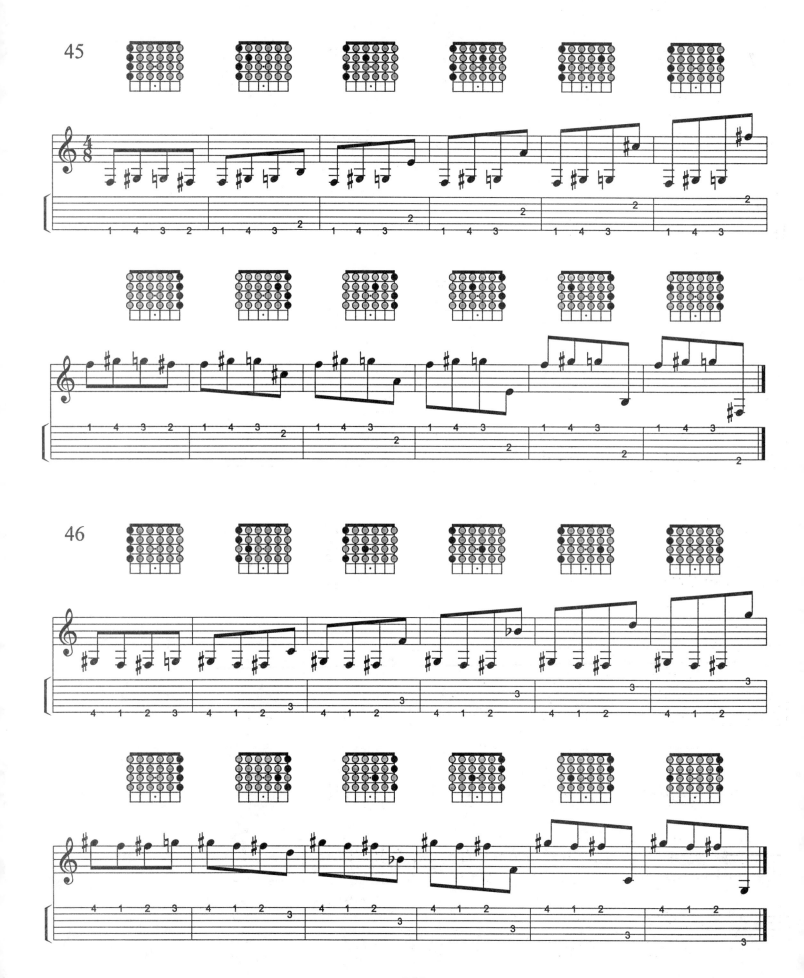

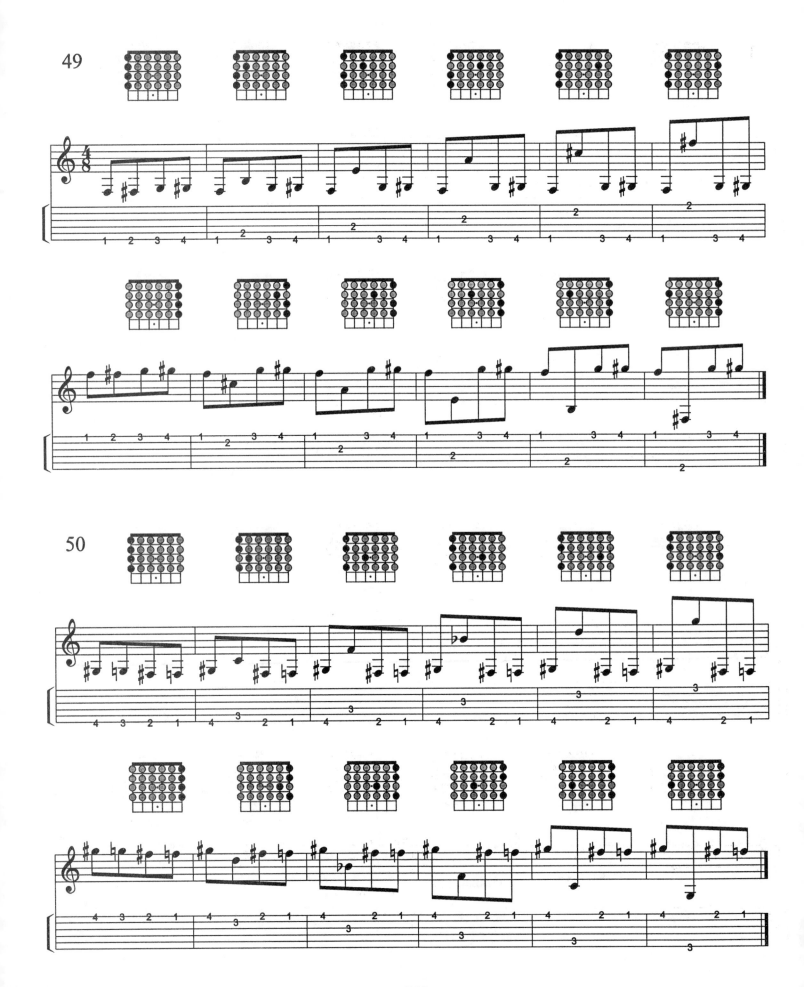

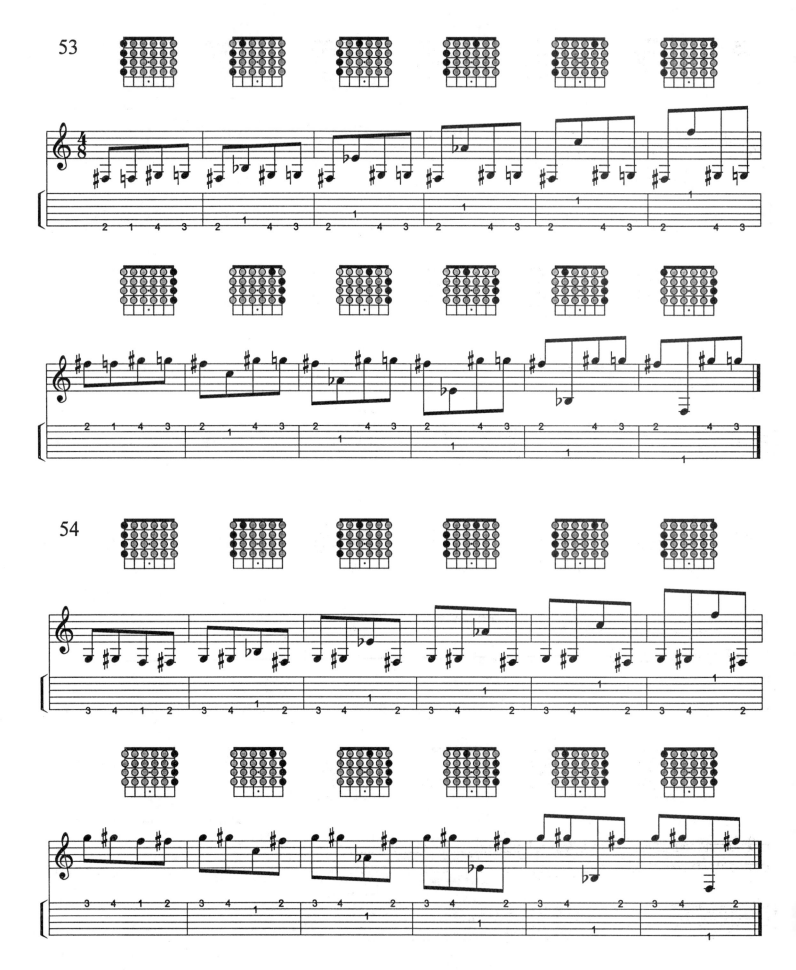

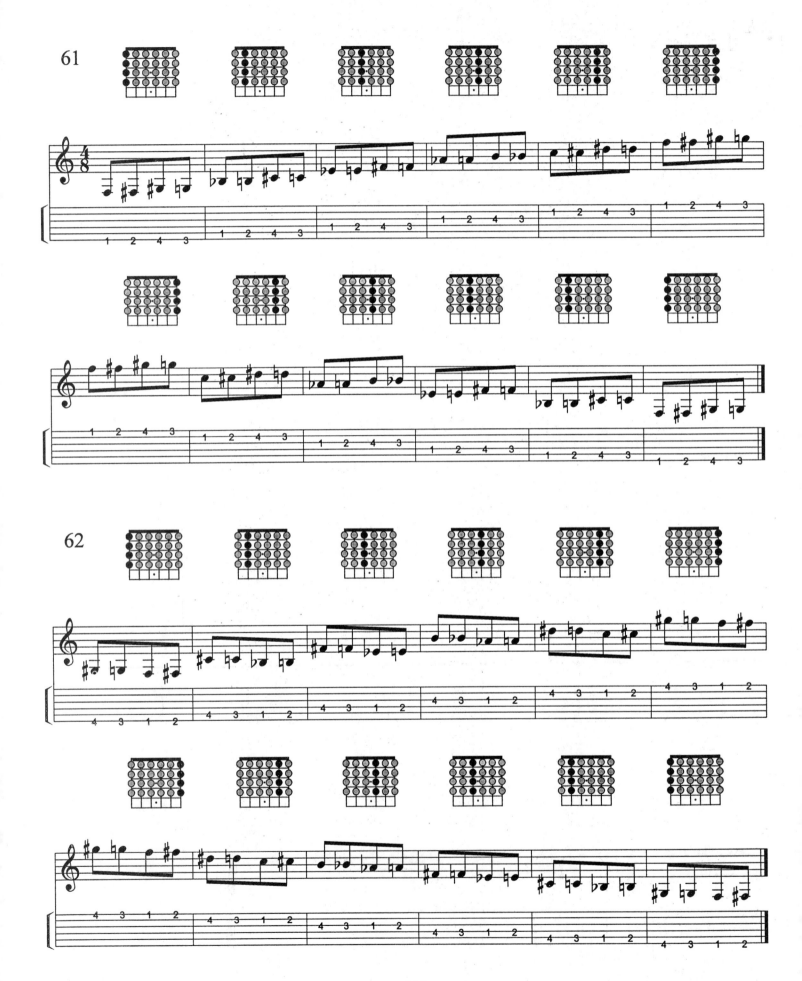

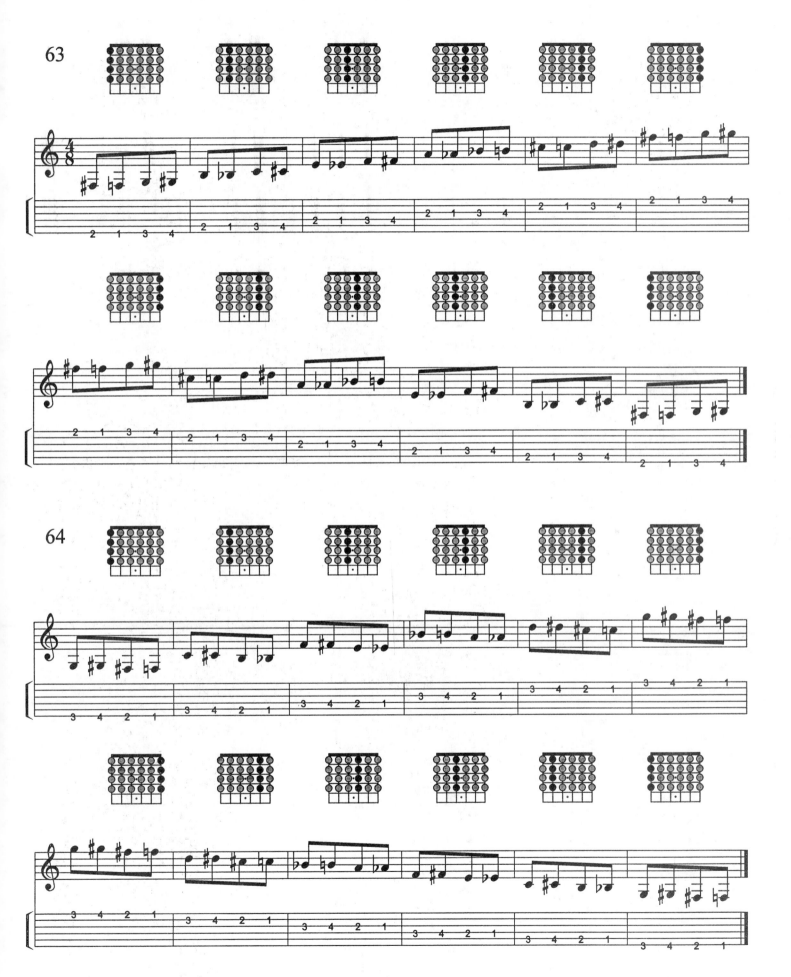

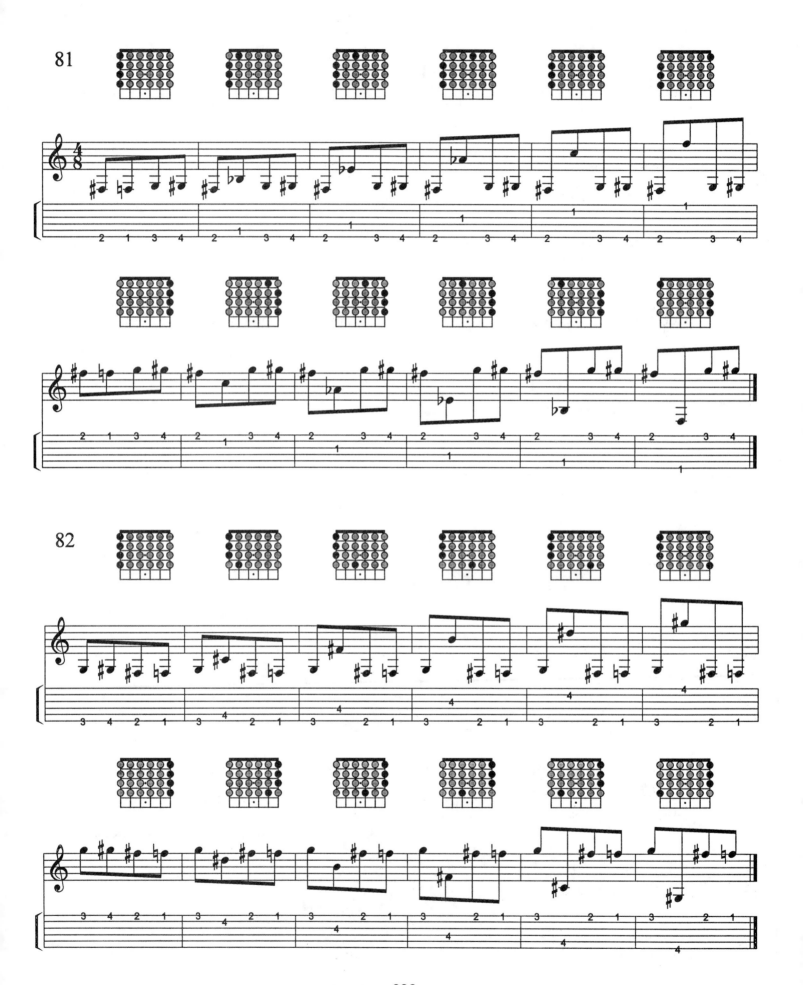

228

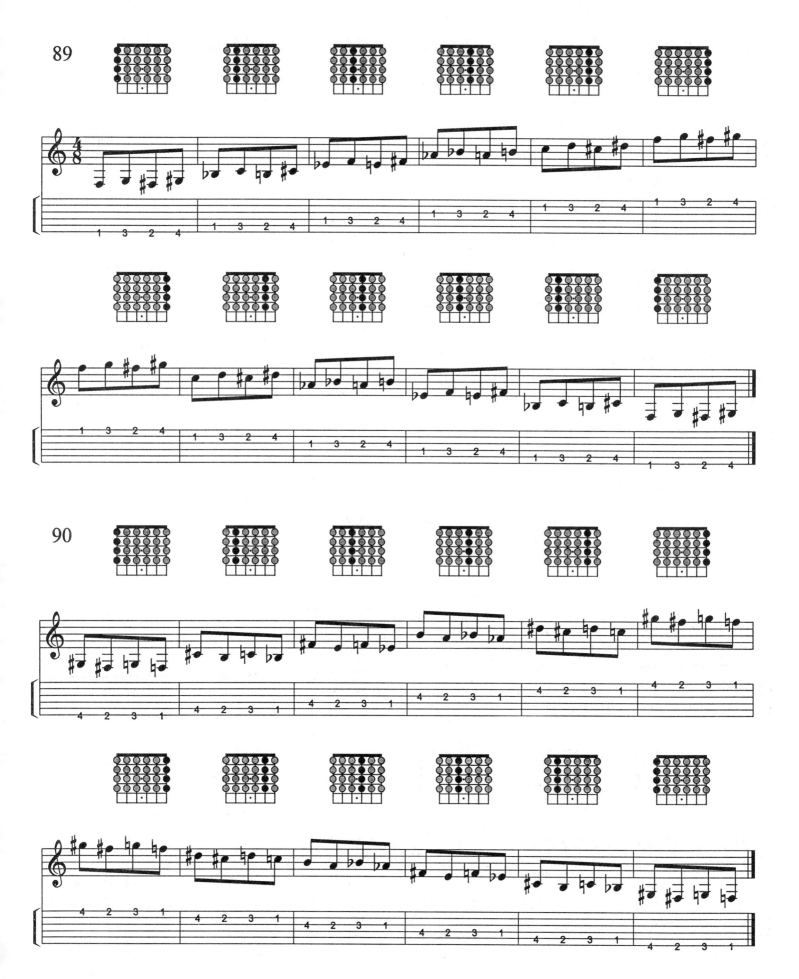

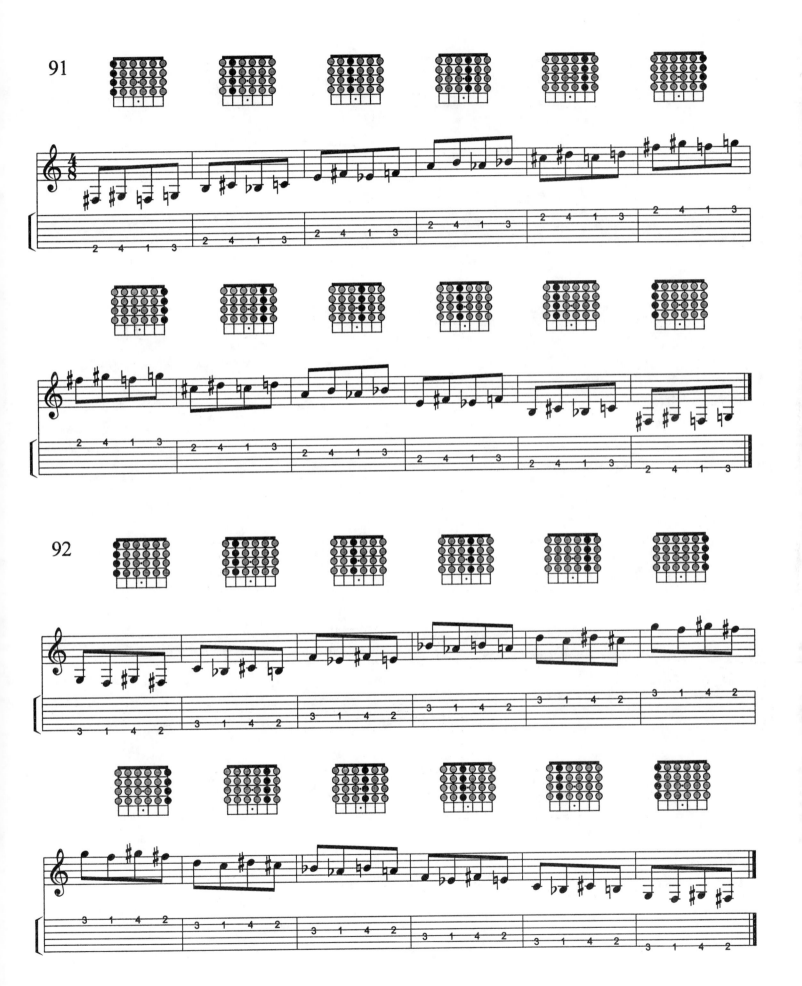

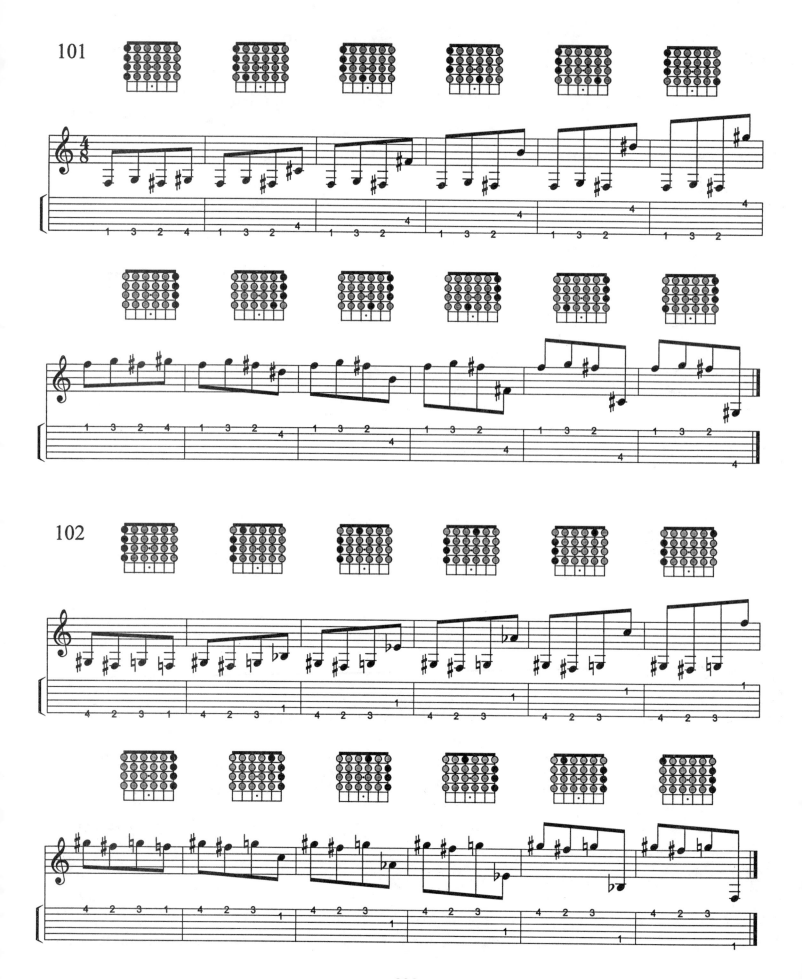

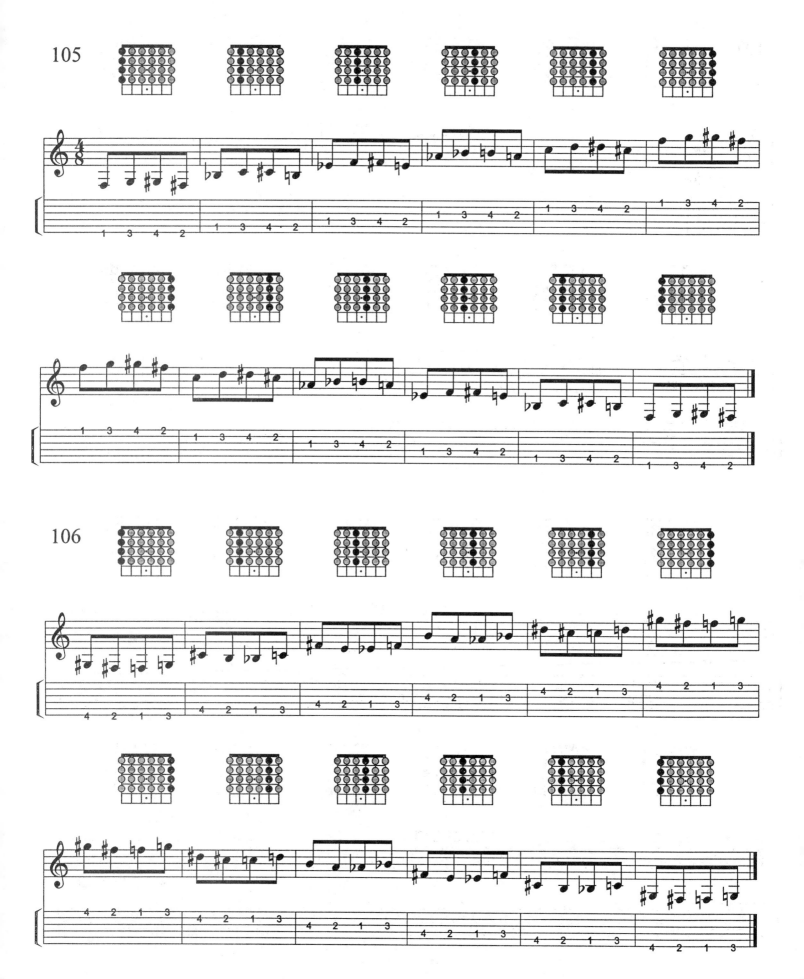

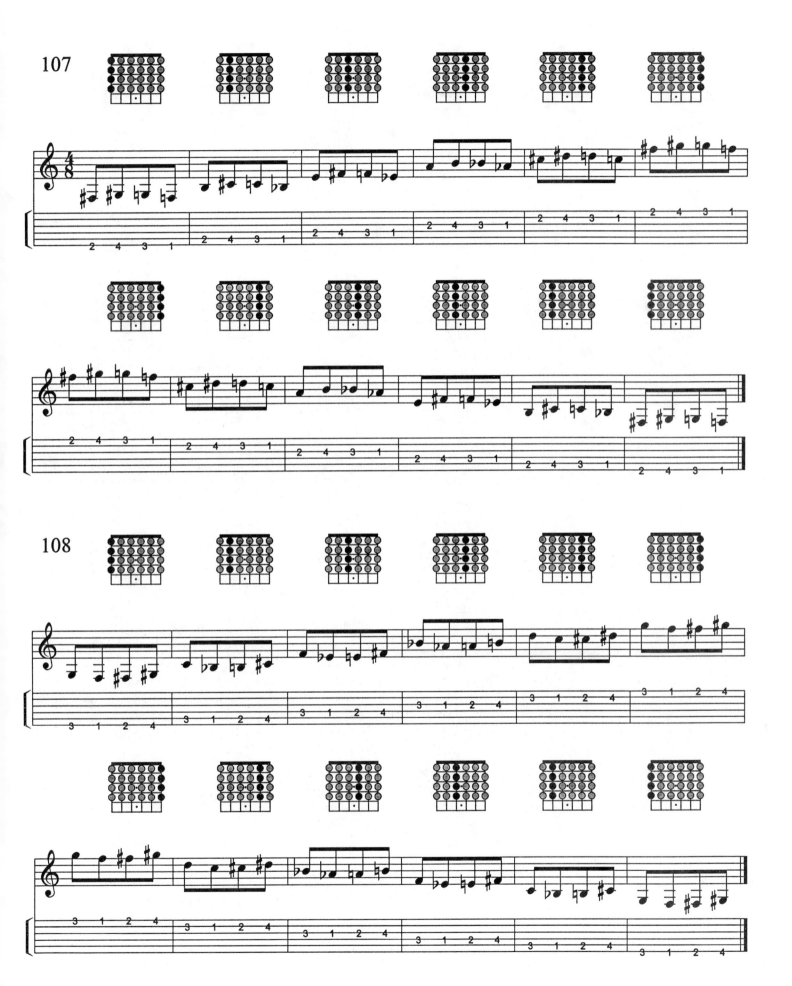

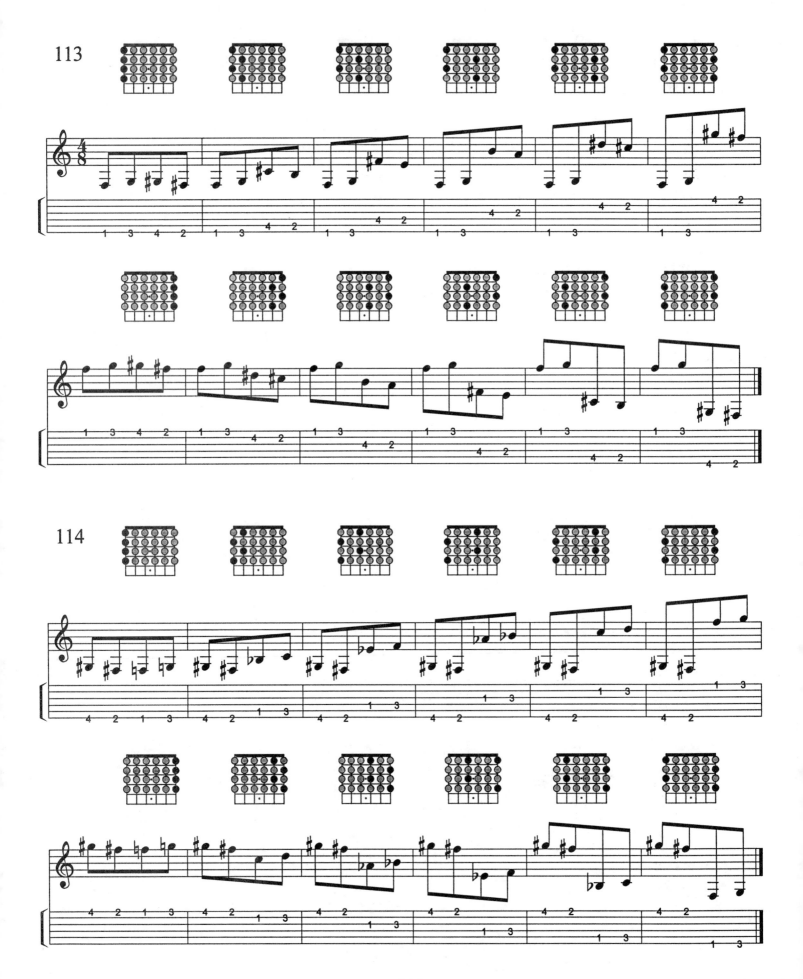

245

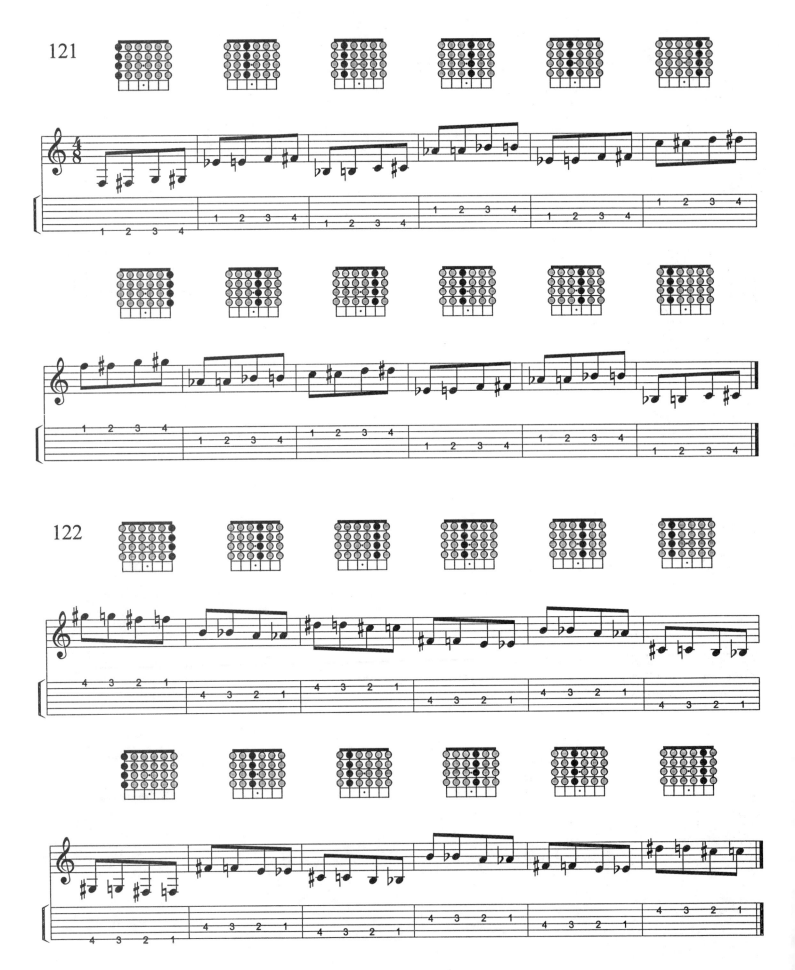

Ascend to a higher plane

Grimoire®

BY ADAM KADMON

THE EXERCISE BOOK

The Exercise Book offers players a fresh and disciplined approach to attaining mastery of the guitar. Laying out the entire foundation for developing dexterity on the guitar, it includes such unique features as 3 and 4 note scales and chordal "coils" for Major and Minor Pentatonic scales, picking patterns and diagrams for each of the "coils," connection of fingering patterns up and down the fretboard and special exercises designed to strengthen playing capacity. The Exercise Book is a thorough and complete compendium of exercises for the guitar.

GT100

THE QUICK CHORD BOOK

With this book Adam Kadmon has created a concise compendium of the basic guitar chords that are most often used by players in all styles, at all levels of performing ability. This book, designed for the novice guitarist, will show beginning players the essential chords quickly and facilitate mastery of a basic repertoire of chords in minutes. Each key is represented by 75 different chords from major and minor chords to thirteenth chords, shown in both fretboard position diagrams and traditional staff notation.

GT102

THE FINGERPICKING BOOK

Starting with basic fingerpicking chord patterns and expanding to major and minor scales and bass ostinato variations, this book uses thousands of fingerboard diagrams, charts and musical examples (conventional staff and tablature) to guide and instruct players in the best way to master the techniques of playing finger-picking guitar and enhance their playing facility. Practical applications are suggested to make use of the material in the creation of original songs and compositions.

GT103

THE RHYTHM GUITAR BOOK

This is a path-breaking new book for a usually overlooked aspect of guitar playing: the special techniques needed for mastering the playing of rhythm guitar. Utilizing his renowned approach to music and the guitar, Kadmon explains and illustrates rhythm, intervals, chord riffs, finger picking and covers much more essential material that rhythm guitarists need to know.

GT104

THE GUITAR BOOK

Drawing on the material he created for the *Guitar Grimoire®*, Adam Kadmon has put together a book that concentrates on the essential material guitarist's need in order to attain mastery of the musical use of the instrument. *The Guitar Book* contains sections on scales, modes, chords, progressions, solo techniques, theory and analysis and other vital topics derived from the highly successful Grimoire folios.

GT101

THE GUITARIST'S KEYBOARD PROGRESSIONS BOOK

With the use of MIDI & Computers, Guitarists today need to become proficient keyboard players. This book offers the guitarist a deeper understanding of Music Theory through keyboard study. Kadmon applies his results-oriented approach by teaching chord progressions and harmony at the keyboard.

In a visually clear format, the book covers chord theory, variations in voicing, a full survey of four-measure progressions and many other approaches to designing individual progressions that will enhance the performer's ability to perform and create.

GT105

- Learn to play any scale in any key on your fret board
- Perfect visual guide to the *Guitar Grimoire* Scales & Modes book
- Pop-up chords and fretboard close-ups
  DVD2 – Scales & Modes – $19.95 (ISBN 0-8258-4906-3)

- Wizard-like details on how to play *any* chord imaginable
- Perfect guide to the *Guitar Grimoire – Chords & Voicings* book
- Includes polychords, chord substitutions, inversions and movable voicings
  DVD3 – Chords & Voicings – $19.95 (ISBN 0-8258-4907-1)

- Learn how standard progressions are created and how to create your own
- Perfect guide to the *Guitar Grimoire Progressions & Improvisation* book
- Learn how to enhance & enrich your solos
  DVD4 – Progressions & Improvisation $19.95 (ISBN 0-8258-4908-X)

◆◆ *Approximate running time 60 minutes each*

The WIZARD SPEAKS!
— On DVD —

AT LONG LAST, THE WIZARD REVEALS, IN PERSON, THE MYSTERIES OF PLAYING THE GUITAR.

This all-new DVD series offers guitar students the opportunity to see and hear Adam Kadmon reveal and demonstrate the techniques and understanding of the underlying structure of music that have helped make the books of *The Guitar Grimoire* among the best-selling guitar teaching publications of all time.

Don't forget these exciting GUITAR GRIMOIRE® titles which correspond to the new DVDs

Scales & Modes (Bk.1)l
GT1 – $21.95 (ISBN O-8258-2171-1)

Chords & Voicings (Bk.2)
GT2 – $21.95 (ISBN O-8258-2172-X)

Progressions & Improvisation (Bk.3)
GT15 – $26.95 (ISBN O-8258-3197-0)